DEALING WITH UNCERTAINTY IN CONTEMPORARY AFRICAN LIVES

Edited by
Liv Haram and C. Bawa Yamba

NORDISKA AFRIKAINSTITUTET 2009

Indexing terms:
  Uncertainty
  Traditional culture
  Anthropology
  Cultural change
  Social change
  Modernization
  Gender relations
  Sexually transmitted diseases
  Economic implications
  Daily life
  Conference papers

Cover: Painting by Kåre Haram
Language editing: Wendy Davies
Index: Rohan Bolton
ISBN 978-91-7106-649-7
© the authors and Nordiska Afrikainstitutet 2009
Printed in Sweden by GML Print on Demand AB, Stockholm 2009

To the memory of Mariken Vaa,
colleague and friend and dedicated Africanist

Contents

Preface and Acknowledgements

This volume is the second publication based on the conference "Uncertainty in Contemporary African Lives", held at the MS Training Centre for Development Co-operation outside Arusha town, in Tanzania, 9–11 April 2003. In the three-day conference the 24 participants – from South Africa, Botswana, Zimbabwe, Uganda, Kenya and Tanzania, as well as from England, Denmark, Sweden and Norway – all presented papers. One caveat is appropriate here. The papers at the conference were overwhelmingly from East and Southern Africa. We believe, however, that the processes they are concerned with are generalisable to and valid for much of sub-Saharan Africa, thus the title. The first publication from the conference appeared in African Sociological Review, Special Issue, No. 8 (1). It contained eight of the 24 conference papers and an introduction, 'Visiting the Issue of Uncertainty in Contemporary African Lives' (Haram and Yamba 2004). This present volume comprises the nine remaining papers.

The conference had its origins in Haram's project at the Nordic Africa Institute on 'Modernisation and Distress in Men's and Woman's Lives: African Experiences', initiated in January 2000. The project dealt with societies undergoing rapid transformation, brought about by forces such as modernisation and globalisation, and the way such processes increase stress and uncertainties in the lives of young men and women. The conference focused on uncertainty, which was one of the central themes of the project, and all papers implicitly or explicitly sought to explore and understand how people in contemporary Africa experience situations of great upheaval, stress, and uncertainty in their everyday lives. The approach was grounded in the awareness that it is important to see people not merely as victims of inauspicious circumstances, but as agents actively responding to their situations, however adverse. Do people draw upon specific 'cultural models', techniques or prescriptions and, thus, rely on a specific course of action when they face grave problems in life? Do they feel alienated and helpless in a risky and uncertain world, or do they take a pragmatic approach to suffering and misfortune? These were some of the basic questions we took as a point of departure for the discussions.

Panel sessions dealt with six main themes, namely, 'Agency, Risk and Uncertainty'; 'Veiling Tears: Gendered Equanimity'; 'Control, Hope and Ultimate Despair'; 'HIV/ AIDS Management: Strategies and Intervention';

'Solace and Certainty in Religion?'; and 'Uncertainty, Misfortune and Modernities'.

Professor Sandra Wallman, of University College, London, Professor Susan Reynolds Whyte, University of Copenhagen, and Dr. Todd Sanders, then at the University of Cambridge, were resource persons, who also chaired sessions, as well as presenting papers. Other chairs of sessions were Associate Professor Francis Nyamnjoh, then at the University of Botswana (currently Head of the Department of Publications and Communications at CODESRIA), and Dr. C. Bawa Yamba, then at the Nordic Africa Institute (currently Associate Professor at Diakonhjemmet University College, Oslo), and Associate Professor Liv Haram (now at the Norwegian University of Science and Technology, Trondheim).

The particular nature of the conference topic led to scholarly explorations of themes, such as the anthropology of religion, medical anthropology, as well as indigenous notions of what constitutes modernity in its various manifestations. The diverse discussions soon revealed a fruitful divide between one group of scholars who saw as their task the need to use research to do something about the situations on the ground, and another group who expounded on theoretical themes, without seeing the ameliorating of the situations on the ground as a necessary corollary of the researcher's endeavour. Thus, while the former were more concerned with the sources of uncertainties, what resources would be required to control them, and the possibility of changing people's behaviour so as to improve their life situation, the latter group was more interested in demarcating uncertainty as a social phenomenon, and establishing its relationship to 'certainty' in people's lived experience. Both positions brought a refreshing vitality to the proceedings. The closing session, 'Certainty – Uncertainty: Life on an Even Keel?' facilitated by Professor Sandra Wallman, revisited some of the central issues and spurred lively and involved discussions.

We wish to thank two anonymous reviewers who scrutinised the volume for their incisive and detailed comments on how the book could be improved. We believe the volume has improved immensely from their advice. Needless to say, however, that any remaining shortcomings are our own, something that we must, to some degree, share with the authors of the papers for insisting on maintaining the specificity of their data and the conclusions derived therefrom.

As convenor and the person responsible for the conference, Haram would like to take this opportunity of expressing her deepest gratitude to all the resource persons who helped with chairing, to all the participants, and to the presenters whose papers have not appeared in this book. Thanks also go to the MS Training Centre for Development Co-operation for their hospitality. Very special thanks go to Ingrid Anderson, at the Nordic Africa Institute, for excellent organisational assistance. Finally, but not least, we wish to thank the Nordic Africa Institute for financial support, and by extension, the Foreign Affairs Ministries of Denmark, Finland, Norway and Sweden who jointly funded the activities of the above-mentioned research project.

Liv Haram
C. Bawa Yamba

Reference

Haram, Liv and Bawa Yamba (eds), 2004, "Visiting the issue of uncertainty in contemporary African lives", *African Sociological Review* 8 (1):1–10.

Areas covered by the authors

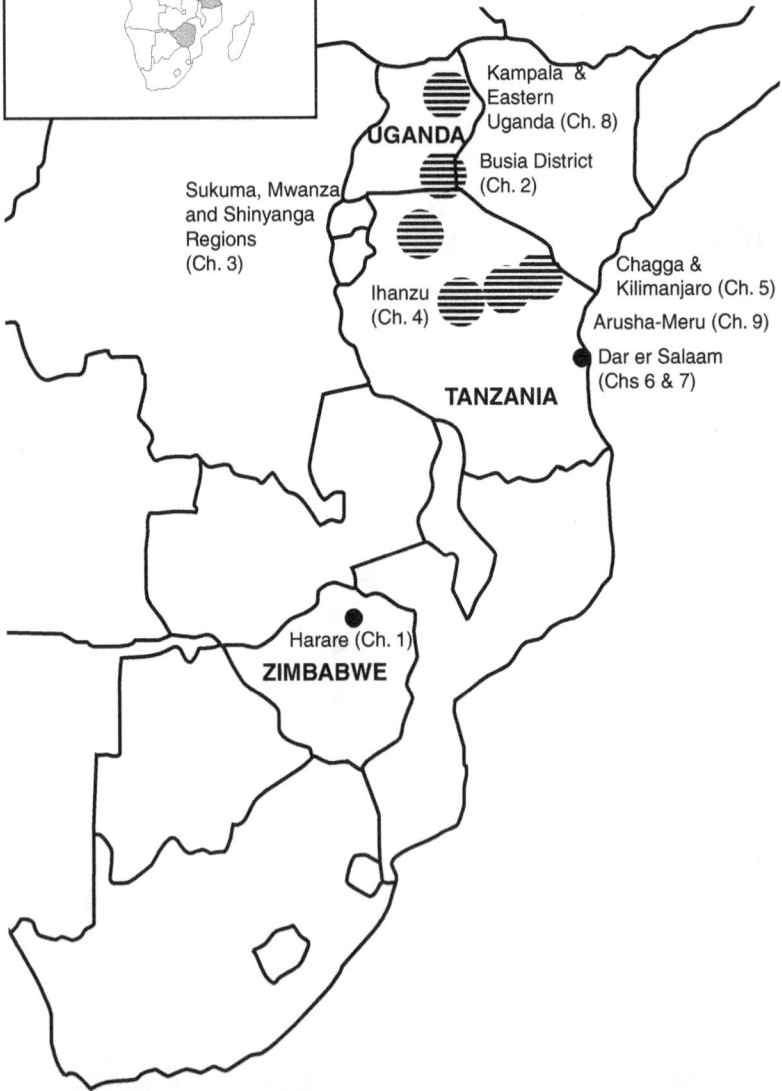

Kampala & Eastern Uganda (Ch. 8)

UGANDA

Busia District (Ch. 2)

Sukuma, Mwanza and Shinyanga Regions (Ch. 3)

Chagga & Kilimanjaro (Ch. 5)

Ihanzu (Ch. 4)

Arusha-Meru (Ch. 9)

Dar er Salaam (Chs 6 & 7)

TANZANIA

Harare (Ch. 1)

ZIMBABWE

Situating Uncertainty in Contemporary Africa: An Introduction

Liv Haram and C. Bawa Yamba

The central theme of this volume is that of uncertainty in the lives of contemporary Africans mainly in eastern and southern Africa. Haram, who convened the conference from which the volume is the outcome, opted for a strategy that did not impose a rigid framework on how the concept of uncertainty should be interpreted; nor were the papers expected to grapple with the ontological implications of the concept. At the conference, the authors dealt explicitly or implicitly with uncertainty, primarily, using their different ethnographies as the point of departure. They sought to explore and explain how people in contemporary Africa experience and cope with uncertainty in everyday life. What emerges is a diversity of approaches, focusing on issues that can be subsumed under a distinct set of problems areas, such as: the minimisation of uncertainty through religion; grappling with the perceived threat of the malevolent witches and sorcerers; facing the distress of mental health issues; and managing the ever-present HIV and AIDS pandemic. Uncertainty in these contexts appears to be somehow correlated with modernity, which impinges, not always positively, on local climes. This correlation is not only at the level of analysis, but often cited by the people themselves as part of the cause of their current strife.

While we cannot hold that uncertainty is something specific to Africa alone, the scale and impact of various kinds of catastrophes on the continent has been disproportionately huge in recent times. Examples are legion, but we have in mind, on the one hand, contingent sets of recurrent phenomena across the continent such as drought, famine, and epidemics of various kinds; and on the other hand, the predictable consequences of poor governance and civil wars which have resulted in large-scale displacements of people. Both types of phenomena have, of course, resulted in a weakening of the social fabric and traditional support networks, making life uncertain for the majority of Africans. More than this, these changes have coincided with the impact of those processes often described as modernisation and globalisation which, while sometimes equated with progress, have also contributed to social distress and insecurity, and have compounded the uncertainties in the daily lives of people.

Following the economic crises of the late 1970s and early 1980s, most African countries were compelled to implement Structural Adjustment Programmes (SAP), as required by the International Monetary Fund (IMF), a corollary of which were the all-encompassing reforms in the public sector and local government, along with increased democratisation and multiparty forms of government (Mkandawire and Olukoshi 1995).[1] Economic systems were restructured in order to facilitate integration into the world economy. Market liberalisation was to lead to privatisation of the economy and a relatively free flow of goods and commodities. Although this strategy was expected also to achieve poverty reduction, economic progress hardly trickled down to a majority of the people in most countries, who remain extremely poor (Booth et al. 1999), but might be regarded as generalisable to much of south Saharan Africa (Comaroff 2007; Hansen and Twaddle 1995, for the case of Uganda).

While many imported commodities were available and on display even in the most remote villages, something local people often cited as an indication of improved conditions, such goods were often beyond the reach of the majority of the people, many of whom lived on less than a dollar a day. Thus, the ramification of neoliberal economics and its effects on everyday life have contributed to increased economic disparities, marginalisation and social suffering (Kleinman et al. 1997). Many Africans continued to struggle with high unemployment, economic decline and rising inflation rates. Access to health services were also undermined by the implementation of cost-sharing policies and 'user fees' policies, which were also part and parcel of the efforts to improve failing economies and provide sustainable health care. One indicator of such deterioration is, for instance, the fact that whereas under-five mortality decreased between 1960 and 1985, it has been increasing ever since. Take, for example, the case of Tanzania, the country in which six of the authors in this volume conducted their research: the change from African socialism to a free-market policy, marked a sharp turn from Nyerere's politics and the Arusha Declaration – which was a policy that strove for egalitarian ideals, self-reliance and a socialist orientation (Tripp 1997).

Changes of this kind have accelerated processes of urbanisation and stratification. In many local rural communities a new entrepreneurial class

---

1. SAP were implemented by the World Bank and the International Monetary Fund in response to the African crises, so as to impose financial and fiscal order as well as to reduce state control and promote the free market (Chabal and Daloz 1999).

has emerged, resulting in an even higher gap between a minority of the people, who are relatively well-off, and the majority that constitute the poorest sections of the population.

In present day Tanzania, it is estimated that more than 50 per cent of the population lives in poverty. Social indicators show that the situation is still deteriorating for the majority of the people (WHO 2006). Although new opportunities now exist, the capacity to make use of these new opportunities is unevenly distributed among people. It is thus clear that the economic reforms of the past few decades have created expectations for a better livelihood for the majority of the population, yet delivered little in terms of reduction in poverty. The situation is not very different in Zambia, which was once one of the more prosperous countries in the southern African region (Saasa and Carlsson 2002).

Brief notes on this concept of uncertainty

The above discussion shows the kind of conditions that have increased uncertainty in the lives of contemporary Africans. Nonetheless, though an increasingly common concept in the social sciences, uncertainty somehow lacks a clear semantic denotation; its connotations are as extensive as its denotation is vast and imprecise. We need to clarify our usage. In anthropology uncertainty is often used, undefined, to imply unpredictable outcomes, often of a negative kind that make life precarious, although some would hold that it is precisely such unpredictability that makes life a challenging drama.

First, the notion of uncertainty employed here has no affinity with economic predictions of the (un)likelihood of healthy returns on an investment, nor does it refer to the concept of indeterminacy in physics. Our concern is, first and foremost, with how the people under study deal with the unpredictable outcome of a current situation, which they anticipate with varying degrees of unease and anxiety, or how they face difficult situations in life. We grapple with the concept on two levels: the first is how the authors in this volume conceive of phenomena that result in uncertainty in the lives of the groups they have studied; the second is how the people under study deal with problems of uncertainty. Though the former is entailed in the latter, the emphasis is on the situating of uncertainty in specific social contexts and exploring how it is managed. Anthropologists and, indeed, social scientists have generally treated uncertainty as a concept denoting non-recurrent and unpredictable phenomena that are intrinsically difficult to counteract, but affect the lives of individuals or a given group of people (see, for example, Jenkins et al. 2005; Whyte 1997; Ådahl 2007).

Commonly, when we refer to uncertainty, we choose examples such as accidents, the onset of bad fortune, severe illness, sudden death and other contingent events that are neither predictable nor within one's sphere of control.

Depending on the kind of epistemological context we are situated in, we might dismiss an event as merely an *accident,* something that happened by *chance,* or we might regard such an event as providential and therefore find it unnecessary to devote any energy to finding out the ultimate cause of that particular event. Attributing an event to providence might be a sufficient enough explanation for those who are religiously inclined. Attributing an unpredictable event to the agency of some malevolent force, and seeking some means of preventing and counteracting its negative consequences, is the kind of context in which the chapters in this volume situate their discussion. Some of the chapters volume deal with occurrences that, despite their randomness, are perceived as the outcome of some agency, and thus the ultimate *cause* of that occurrence. Thus the prevailing universe of discourse in any given social context is what determines which kinds of explanations are drawn upon to make sense of such events. Nonetheless, whether people adhere to a model that accepts *chance* and *accident* as sufficient explanation, or whether they hold that a transcendent agency of some kind is what causes something to happen, they are both similarly engaged in logical and rational ways of dealing with uncertainty. Indeed, we might envisage here a continuum of different perceptions of what makes uncertain events occur. At the one end, there would be people who conduct fairly ordinary activities to minimise the chances of mishaps; at the other end would be people who do not entirely accept the idea of a chance occurrence, but see every mishap as having a transcendent cause, and therefore resort to different pragmatic strategies to minimise the adverse effects as well as prevent its future occurrence. The chapters in the volume would appear to cluster at this latter end of this continuum, but they also show the complexity of choice, and the often necessary combination of actions derived from both schemes. We meet people who struggle, against all prevailing odds, to deal pragmatically with uncertainty in everyday life. In this sense the approach of the chapters might be regarded as Whytean (with reference to Whyte (1997) whose award-winning monograph advanced a paradigm for seeing people in adverse states as pursuing pragmatic responses to deal with life).

The impact of the unpredictable always shakes the very foundation of human existence. Regularities are what we prefer, be they something we infer from nature, as, for example, the inevitable sequences of the seasons; or something we impose on nature and other phenomena through a simple activity as the assigning of names to things that would appear to be intimations of such order. We need to explain unpredictable occurrences, in an effort to manage or control them, or, perhaps we even hope thereby to be able to prevent their future occurrence. The Azande oracles, as Evans-Pritchard (1937) has shown, sought not only to explain unfortunate events through the assigning of agency to particular witches, but also conducted rituals to prevent their future occurrence. This was quintessentially a pragmatic effort to minimise uncertainty. In the ethnographic contexts from which the contributions to this volume are derived, something similar is at play. People resort to various means to ensure some certainty in their lives, and thereby to minimise risk and danger.

The first two chapters, by Chitando and Christiansen, respectively, deal with the reliance on Charismatic Christianity in the search for some kind of existential constancy, as it were: a quest for certitude and, we might add, certainty, although the achievement of the latter itself entails some degree of uncertainty. Chitando (Chapter 1) shows how the uncertainties following the failure of neoliberal economics, combined with the oppressive governance that has plagued Zimbabweans in the last couple of decades, have partly led to the rise of Pentecostal churches, whose leaders and prophets provide some certainty in the everyday lives of people. Although the rise in Charismatic Christianity has been reported in other parts of Africa, with other origins or a different raison d'être, the upsurge in Zimbabwe appears to be correlated with the difficult recent developments in the country. One striking example of this way of managing uncertainty is the sanctifying of passports, to imbue them with some indeterminate force that would facilitate border crossing. Christensen's chapter (2) deals with the local constructions of certainty. Taking her point of departure in a phenomenological conceptualisation of intersubjectivity, she argues that the relationship between the individual and God constitutes a key for understanding the Charismatic claims to and experiences of certainty. All the chapters, as is clear in the following sections below, similarly deal with how people manage uncertainty whether it is caused by witchcraft (Mesaki, Chapter 3; Sanders, Chapter 4; Myhre, Chapter 5), or by mental illness (Mhina, Chapter 6), whether it is part of a complex set of factors that drives women to commit suicide (Ndosi, Chapter 7) or underlies the existential dilemmas of HIV and AIDS (Mogensen, Chapter 8), or the uncertain aetiologies of HIV and AIDS (Haram, Chapter 9).

Uncertainty is a slippery concept; too much preoccupation with it results inevitably in a teleological warp of some kind: it is not merely a quibble to hold that what is certain about uncertainty is the fact that it is uncertain. It is often closely linked to the concept of risk, which conveys, in its extensive sense, intimations of certainty, particularly if it is allowed that some necessary calculation and choice would lead to a predictable outcome. However, in this present context, what is more interesting is the fact that uncertainty presupposes the contrasting notion of certainty, the striving for which both provides the schema, as it were, and constitutes the course of action people follow in dealing with what is uncertain.

The important issue, then, is how people make sense of everyday afflictions which compound uncertainty and mar their existence, since how they perceive and understand such phenomena also shapes their responses. These issues become crystallised when we see them as underlying any human attempt to manage and deal with the ontological insecurities (cf. Giddens 1990; Giddens 1993) of modern life.

Some trajectories of modern life

Modern life in Africa has been a mixed blessing. In the years following independence there was much improvement in the lives of people. In Tanzania, for example, there was a real increase in the standard of living, as measured by such indicators as increasing enrolments ratios for both sexes in primary and secondary school, rising adult literacy, higher life expectancy and decrease in maternal mortality rates (among others). Such progress was reinforced by a postcolonial rhetoric which engendered expectations of modernity. But development as conveyed in the idea and meta-narrative of modernity (often perceived also as synonymous with progress) did not emerge in Africa. For most Tanzanians 'development' has remained an elusive and imaginary concept, even for many of those who experienced the better times of the 1970s and 1980s. Similar processes, where people's expectations of economic 'development' have never quite materialised, where modest gains have been reversed and hopes for a better future dashed, exist in many parts of contemporary Africa (see, for example, Chabal and Daloz 1999; Ferguson 1999).

A central question then, is: how do people adapt to such a situation? How do they make sense of development? As an elusive concept at the level of policy and propaganda that at some stage has stopped in its tracks? A something that has been appropriated by a minority, while the rest of the people have eked out a living much as they did in the past, a time commonly referred to as the era of 'backwardness'? One consequence of this widespread disillusion with 'development' is that the very concept of development itself has changed in meaning; it is now regarded as something that is also dubious and ambiguous, and is strongly associated with what is immoral and evil in society today. Thus many Tanzanian regard HIV and AIDS as causally connected with the evil effects of modern life (Dilger 2003; Haram 2005; Setel 1999). The majority of people believe that life has become more precarious and more uncertain. This appears to be a common perspective, even if it is allowed that believing 'things were better in the past' may partly reflect a universal human tendency: having nostalgic recollections of the past as better than the present, even though this may not have been true, were it possible to employ some objective indicator(s) to measure such contentions. Nonetheless, it is such subjective perceptions that are important in the way people make choices and devise strategies to get on with life. Thus the chapters in this volume simultaneously convey some of these contradictory processes, as people grapple with daily life: on the one hand, expressing feelings of loss of the past; while, on the other hand, being aware that they now dwell in a world in which, potentially, possibilities and opportunities exist for advancement of some kind, even if access to such possibilities is limited.

Although the Structural Adjustment Programmes were intended to provide security and improve the wellbeing of citizens, the reverse has generally occurred. What emerged in the wake of the reforms were increased disparities in wealth distribution. In many African countries a similar situation prevailed. Furthermore, most countries also saw the emergence of a small elite that succeeded in accumulating extreme wealth and power (see Chabal and Daloz 1999).

For most people, daily life became a perpetual struggle in the search of food, education, employment and medicine, situated within contexts where individual civil rights were weak or non-existent. The disparities were further reflected, for example, in the fact that while private schools had the newest textbooks and (relatively) well-paid teachers, and private medical facilities and clinics stocked the most essential drugs, such pockets of wellbeing were only available to those with purchasing power. The poor had few or no options whatsoever.

The chapters in this volume are drawn from local settings characterised by deprivation and inequalities to show how, notwithstanding the prevailing constraints, people still try to manage to cope with their lives. They situate contemporary East African worlds, certainly a microcosm of much of sub-

Saharan Africa, in landscapes of regressive economies, diseases, migration, social conflict, accusations of witchcraft, and the anguish of mental illness. The underlying theme is that despite such bleak conditions people still try to exert some agency in trying to improve their lives.

Migration – across states and trade in human beings

Modern life in Africa has resulted in the twin phenomena of urbanisation and migration. The attraction of the urban centres where jobs were more available was an important pull factor for economically motivated movement. In addition to such migrations, there were also politically impelled movements, or less disruptive ones such as those resulting from postings of state employees. Even if the push and pull factors influence the nature of life in the new social climate, the migrant is exposed to all kinds of factors that make them more vulnerable than those among whom they now reside. Thus, migration always increases risk and uncertainty for the migrant in the new environment. Migrants are more likely to end up in stranger enclaves with sub-standard housing, and to be made scapegoats for crime and other social ills. Migrants also often have poorer access to health care. More important for our purpose here is that the cause of migrant vulnerability is the inevitable weakening or even severing of traditional social ties after movement. Douglas (1994) expresses this very clearly when she writes:

> To move out of the local community means defying its tyranny. The escapee is often glad to shuffle off its tedious constraints, and makes light of its old compensations. *I would add that liberation from the small community also means losing the old protections.* The markets suck us (willingly) out of our cosy, dull, local niches and turn us into unencumbered actors, mobile in a world system, but setting us free they leave us exposed. We feel vulnerable. (Douglas 1994:15, our emphasis)

Movements of this kind, be they migrations from one local setting to another, or movement across national borders, entail danger at many levels. The essential point we are making here is that many African migrants retain complex ontological ideas of their home and origins, which they, in a sense, perceive as autochthonous (see, for example, Parkin 1991). Movement from their origins, whatever the causes, are perceived with unease and as entailing exposure to increased risk and danger. Maintaining continued contact of some kind with home, through ritual exchange or investing in natal land, are some of the ways that migrants retain contact with 'home' and minimise the uncertainty of life.

We wish to reiterate the point that migration entails leaving a spatial and moral sphere where norms, social obligations and duties are clearly specified for another spatio-moral context where such structures are weak, non-specific or non-existent. Thus such migration involves not only a physical displacement but a mental displacement as well, and this aggravates already existing distress and uncertainty in the life of the migrant.

Zimbabwe epitomises the dire economic hardships experienced by many African peoples, albeit in the severest imaginable form. Millions of Zimbabweans have been compelled to leave their homes in an effort to seek a better life elsewhere. Fantastic inflation levels, a government lacking legitimacy, the unresolved land issue, and HIV and AIDS have generated much anxiety, suffering and despair. Chitando (Chapter 1) shows how the deteriorating conditions over the past few decades has coincided with the increasing rise of the spiritual healers and a booming spiritual market. The unprecedented burgeoning of African independent churches, prophets and spiritual healers clearly expresses the capacity of religion to equip its adherents – the Harare urban poor – with the resources to cope with various challenges of life. One less drastic consequence of the migrating from Zimbabwe, Chitando shows, is it that of ensuring that one is able to successfully cross borders as an illegal migrant. The whole process becomes less risky – or less uncertain – when one's passport is blessed and sanctified by a spiritual healer. Prospective migrants therefore have their travel documents "sanctified" to ensure safe crossing into the new country.

While claiming that the upsurge in religious healing coincides with prevailing economic hardship, Chitando cautions us, nonetheless, about the danger of reducing religion to an epiphenomenon that can be explained in economic terms. Religion and the prophets' ability to alleviate people's anxiety forcefully connect adherents to a realm where new possibilities are perceived to exist.

Displacement and marginality are intrinsic aspects of migration. The migrant, therefore, is often compelled to operate on the margins of what is socially and morally acceptable. Little wonder then that distress, danger and risk appear to increase on the margins of urban space or in illegal settler communities in a foreign country, where the transplanted migrants live. This compounds situations of vulnerability and risk, even if such risk may also be regarded as culturally specific, as Douglas (1994) has shown.

Witchcraft as a means of dealing with uncertainty

Much of recent anthropological work on witchcraft in contemporary Africa has retained the same old view of the phenomenon as a levelling mechanism for redressing the inequalities associated with modern life, as well as an explanatory model for misfortune and uncertainty. Indeed, most problems associated with modern life in Africa, poverty and wealth, illnesses and even the HIV and AIDS epidemic, are treated as causally related to the resurgence of witchcraft beliefs (Bond and Ciekawy 2001 and others; Comaroff and Comaroff 1993; Geschiere 1997; Moore and Sanders 2001).

Anthropologists have traditionally approached witchcraft and occult practices in Africa as an explanation of misfortune, or one of the means through which society regulates social and economic accumulation; phenomena that function, as mentioned above, as forms of levelling (see classics such as Douglas 1970; Evans-Pritchard 1937; Mitchell 1956; White et al.). Recent approaches to the analysis of witchcraft appear to have become concerned with its epistemic legitimacy. How can anyone believe in the kind of causality it postulates? Not surprisingly there appears to be now a tendency on the part of some contemporary Africans to view the phenomenon as something "primitive", something that is out of tune with modernisation, an anachronistic remnant of the past. This might account for the reason why some perceive the phenomenon as an aspect of African modernity, albeit one that is relegated to the conceptual fiefdom of the discontented (Comaroff and Comaroff 1993; Geschiere 1997). We believe this is partly the reason why most anthropologists sidestep the issue of witchcraft as essentially located at the level of belief and instead focus their analysis at the level of practice (cf. Kapferer 2002). The same cannot be said of Myhre (infra), whose analysis in this volume constitutes an interesting heuristic approach, focusing on how such beliefs emerge from the ambiguities of social relationship.

Nonetheless, the Weberian assumption that "magical" practices became less socially relevant with increased education, urbanisation and other contexts of modernity, has proved to be not quite correct. Witchcraft belief and practices in contemporary modern Africa have not only remained, but, as much of the literature shows, have even increased with modernity/modernities (see also, Comaroff and Comaroff 1993; Geschiere 1997; Moore and Sanders 2001; Yamba 1997). Much in line with the Comaroffs'(1993) thesis on witchcraft as correlated to modernity in Africa, Geschiere (1997) argues that people's understanding of "witchcraft" has shifted from a concern about social and economic levelling to a concern about "accumulation". This is a point earlier elaborated by Bayart (1993) who shows how the African elite maintain their hegemony through accumulation and access to natural resources, which he conveys through the metaphor of "eating", thereby implying an association of this kind of behaviour with occult powers and witchcraft (see also Geschiere 1997:14). The chapters by Mesaki, Myhre and Sanders in this volume explore practices of this kind, and ask how we, as social scientists, should approach such complex phenomena without reducing them to mechanistic African responses to rapid change, or just to refractions of modernisation and new forms of globalisation (cf., for instance, Kapferer 2002).

Mesaki's chapter deals with what is undoubtedly one of the most extreme expressions of witchcraft practice in contemporary Africa: the murders of alleged witches, often old women, among the Sukuma of northern Tanzania. He traces the practice from the pre-colonial, to colonial and postcolonial times, to show how it has evolved into something much more sinister than a mere mechanism for social levelling. He describes how elderly people and widows, in particular, are brutally murdered by hired thugs at night. Mesaki shows how, despite strong statements from the highest levels of government, the police and the authorities are unable to prevent the killings. Mesaki attributes this to the impotence of the institutions of law enforcement and of the state itself. A worrying element in the cases Mesaki presents is that the killing of alleged witches might well be an epiphenomenon of greed, not just something propelled by belief in witchcraft. Often, the intended victims are targeted by their own younger relatives who hope to benefit from the death of those who stand in the way of their rightful inheritance. It seems clear from Mesaki's account that such accusations are pretexts that legitimate getting rid of purported witches, the whole practice being made possible by the generally accepted discourse and framework of the belief and practice of witchcraft. However, another plausible explanation as to why this cruel behaviour persists may be that, the longer the old grandparent lives on, the more delayed the inheriting of farming land and similar properties by their legitimate heirs. It is also plausible to assume that the killing of people and conflict over wealth probably favour the wealthier segments of the Sukuma people, thus resulting in yet greater disparities, which in turn reproduce this practice of witch killings.

Sanders (Chapter 4), on the Ilhanzu of Tanzania, argues that the proliferation of witchcraft in postcolonial Africa is directly related to the penetration of neoliberal capitalism and the inter-articulation of the local and the global forces. More particularly, he argues that the various forms of witchcraft among the Ilhanzu appear to express people's hopes of actively participating in a world of material abundance, while at the same time acknowledging their apprehensions about the vast inequalities that such material accumulation implies. Myhre (Chapter 5), on the other hand, critiques the very thesis that witchcraft is a modern phenomenon. Although people at times explain such evil practices as consequences of modern life, it does not necessarily mean that they consider the practice as particularly modern or as constituent of the modern. In a fine-grained ethnographic analysis, he shows that witchcraft practices among the Chagga of Kilimanjaro in northern Tanzania has a long and continuous history and cannot, therefore, be fully explained in terms of societal "needs" arising from modern social change. Analysing the connections between vernacular conceptual meanings and social relationality, Myhre describes witchcraft as a local representation of social fragility and uncertainty.

The chapters by Mhina and Mogensen (6 and 8, respectively), deal with some of the consequences of the weakening of supportive, but also demanding, bonds of kinship. Mhina uses narratives by people with mental illness and their relatives, to illuminate their life situation, where care is provided by kinsmen with little support from a weak health and psychiatric care system. Mhina's material from Dar es Salaam illustrates how an already marginalised group of people – the mentally ill – are further marginalised by the state, which is unable to provide proper health care or appropriate treatment to the mentally ill. The accounts by people affected by mental illness that Mhina examines reflect a complex reality in which people pick and choose from a variety of therapeutic options, but are, for the most part, let down by all of these.

Mhina's chapter constitutes a disturbing and powerful censure of the health care system, which is perhaps representative of the situation in other parts of sub-Saharan African as well. It also shows how the mentally ill have to resort to medical pluralism in the hope that one of the systems will work.

Mogensen explores how the recent availability of drugs for the management of HIV infection, antiretroviral (ARV) treatment, has heightened the discrepancy between availability and accessibility. Though these life-prolonging drugs are available, they are not easily assessible to a majority of the infected. The gap between availability and accessibility constitutes fertile ground for moral dilemmas between the demanding bonds of kinship and the real constraints of the marginal household economy. Indeed, the existence of options is a very important factor in the perception of uncertainty. As Whyte points out, the very existence of alternatives is also important for the issue of uncertainty (1997: 23). Increased knowledge about HIV and AIDS, the possibility of taking a test and the existence of the ARV treatment may thus also be sources of increased stress and uncertainty. Another subtle issue that can be extrapolated from Mogensen's ethnography is that of the consequences and the uncertainty generated when one articulates what should remain unsaid. The illocutionary force of saying what was known but not said appears to have sparked off a trajectory of action and commitment by the family of the main informant – Kate – that must have been quite demanding, and might also be regarded as causing increased distress and uncertainty for the whole extended family. This, of course, had wide implications beyond this specific case. Another particularly interesting issue in Mogensen's sensitive ethnography is her reflective discussion of her role in the encounter between anthropologist and those studied.

Seeking certainty and solace in religion

Many chapters in this volume address the importance of religion as a compass, as it were, for creating some degree of certainty and providing some meaning in an otherwise uncertain world. As well illustrated in the chapters by Chitando, Christiansen and Myhre (Chapters 1, 2 and 5 respectively), Charismatic Christianity and spirit possession cults have become increasingly popular across contemporary Africa during the last decades.[2] African independent churches and the old mission churches have lost much ground to the Charismatic churches – particularly the Pentecostal churches, which are now mushrooming throughout much of Africa (cf., for instance, Gifford 1994; Meyer 1992; Meyer 1998). An increasing body of research has emerged that links these trends to processes of increasing uncertainty in people's everyday life and the ability of such churches to address people's everyday concerns locally. Birgit Meyer's study of Pentecostalism (1992), for example, shows how Pentecostal churches, in contrast to the mission churches, not only accept local causal explanatory models of affliction and misfortune – which include witchcraft – but are also able to incorporate them into local cosmologies and practices. They are thus able to address people's everyday concerns in a locally meaningful way by giving them practical guidelines to live by. Much research from Africa underscores people's pragmatic approach to religion (Beidelman 1993 (1986); Evans-Pritchard 1937; Whyte 1997, to mention some) and the power of the churches to address and heal their members' afflictions, offering them new hope and, above all, equipping them with practical guidelines for life in an uncertain

---

2. These churches are proliferating the world over, not only in Africa (Dijk et al. 2000; Meyer 1998).

life situation. The chapters by Christensen and Chitando particularly illustrate this unique ability to meet the specific needs of their followers (Chapters 1 and 2, respectively).

Based on anthropological fieldwork in south-eastern Uganda, Christensen describes how the members of the Charismatic Christian churches live and deal with hardship, by exchanging their "old" traditional ways of life for a new way of living in the world. Thus, in contrast to Meyer (1998), Christensen illustrates how the "Savedees" are seeking not only solace but also practical solutions to their everyday problems and uncertainties through a Christian way of living.

To many in the Western world, turning to religion for solace and spiritual support is often a last resort in life's most difficult and uncertain situations. In this volume several chapters illustrate how in Africa people's everyday life is strongly embedded in religion. It is both a belief and a practice that is always present; it is the one virtual constant of life that underlies everything. "Faith-practices", or to borrow Bourdieu's concept, "practical knowledge", constitute one of the "enabling agents to generate an infinity of practices adapted to endlessly changing situations ..." (1993:16). Religion is both the ontological basis for their lives and the meaning of life, as well as that which provides prescriptive guidance for how to live in the world.

Agency and ultimate despair?

Our discussion thus far may seem to have centred on the precarious conditions that aggravate uncertainty and difficulties in the lives of people in Africa. This is, of course, inevitable, given the theme of this volume. We also wish to point out that the issue of agency arises when people act upon their situation by trying to control it, in an effort to minimise the levels of uncertainty in their lives. The scope of possibilities for making a difference through their own action may be quite limited. However, the fact that they do act at all is significant. As most chapters in this volume illustrate, people engage very actively in the negotiation of their position in the world.

Agency may be seen as a parallel concept to risk and uncertainty, but it could also be argued that agency is, in effect, the counterpart of those concepts. It is through agency that a person makes and executes choices – rational or irrational, depending on the particular type of logic we apply to others' choices – in order to minimise uncertainty in everyday life. However, as explored in some of the chapters, there are limits to our/human agency. The very fact that our agency might not always be adequate to deal with a situation we encounter is explored in some depth in the chapters by

Mhina (Chapter 6), Ndosi (Chapter 7), Mogensen (Chapters 8) and Haram (Chapters 9).

Ndosi, one of the 12 or so psychiatrists in the whole of Tanzania, writes from a medical perspective. His chapter is based on research from Dar es Salaam in which he explores the troubled life of women who have committed suicide (Chapter 7). By interviewing some of the surviving relatives of the deceased, the author traces perceived factors that might have triggered the decision to commit suicide, often executed through self-poisoning. Male infidelity and other partner-related problems were the underlying causes. These found their expression in distrust between the partners, which led to psychological and/or sexual abuse of the women, culminating in the suicide of the female partner.

Some people are predisposed to depression, but living in contexts where resources are scarce there is no help in terms of anti-depressants, which have improved life for people of similar dispositions in the richer parts of the world. In Africa, in the absence of medication and appropriate therapy, taking one's own life appears to be increasingly becoming a perceived option. Perhaps, in another context with more congenial conditions, those who are driven to such ultimate despair might have opted for life. The reasons as to why some people choose self-destruction are difficult to explain, if not incomprehensible. This is what prompts Ndosi, following Camus, to characterise suicide as a truly philosophical dilemma. Ndosi shows that the reasons behind the suicides are complex. It would seem, however, that economic problems are also one of the significant set of factors that trigger off the "decision". Many of the suicidal women had also lived in very distressing relationships with their (male) partners and two-thirds of them had experienced grave violence from their partners.

Violence against women, commonly male violence against women, is a topic that runs through most chapters in this volume. Recall Mesaki's chapter (3), where old widows accused of witchcraft and killed by their own kin (cf. also Myhre's chapter in this volume).

Haram's chapter also underscores the worrying phenomenon of violence against women. Young women, in their quest for independence often find themselves the easy victims of sexual harassment and rape. Perceiving their mothers' ways of life as outdated, they seek new and modern ways of living by leaving their homes and thus not only cross spatial borders but also go against the male-biased moral order. This not only aggravates uncertainty in their lives, but increases the likelihood of their becoming infected by HIV and other sexually transmitted infections, which in turn reinforces stereotypical notions that women are the transmitters of diseases. Violence against women only becomes more frequent and cruel when men – often HIV positive themselves – learn that their female partner is infected (see Ndosi's chapter in this volume; cf., for instance, also Maman et al. 2002). Violence against women has received much recent attentions through media coverage of graphic occurrences in many parts of Africa – Congo and Darfur constitute good examples. But gender violence is not something that is confined to Africa. It is a major global issue and common in other parts of the world (Green 1999). In the African context its specificity is situated in the fact that women are increasingly struggling for independence and a modern life, and this has proven to be a mixed blessing, as shown in Haram's chapter.

In this introduction we have only been able to touch on a number of vital themes, which we believe no researcher interested in present day African life can avoid. We hope our sweeping statements will spur the reader to explore the interesting contributions in the present volume carefully. We wager that the chapters will not leave the reader unmoved, and if that turns out to be the case, the volume and the conference from which the chapters are derived, will not have been in vain.

References

Bayart, Jean-Francois, 1993, *The state in Africa: the politics of the belly.* Harlow: Longman.

Beidelman, T.O., 1993 (1986), *Moral imagination in Kaguru modes of thought.* Bloomington: Indiana University Press.

Bond, George Clement and Diane M. Ciekawy (eds), 2001, *Witchcraft dialogues: anthropological and philosophical exchanges.* Athens, Ohio: Ohio University Center for International Studies.

Booth, David, Melissa Leach and Allison Tierney, 1999, *Experiencing Poverty in Africa: Perspectives from Anthropology.* Originally appeared as "Background Paper No. 1(b)" for the World Bank Poverty Status Report 1999.

Bourdieu, Pierre, 1993, *Outline of a theory of practice.* Cambridge: Cambridge University Press.

Chabal, Patrick and Jean-Pascal Daloz, 1999, *Africa works: disorder as political instrument.* Bloomington: Indiana University Press.

Comaroff, Jean and John Comaroff, 2007, "Law and disorder in the postcolony", *Social Anthropology,* 15(2):133–152.

Comaroff, Jean and John L. Comaroff, 1993, *Modernity and its malcontents: ritual and power in Postcolonial Africa.* Chicago: University of Chicago Press.

Dijk, Rijk van, Ria Reis and Marja Spierenburg, 2000, *The quest for fruition through ngoma: the political aspects of healing in South Africa.* Athens: Ohio University Press; Oxford: James Currey.

Dilger, Hansjörg, 2003, "Sexuality, AIDS, and the lures of modernity: reflexivity and morality among young people in rural Tanzania", *Medical Anthropology,* 22(1):23–52.

Douglas, Mary, 1970, *Witchcraft: confessions & accusations.* London: Tavistock Publications.

—1994, *Risk and blame: essays in cultural theory.* London: Routledge.

Evans-Pritchard, E.E., 1937, *Witchcraft, oracles and magic among the Azande.* London: Oxford University Press.

Ferguson, James, 1999, *Expectations of modernity: myths and meanings of urban life on the Zambian copperbelt.* Berkeley and London: University of California Press.

Geschiere, Peter, 1997, *The modernity of witchcraft : politics and the occult in postcolonial Africa.* Charlottesville, VA: University Press of Virginia.

Giddens, Anthony, 1990, *The consequences of modernity.* Cambridge: Polity Press.

—, 1993, *Modernity and self-identity: self and society in the late modern age.* Cambridge, UK: Polity Press.

Gifford, P., 1994, "Some Recent Developments in African Christianity", *African Affairs,* 93(373):513–534.

Green, December, 1999, *Gender violence in Africa: African women's responses.* New York: St. Martin's Press.

Hansen, Holger Bernt and Michael Twaddle, 1995, *Religion & politics in East Africa: the period since independence.* London: James Currey.

Haram, Liv, 2005, "AIDS and risk: the handling of uncertainty in northern Tanzania", *Culture, Health & Sexuality,* 7(1):pp.1–13.

Jenkins, Richard, Hanne Jessen and Vibeke Steffen, 2005, *Managing uncertainty: ethnographic studies of illness, risk and the struggle for control.* Copenhagen: Museum Tusculanum press, University of Copenhagen.

Kapferer, Bruce, 2002, *Beyond rationalism.* New York: Berghahn Books.

Kleinman, Arthur, Veena Das and Margaret M. Lock, 1997, *Social suffering.* Berkeley: University of California Press.

Maman, Suzanne, et al., 2002, "HIV-positive women report more lifetime partner violence: findings from a voluntary counselling and testing clinic in Dar es Salaam, Tanzania", *American Journal of Public Health,* 92(8):1331–37.

Meyer, Birgit, 1992, "'If you are a Devil, you are a Witch, and if you are a Witch, you are a Devil': the Integratoin of 'Pagan' Ideas into the Conceptual Universe of Ewe Christians in Southeastern Ghana", *Journal of Religion in Africa,* 22(2):98–132.

—, 1998, "Make a Complete Break with the Past: Memory and Post-colonial Modernity in Ghaneian Pentecostalist Discourse", *Journal of religion in Africa*, 27(3):316–349.

Mitchell, J. Clyde, 1956, *The Yao village: a study in the social structure of a Nyasaland tribe*. Manchester: Published on behalf of the Rhodes-Livingstone Institute, Northern Rhodesia by Manchester University Press.

Mkandawire, Thandika and Adebayo O. Olukoshi, 1995, *Between liberalisation and oppression: the politics of structural adjustment in Africa*. Oxford: CODESRIA.

Moore, Henrietta L. and Todd Sanders, 2001, *Magical interpretations, material realities: modernity, witchcraft, and the occult in postcolonial Africa*. London: Routledge.

Parkin, David,1991, *Sacred void: spatial images of work and ritual among the Giriama of Kenya*. Cambridge: Cambridge University Press.

Setel, Philip Wittman, 1999, *A plague of paradoxes: AIDS, culture, and demography in Northern Tanzania*. Chicago: The University of Chicago Press.

Saasa, Oliver S. and Jerker Carlsson, 2002, *Aid and poverty reduction in Zambia: mission unaccomplished*. Uppsala: Nordiska Afrikainstitutet.

Tripp, Aili Mari, 1997, *Changing the rules: the politics of liberalization and the urban informal economy in Tanzania*. Berkeley: University of California Press.

White, G.D., K.C. Househam and D. Ngomane, 1976, "Child abuse among rural blacks", *South African Medical Journal*, 50(39):1499.

WHO, 2006, *Country Health System Fact Sheet 2006, United Republic of Tanzania*, p. 8. World Health Organisation, Africa.

Whyte, Susan Reynolds, 1997, *Questioning misfortune: the pragmatics of uncertainty in Eastern Uganda*. Volume 4. Cambridge: Cambridge University Press.

Yamba, C. Bawa, 1997, "Cosmologies in Turmoil: Witchfinding and AIDS in Chiawa, Zambia", *Africa. Journal of the International African Institute*, 67(2):200–223.

Ådahl, S., 2007, "Good Lives, Hidden Miseries. An Ethnogrpahy of Uncertainty in a Finnish Village". Doctoral dissertation, Department of Social and Cultural Anthropology, University of Helsinki.

CHAPTER I

Deliverance and Sanctified Passports: Prophetic Activities amidst Uncertainty in Harare

Ezra Chitando

Introduction

Since the late 1990s, Zimbabwe has been undergoing a social and economic crisis. After a period of relative prosperity in the early 1980s, the government embraced the Economic Structural Adjustment Programme (ESAP) in 1991. Instead of instigating an economic revival, ESAP resulted in an increase in suffering for vulnerable groups such as the working poor (Gibbon 1995). The social and economic implications due to the spread of HIV/ AIDS wreaked havoc and threatened to wipe out gains that had been made in education and health. Political violence, efforts to resolve the emotive land question and galloping inflation have generated anxiety, pessimism and despair especially among the young generation. Thus, as argued by Trudell in reference to young people in Africa, "The institutions of education, socialization and authority which provide shape to their lives are being assailed as never before by war, HIV/AIDS, cultural and political change" (Trudell 2002:1). Although young Zimbabweans are not experiencing a physical war, they are encountering many psychological and economic "wars".

Considering the harsh economic situation in contemporary Zimbabwe and especially the difficult and unpromising life situation among the young, one would assume a certain causal link between the poor economic situation and an increase in religious expressions. As the Zimbabwean economy failed to satisfy the basic needs of the majority of the people, the spiritual market experienced a remarkable boom. In the 1990s, Pentecostalism became a popular mode of religious expression. Many new churches, ministries, fellowships and other models of religious organisation emerged. Gospel music gained ascendancy (Chitando 2002:7), while religious innovation scaled new heights. Amidst this anxiety, groaning and groping for spiritual support, the various types of "prophets" (referred to as *maporofita* in the Shona language) – a phenomenon I will soon turn to – promised people help in overcoming all negative forces. Joining the growing band of religious entrepreneurs that included pastors, musicians, publishers, bible teachers and others, these prophets offered their services to anxious clients.

This chapter examines the role of prophets from African independent churches (AICs), also referred to as African instituted and indigenous churches, in the context of anxiety in contemporary Harare, the capital city of Zimbabwe. Prophets are men and women who claim to be agents of the Holy Spirit in alleviating human suffering. They are believed to combat illness and misfortune through the power of the Holy Spirit. Prophets encompass a broad category that includes individuals who utilise diverse healing practices. Some of them use symbolic objects like rods, holy cords and blessed water, while others heal through prayer only. They also belong to different churches, but the term *muporofita* (singular) is used to refer to their putative power to identify and overcome negative spiritual forces. Consequently, the prophet is sometimes referred to as a spiritual healer or *munhu waMwari* (which can be translated as "God's servant").

This study highlights the upsurge in prophetic activity in Harare and links it to the need to counter uncertainty. The vulnerability of women, as shown by their being the major clients, receives considerable coverage. The study also explores the role of religion in the struggle for survival and in mitigating anxiety in an African urban context. It seeks to contribute to discourses on the importance of religion in negotiating uncertainty in human existence. While previous studies on prophets in Southern Africa have dwelt with healing as a recruitment technique, this study puts emphasis on the role of prophets in addressing contemporary urban challenges. It shows how prophets attend to clients from diverse religious backgrounds. It illustrates the capacity of religion to give meaning to human life, while simultaneously equipping its adherents to be resourceful in meeting diverse challenges.

The material being drawn upon in this chapter was collected between 2000 and 2002 as part of a larger study on urban religion in Zimbabwe. It was collected through extensive interviews with 30 prophets, 10 ministers of religion, five medical personnel, five traditional healers and three politicians. Due to the continuing fragmentation of AICs, many prophets and clients kept changing their affiliation, making it difficult for the researchers to establish their denominational allegiance. We also experienced some difficulties in data collection among female respondents who, at times, were hesitant to share their experiences with researchers of the opposite sex. However, by utilising the services of a female research assistant, we managed to create an environment in which female informants gave us valuable information.

Prophets were identified through advertisements in the city centre, by visiting them at their healing places, and by participating in the services at the various "sacred" spots in Harare. The main form of specific data sought, included the actual healing ceremonies, the testimonies of people who have sought the services of prophets, the marketing strategies of prophets, and the perceptions of members of the public concerning prophetic healing. The section on women and healing seeks to draw attention to the gendered aspect of uncertainty in Harare. The following section seeks to describe the context in which prophets are operating.

Defeating principalities and powers: Prophets in Harare

Religious beliefs and practices do not occur in a vacuum, and in order to appreciate the rise in prophetic activities in Harare, it is necessary to briefly highlight the changing economic, social and political conditions. Urban poverty has threatened to make political independence a nightmare for most Zimbabweans. Although Harare was built as an outstanding colonial city, it has faced numerous problems, such as overcrowding, inadequate sanitary and health facilities, and an increasing crime rate. The congested suburbs were originally built as sources of cheap labour for the white minority during the colonial period. It was assumed that blacks were only temporary residents. However, the attainment of political independence did not transform the status of the black majority in any radical manner. Emerging class interests ensured that these high density areas continued to have high incidences of poverty (Zinyama, Tevera and Cumming 1993). The only major transition that occurred upon the attainment of independence was that the African townships were renamed high density suburbs.

The adoption of ESAP in the 1990s saw an increase in retrenchments, hyperinflation, and a decline in the provision of social services. The phenomenon of children on the streets, orphans and other vulnerable children, became pronounced. Destitute women begging on the streets of Harare also increased in number (Chitando 2000:41). As their livelihoods came increasingly under threat, urban workers became more militant in their confrontation with the state. The Zimbabwe Congress of Trade Unions (ZCTU) staged a number of successful "stayaways" in its efforts to gain concessions from the state. For instance, the labour movement encouraged its members to stay at home during working days, thus hurting industry and commerce, as a method of forcing the state to accept its demands. The opposition Movement for Democratic Change (MDC), formed in 1999, enjoyed a lot of support from urban dwellers, underlining their frustration with the ruling party. Thus, as argued by Kamete, "Zimbabwe's urban residents have

31

staged a mass rebellion against the party to which they had owed their allegiance for two decades" (Kamete 2002:31).

It is within this context of suffering and despair in the late 1990s that Harare witnessed a marked increase in prophetic activities. Some members of AICs put up posters on public buildings, trees, bus stations, street lamps, and in other strategic places, announcing the presence of spiritual healers who promised to stop people's suffering (Chitando 2001:61). They issued an open invitation to individuals who suffered from various spiritual, social and economic problems to come and witness the power of the Holy Spirit. Some of the advertisements showed the prophet or prophetess in sacred regalia. The more enterprising ones claimed that they came from Chipinge, an area acclaimed for producing effective traditional healers. Chipinge is located in the eastern province of Manicaland, close to the border with Mozambique, a country reputed for having outstanding indigenous herbalists. However, the distinction between "prophets" (*maporofita*) and "traditional healers" (*n'anga*), remained contested by members of the public since they both appealed to the transcendent realm and treated similar cases. Both prophets and healers belong to the Zimbabwe National Traditional Healers Association (ZINATHA), a body responsible for the legitimisation and use of traditional medicine. However, prophets have sought to distinguish themselves from the traditional healers by emphasising their Christian identity. Their ZINATHA certificates have the Bible as a distinctive symbol, while they claim to be operating under the guidance of the Holy Spirit. This insistence on a Christian identity is meant to separate them from traditional healers and to counter accusations that they are indulging in African traditional religions. Due to the attacks on African traditional religions by most missionaries during the colonial period, many Zimbabwean Christians still seek to distance themselves from indigenous beliefs and practices.

My findings in Harare show that most prophets come from "spirit type" churches. These are churches that emphasise the role of the Holy Spirit in healing and religious experience. Although the typology continues to be the source of scholarly debate, it is possible to locate these churches within the broader context of Pentecostalism. Harvey Cox (1996:246) argues, "The African independent churches constitute an expression of the worldwide Pentecostal movement." In the context of uncertainty and struggle for meaningful existence, Pentecostalism encourages its adherents to approach life with optimism and hope. Thus, a recurrent theme found in most of the Pentecostal church services in Harare was, "in all these things we are more than conquerors through him who loved us" (Romans 8:37).

It requires a longer narrative to trace the rise of AICs in Zimbabwe (Daneel 1971). As noted by Daneel, these churches were mainly started by migrant workers from South Africa in the 1920s and operated in the rural areas. However, due to rural-urban migration, they gained footholds in urban areas and became popular amongst the lower classes. Today AICs have become an integral part of the urban landscape in Southern Africa, their adherents wearing distinctive attire and hairstyles. Zionist and Apostolic churches are highly visible in countries like Botswana, South Africa and Zimbabwe. Members of these churches are actively involved in the informal sector, and particularly cross-border trading. AICs constitute a very vibrant wing of African Christianity, although the younger Pentecostal/Charismatic churches have overtaken them in terms of expansion and growth. Central to the missionary efforts of AICs is the prophetic office, which I now will turn to, with a focus on the role and work of the prophets.

Prophetic activities in Harare

All the prophets who were interviewed claimed to be affiliated to specific churches. They maintained that independent prophets tend to be motivated by financial considerations and were largely false. Independent prophets do not operate under any religious authority. They manage their own affairs and are not answerable to any higher offices. They are free to charge their own consultation fees. Prophets affiliated to churches claim that independent prophets are not inspired by the Holy Spirit. One such prophet, Tatenda Mabhachi, argued, "Independent prophets are only concerned about making money." The ideology of prophetic calls in both the Old Testament and African traditional religions is that the individual, who has been chosen by the sacred, undergoes numerous trials. Furthermore, he or she does not derive any material benefits from undertaking sacred functions. In a harsh economic environment, any individual who claims to be guided by the Holy Spirit but makes financial gains is open to the charge of abusing religion.

Prophets who belong to AICs claim that church affiliation ensures that their services are supervised. Most of the churches I came across have vernacular names and describe themselves as Apostolic,[1] and thereby seek to cap-

---

1. Some of the churches include Signs of the Apostles (Zviratidzo ZvaVapostori), John the Baptist Apostolic Church (Johane Mubhabhatidzi Apostolic Church), Revelation Apostolic Church (Ruvheneko Apostolic Church) and Holy Angel Apostolic Church (Ngirozi Inoyera Apostolic Church). These names seek to portray the various splinter groups as authentic Christian movements based on apostolic succession.

ture particular revelatory experiences of the founder, as in Johane Masowe of the Seven Stars (Johane Masowe YeNyenyedzi Nomwe). All these churches have prophets who seek to ameliorate human suffering through spiritual healing.

Most of the prophets and people who utilise their services have a Shona cultural background.2 Shona traditional religious practices consist of interacting with *midzimu* (which can be translated as "ancestors") who are believed to reward and punish the living. Although Mwari, "the high God", is significant, traditional healers play an important role in ensuring people's health and prosperity. These traditional healers are believed to have the ability to interpret the spiritual world and to guide the living. The Shona, like many other people, do not make a rigid separation between physical and spiritual health as these are regarded as being inextricably intertwined (Bourdillon 1987). It is held that misfortune, disease and death emanate from unhealthy relationships between the realms of the living and the dead. My research findings show that respondents have been heavily influenced by such religious ideas, despite the impact of Christianity and its attack on indigenous knowledge systems.

Most of the respondents indicated that they regarded the prophets as specialists in illnesses emanating from *chivanhu* (the traditional worldview). They believe that these are issues that relate specifically to what they regard as peculiar Shona cultural demands such as appeasing the ancestors, fighting avenging spirits, exorcising the spirit of witchcraft and related phenomena. One respondent, a 34-year-old woman, who suffered from ulcers, illustrated this conviction when she said, "Prophets are able to address African problems, unlike medical doctors in the hospitals." Like the traditional healers, prophets are regarded as individuals who have privileged access to the spiritual realm, and thus are able to understand and treat "African problems".

Prophets therefore tend to handle illnesses that are considered unnatural or cultural. According to Gordon Chavunduka (1994:69), a Zimbabwean sociologist who conducted his studies in the 1980s, ancestor spirits, angered spirits, alien or stranger spirits, witches and sorcerers are held to cause "unnatural illnesses",3 such as mental illness and persistent headaches. In the advertisements, prophets claim that through the power of the Holy Spirit,

---

2. Although it could be argued that the term Shona is an invention that masks considerable diversity, it remains possible to use it to refer to people who speak related dialects and who share common cultural beliefs and practices.
3. "Unnatural illnesses" are believed to be caused by spiritual agents and cannot be treated, as opposed to "natural illnesses", which can be treated.

they are able to overcome all negative spiritual forces and to restore health. The prophets respond to the beliefs of their clients by upholding the existence of various spiritual forces that threaten prosperity. They adopt a communication strategy that suits the urban environment, namely the written word, to reach out to their potential clients. They also promise better employment opportunities and financial security to people who utilise their services.

The historical mission churches, also referred to as mainline churches, such as the Catholics, the Anglicans and the Methodists, have not been as creative in meeting the religious needs of African converts as the indigenous churches. Thus, members of the mainline churches sometimes utilise the services of the prophets, although they do so discreetly. The mainline churches were built by missionaries during the colonial period; they tend to follow the example of their mother churches in Europe and North America. The main difference between AICs and the mainline churches lies in the fact that the former are a result of African initiatives in mission, while the latter are a result of foreign missionaries. In addition, AICs tend to take the African worldview seriously, offering answers to issues such as witchcraft and other spirits. My research findings show that many members of mainline churches seek the services of prophets. Paul Garai, a member of the Seventh Day Adventist Church argued, "There are some spiritual issues that my pastor is unable to handle, therefore I take these to the prophets."

Alongside members of the mainline churches, some members of the newer Pentecostal churches also visit the prophets, albeit in a clandestine manner. These churches are characterised by their emphasis on faith, prosperity and modernity. They utilise contemporary communication strategies like the internet, radio and television. Attracting graduates and young professionals, the younger Pentecostal churches regard AICs as unsophisticated and emerging from an insufficient understanding of the biblical text. Preachers from the more recently established Pentecostal churches, condemn the prophets and ridicule some of their members who visit the prophets for help. Most of these younger Pentecostal churches were established in Harare in the 1990s. Rijk Van Dijk, who studied these churches in Malawi and Ghana in the 1990s, maintains that they have "created a kind of reflexive distance from the other independent churches, proclaiming their dissociation from syncretism by rejecting a whole array of traditional practices, purification and protection rituals and symbolic repertoires" (Van Dijk 2000:12). My findings in Harare confirm Van Dijk's observation as preachers from the younger Pentecostal churches, such as Christ Ministries, tend to caricature AIC prophets and project them as charlatans. These newer Pentecostal churches also discourage the use of prophetic healing objects, arguing that the Holy Spirit does not require symbolic attire for healing to occur. For their part, AIC prophets do not discriminate between clients on the basis of religious affiliation, but render their services to all those who require help in trying economic times.

Apart from handling cases that are physical and spiritual, such as bad luck, prophets also claim to have the ability to transform their clients' economic fortunes since it is argued that spiritual forces are responsible for urban poverty. A number of advertisements asked, "Does your money disappear without explanation? Are you failing to use money properly?" In many cases prophets allege that angry ancestral spirits cause their descendants to lack financial discipline. Alternatively, one's enemies can send a "mystical being", called a *chikwambo*, to drain one's finances. In an economy with four-digit inflation such as that of Zimbabwe, it is understandable that some individuals suspect that spiritual forces are responsible for the rapid depletion of their financial resources.

It is therefore possible to regard inflation in Zimbabwe as the contemporary *chikwambo* who mysteriously squeezes wealth from people. These objects and forces are believed to have the capacity to frustrate people and cause misfortune, such as ill-health, and loss of prosperity. It is held that ambitious individuals visit traditional healers to purchase the *chikwambo* whose duty is to bring wealth to its owner. However, in this process, the *chikwambo* destabilises the finances of the owner's relatives and while it causes rapid depletion of family resources for some family members, its owner, on the other, will gain wealth and prosperity in life. It is also argued that a *chikwambo* feeds on human blood, and this type of behaviour is used to explain any frequent deaths within the extended family. Sudden deaths or successive deaths within the family often give rise to suspicions that a *chikwambo* is at work. Individuals whose businesses used to be prosperous but have since collapsed are often accused of having owned a *chikwambo*. Prophets in Harare maintain that they can exorcise these negative spiritual forces through the power of the Holy Spirit. Through prayer, medicated water, spiritually charged fine stones, milk, holy threads, and various mixtures, they claim to overcome spirits bent on promoting poverty for some, and consequently, according to this cultural logic, wealth for others. In some instances, they prescribe cleansing rituals at one of the many "River Jordans" (*Jorodhani*) – rivers which, with reference to the Bible, are likened to the River Jordan – found in the city.

Clients who visit the prophets are clearly anxious about their survival in a stifling urban context. Although social status has some bearing on whether one seeks the services of the prophets, my findings show that individuals from the various social groups interact with prophets. While the three medical systems of traditional medicine, hospital health care and faith healing appear exclusive (Dahlin 2001:113), clients are constantly moving back and forth between treatment options in search of better health and prosperity and wellbeing. Business executives, medical doctors, priests from historic mission churches, nurses, computer experts and other professionals consult prophets. One prophet, Edgar Tapera, operating just outside the entrance of the University of Zimbabwe, claimed that university students and staff, employers and domestic workers from the neighbouring Alexandra Park, as well as European tourists, sought his help on various issues.

In search of a better life situation many people in Harare turn to the prophets. Although all the prophets interviewed acknowledged the challenges posed by the HIV/AIDS epidemic, they maintained that the Holy Spirit can effect miraculous healing – even of HIV/AIDS. They attend to people infected with the virus and pray for healing. Both the prophets and clients interpreted healing holistically to include the possibility of miracles and spiritual restoration. This interpretation of healing is proffered by other Christians in Zimbabwe, such as the Catholic women's groups who pray for the many who are suffering and dying of AIDS. The near-collapse of the health delivery system in Zimbabwe has also facilitated the rise in popularity of the prophets. Concerned relatives and friends have sometimes been forced to take patients to prophets after failing to raise hospital fees. The shortage of drugs and the exodus of qualified health personnel to other countries have had negative consequences for the health sector. Most prophets do not demand high fees from their clients, but commonly only ask for a token of appreciation. Their ideology, relying on the power of the Holy Spirit, also generates confidence in a community whose faith in the effectiveness of Western medicine has been shaken by the failure to find a cure for HIV/AIDS.

Overall, the hostile social and economic conditions prevailing in Harare since the late 1990s have been favourable to the increase in prophetic activities. Prices of essential commodities soared, while retrenchment was a constant threat for the poorly paid workers. The critical shortage of foreign currency threatened the viability of many businesses. As a response, many men and women felt called by God to mitigate the suffering. They also felt empowered by the Holy Spirit to defeat all principalities and powers that reduced the possibility of living full lives before death. A study conducted by Paul Gundani in Harare in the late 1990s summarises the prophetic activities thus:

> The posters and metal plates appeal to all who suffer from a myriad of physical, spiritual, social and psychic problems to come to the prophet for treatment and healing. The prophets claim to be able to treat patients suffering from all manner of illness caused by witchcraft and sorcery, chronic headaches, barrenness, impotence, stomach-ache, sexually transmitted infections, and a variety of cancers. Apart from these diseases the prophets also claim to be able to put an end to bouts of bad luck, which they claim to be responsible for a variety of misfortunes, ranging from unemployment, victimization at work, complicated pregnancy, family feuds, and loss of property through burglary and theft (Gundani 2001:137).

As prophetic activities increased in Harare in the late 1990s, people at various social locations utilised their services. However, my findings indicate that women constitute the majority of clients. It is mainly women who frequent the various healing places where prophets operate. The following section dwells on the interaction between women and prophets in Harare and highlights some of the reasons why women seek the healing services of the prophets.

Carrying multiple burdens: Women and prophetic activities

The category of gender has been firmly put on the agenda of the academic study of religion since the 1990s (see, for instance, King 1995). Many of these studies argue that women's low socio-economic status is largely responsible for their utilisation of the services of the prophets. It is crucial to pay attention to the dynamics of gender when analysing prophetic activities in Harare as women's and men's experiences of uncertainty are not similar.

Suffocated by patriarchal values and norms, many women turn to the prophets in the hope of getting spiritual support. Carrying multiple burdens, women congregate at the prophetic office anticipating that their loads will be made lighter. Trampled upon in the urban space where negative labels like *hure* (prostitute), *chirwere* (diseased), *ngozi* (dangerous or vengeful spirit) and others are ascribed to them (Mashiri 2000), women turn to the sacred realm for a sense of value and dignity. These negative Shona terms are used to portray urban women as carriers of dangerous diseases.

Many female respondents indicated that they visited prophets on matters relating to their fertility and reproductive health. Married women in particular were worried about barrenness. The pressure for women to have children was acute for women in both rural and urban areas. In most cases, they felt that the viability of their marriages depended on their ability to bear children. Prophets who claimed that they were able to restore women's fertility were therefore popular. So too were those who argued that they were able to facilitate the birth of a son. The vulnerability of women to male dominance and a system of inheritance which mainly favours men in the distribution of resources is brought out in such cases.

In the cause of seeking relief, some women have been sexually abused by prophets who prescribe sexual union as part of the "mystical transfer of the power of the Holy Spirit". Although some prophets, including prominent faith healers, have appeared in court over allegations of rape, this is only the tip of the iceberg. The prophetic claim of having unlimited spiritual power has forced many women to suffer in silence. The treatment of women as objects for male sexual pleasure is seen in these instances. In their anxiety to have children, many women have become dangerously exposed to sexual abuse. One woman, aged 21, summarised her situation thus: "These prophets use their spiritual powers to demand sexual favours from us." Another woman, 26 years old, narrated how a young prophet claimed that healing could only be effected if she would take off all her clothes. He subsequently raped her. "I carry heavy scars in my heart," she said. Many women also narrated cases about other women who had been sexually assaulted by prophets. Thus, it seems to be rather common for women to have such shocking experiences.

It seems that the spirit-type churches attract more women because they address their needs in a direct and vivid manner compared to men. The question of fertility is a burning one, and society continues to pressurise women to bear children. In their quest for children, many women have fallen prey to sexual violence. Many respondents noted that prophets encourage women to visit their healing cubicles alone during the night. Other prophets insist on retreating to sacred groves on the outskirts of Harare. In such circumstances the vulnerability of women increases. Furthermore, prophets threaten to cause the death of women who resist their moves. They claim to have unlimited spiritual powers that will allow them to punish the women should they expose them. There are also some women who consult prophets because they fear that they might be possessed by evil spirits. Still others are anxious that they might have inherited the spirit of witchcraft and fear that it soon will become active. Such is the case of a young university student, aged 21, who told me, "I dream about my deceased aunt who is bringing men an assortment of traditional medicines and I have therefore been visiting prophets for help." The young student interpreted these dreams as a sign that the spirit of witchcraft was coming upon her. In such instances the prophet may prescribe exorcism. The evil spirit that seeks to possess the woman is banished through the agency of the Holy Spirit. Prophets also encourage women to retreat to the *sowe* (sacred wilderness) in order to increase their spirituality. The *sowe* is a secluded place for intense prayer and interacting with God. It is a sacred space where adherents seek to be in contact with the sacred. Dressed in flowing white garments, these women have become a familiar sight in Harare. They regularly move away from the hustle and bustle of the city to have moments of prayer, solitude and meditation in the wilderness. Carrying multiple burdens, these women are empowered by their God – the one who, with reference to the Bible "chose what is weak in the world to shame the strong" (1 Corinthians 1:27).

Women constitute the majority in spirit-type churches in Harare. They face multiple challenges in a hostile urban context. Women also worry about their vulnerability to HIV infection.[4] In most instances, they have to find ways of feeding their families in a situation where essential commodities are scarce. While men have not been actively involved in providing care for the sick, women have taken the main burden and are the main caretakers of people living with HIV and AIDS. It is also women who sing into the night at the endless funeral wakes in Harare. Carrying their heavy crosses, women at varying social locations take time out by retreating to the sacred wilderness. It is therefore accurate to note that women in Zimbabwe "took to the wilderness church because of too much suffering" (Mukonyora 2000:6). The wilderness church refers to the tendency to retreat to the sacred groves and mountains, away from the mainstream activities.

However, women who utilise the services of the prophets do not regard themselves as helpless victims. Although they have been negatively affected by notions of domesticity, or lack of access to education, they are resolute and creative. Some female respondents indicated that prophets empowered them to start income-generating projects by praying for their ventures. Other women received holy water which they sprinkle on their goods/commodities for the cross-border trade. Enterprising women who are active in the informal sector visit prophets in the hope of boosting their sales. Through numerous strategies designed to ensure survival, women in Harare seek to tap sacred forces in their quest for better life.

---

4. Zimbabwe has some of the highest figures of infection in Southern Africa. The estimates are that one in every four adults is infected with HIV.

The prophetic ministry allows women to act as points of contact between women and the sacred. Vongai Mugeyi of the Holy Cross Apostolic Faith Church, for instance, specialises in mitigating the suffering of fellow women. She maintains that she started experiencing visions from an early age. When Vongai was 10 years old, a heavenly being ordered her to liberate women and to assist them when they are in labour and to resolve complicated pregnancies. Another woman, still in her teens, Kudzanai Mavhunje of the Johane Masowe WeChishanu Church, is well known in the Budiriro high-density area in the outskirts of Harare for being an expert in easing "period pains" through prayer and fasting. Yet another woman, Faith Mtwaro of the Johane Masowe Yenyenyedzi Nomwe, attends to mothers whose children may be suffering from various ailments. Mary Nhau of Ruvheneko Apostolic Church treats women with "painful wombs" and those who suffer from sexually transmitted infections. And still another woman, Janet Muhwati of Zviratidzo ZveVapostori Church, claims to heal women with cancer (*nhuta*, in Shona), as well as those with "bad luck" (*munyama*).

Thus, as indicated in the above examples, prophetesses appear to be more sensitive to the needs of women than male prophets are. Although criticisms relating to false prophets, and especially their sexual abuse of women, were directed at the prophetic office, there were fewer cases involving female healers. The general perception appeared to be that the prophetess was an authentic medium of the Holy Spirit. Her central task was to ameliorate human distress. Prophetesses attended to women from diverse social, economic and religious backgrounds. As female representatives of the divine, they equipped other women with the strength to face their challenges with optimism and courage. They brought out the extent to which religion is a helpful resource in the search for a meaningful existence. The following section discusses the importance of prophetic healing in Harare in relation to uncertainty.

Religion and anxiety in an African urban context: A discussion

The rise in popularity of prophets in Harare coincided with deteriorating social and economic conditions in the late 1990s. As individuals and families became more anxious about their prospects in a harsh economic environment, prophets assuaged their concerns. Proclaiming that "the name of Jesus defeated all wars" (*Zita raJesu rinokunda hondo dzose*), prophets sought to equip their clients to live for another day. As people developed phrases to describe their situation, such as "things are tight" (*zvakapressa*), and sought

41

to "solve their troubles" (*nhamo* or *zvinetswa*), many resorted to the prophets for help and support. From the sacred space within the prophet's wooden cabin, individuals and families emerged with their spirits renewed. Prophets empowered individuals to face the world. Familiar "No Work" signs adorning Harare's industrial areas are read differently by an individual armed with blessed stones from the sacred wilderness. News that a company is undertaking a massive retrenchment exercise does not alarm one who has taken a bath in holy water.

There seems to be a clear correlation between people's poor living conditions, joblessness and high inflation rates, on the one hand, and their tendency to seek relief in religion, on the other. It is, however, necessary to resist the danger of reducing religion to an epiphenomenon that can be explained completely by social and economic conditions. Phenomenologists of religion insist that religion may not be wholly explained by non-religious factors. They emphasise the insider's perspective.

In interpreting the role of prophets and their ways of addressing people's anxiety, it is possible to utilise insights from both phenomenology and the social sciences. From the phenomenological tradition, the notion of intentionality on the part of the prophets and their clients is of prime significance. They are not unconscious victims of a vicious economic system who helplessly turn to religion for support. The gods do not enter through human wounds, as some psychological reductionist theories of religion claim. Prophets and their clients are mentally balanced individuals who mount concrete economic strategies to make a living. These include such activities as basket weaving, running flea markets, and forming social clubs, to mention some. As noted earlier, some highly educated professionals are actively involved in the prophetic activities. Expensive vehicles are sometimes seen at a prophet's modest "surgery" as people of a high social standing seek the services of prophets.

Religion is a powerful resource that people use in negotiating uncertainty in an African urban context. Without reducing its practitioners to helpless individuals, it connects them to a transcendent realm where new possibilities abound. Through regular retreats to the wilderness, prophets and their clients seek to have time to be away from pressing everyday issues. This temporary respite, characterised by intense religiosity, is curative in both the physical and spiritual senses. Uncertainty about health and wealth are momentarily banished in the ecstatic seizures instigated by the Holy Spirit. The common white garment obliterates differences emerging from class, sex and education. In an environment characterised by grinding poverty, a high death rate – partly due to AIDS – and social strife, religion empowers its practitioners in unique ways. Prophets play an important role in providing holistic healing. Unlike hospital health care where the focus is exclusively on physical ailments, prophets endeavour to restore health in a comprehensive sense. They are concerned about their client's financial problems, marital tensions, demanding ancestors, and spirits that deplete family resources. Uncertainty relating to finding suitable marriage partners, or retrenchment and prospects for promotion, are banished through the intervention of the Holy Spirit. Religion has therefore been instrumental in allowing people to choose life where the chances of simply giving up are quite high.

It would appear that there is a contradiction between the sociological emphasis on the deteriorating economic conditions and the rise of prophetic activities, on the one hand, and the phenomenological insistence on the empowering role of religion, on the other. However, it is possible to regard the interpretations as complementary. In Harare, the worsening social and economic environment in the 1990s influenced many people to seek the services of prophets. To underscore this point, some highly educated individuals also sought spiritual guidance from the prophets.

Sanctified passports: Taking the exit option

While many people have chosen to continue the struggle for a better life in Harare, some have left the country in pursuit of better livelihoods. In her study of migrant Zimbabwean nurses and doctors in the 1990s, Rudo Gaidzanwa (1999) notes that the quest for better remuneration outside the country has seen the exodus of skilled personnel. The educated elite has been quite mobile, with many getting well-paid jobs in economic exile. They have been joined in the exodus by their less qualified compatriots. The Zimbabwean presence in Botswana and South Africa is pronounced. Others have gone to Europe, North America and wherever else they have been able to penetrate. Many congregations of Zimbabwe-based churches like the Family of God and the Apostolic Faith Mission are found in the United Kingdom. In an informative study, Gerrie Ter Haar (1998) maintains that such African Christians in Europe are "halfway to paradise". However, a lot of uncertainty haunts the prospective immigrant while still in Harare and a number of Zimbabweans have been deported while trying to enter the United Kingdom. The government of Zimbabwe gives maximum publicity to such cases as it desperately seeks to hold on to its human resources. The fear of deportation and anxiety surrounding life in economic and political exile has seen many prospective immigrants seeking the services of the prophets in Harare. Being the flexible sacred practitioners that they are, prophets have met the challenge in creative ways. In some instances, prophets take their clients to sacred pools, in one of the many "River Jordans", for cleansing rituals. The prospective immigrant is liberated from misfortune and "unprogressive lineage spirits" (*mweya yemadzinza*) that may prevent him or her from reaching the desired destination. Prophets may also pray over holy cords to be worn around the waist, or special sweets to be sucked just before meeting immigration officials. Or, in order to ensure a safe passage to economic exile, some prophets in Harare sanctify passports. They pray over passports and bless them in an endeavour to ensure that the owners do not get deported. Spiritually charged passports give peace of mind to their bearers as they seek to get to another country to change their economic fortunes. Zimbabweans based in Europe and North America have taken advantage of the acute shortage of foreign currency to emerge as leading investors. They have been particularly active in the purchase and building of beautiful mansions in the low-density areas of Harare.

Within the context of social and economic challenges in Harare, a passport ceases to be an ordinary document, but signals mobility and new opportunities. It potentially unlocks new worlds and promises economic liberation. In Harare, long and winding queues form at the passport offices as individuals and families seek new beginnings. Thus, when prophets pray over passports, they sanctify a mystical vehicle that transports one from the "House of Hunger" (Marechera 1978) to the "House of Plenty". Migration from Harare is seen by some as the great escape from an enervating environment to one of boundless opportunities.

By allowing clients to cope with deteriorating social and economic conditions, as well as blessing the passports of those opting out, prophets demonstrate their versatility. They highlight how religion speaks to adherents in different situations while reducing uncertainty. Prophets emerge as consultants for people in diverse circumstances. Through their appeal to the Holy Spirit, they minimise angst and suffering in an African urban context. They empower the dispirited and reinvigorate the drained worker. They resurrect dying hopes while vivifying the dreams of expectant immigrants. Prophets in Harare illustrate how the quest for ultimate wellbeing is at the core of religion (Prozesky 1984). In his analysis of the central concern of religion, and on the basis of his analysis of the key teachings of the various religions of the world, Prozesky concluded that religion seeks to ensure wellbeing. By addressing pressing social and economic problems in Harare, prophets demonstrate the extent to which religion equips adherents to face life with optimism and courage.

Conclusion

Residents of Harare have faced numerous challenges since the 1990s. They face great uncertainty in the various spheres of life. Prophets have emerged to counteract disillusion and despair. Although they do not proffer any radical political programme of action, they help individuals and the community to soldier on. Prophets address an array of issues that threaten prosperity in an urban context, by offering religious and practical solutions to the many uncertainties in the contemporary life of Harare urban dwellers.

In this chapter I have shown that the role of prophets in Harare is to assist their clients to face contemporary challenges in a harsh everyday life situation. I have also highlighted the fact that religious people are not passive and helpless but, rather, act upon their many troubles by engaging in concrete projects in an attempt to improve their lives. In the case of those who take their passports to the prophets for the document to be imbued with sacred power, the creativity is striking. These are individuals who are trying to ensure a safe passage to spaces that promise better opportunities. While other studies on prophets in Southern Africa have analysed the healing activities of the prophets in terms of recruitment strategies, this chapter illustrates how the prophets have diversified their activities to meet contemporary challenges. Cognisant of the pressing need for documents that radiate the power of the sacred, prophets have responded accordingly. Religious ideas from African traditional religions and Christianity are creatively blended in this exercise of sanctifying passports.

The upsurge in prophetic activities in Harare in the late 1990s also indicates the significance of religious responses in contexts of uncertainty. Through its ritual dimension, religion equips its followers to feel confident that they are doing something about their situation. Amidst social and economic upheavals, prophets empower their clients to face life with a sense of optimism. In an environment where life appears to be a long and arduous struggle, religion whispers words of comfort and encouragement. Prophets from spirit-type churches in Harare illustrate how religion seeks to challenge uncertainty in contemporary African lives.

Acknowledgements

I would like to thank the University of Zimbabwe Research Board for having awarded me a research grant that allowed me to undertake research for this chapter. I am also grateful to Deborah Tsveture who worked as a student research assistant.

References

Bourdillon, Michael F.C., 1987, *The Shona Peoples: An Ethnography of the Contemporary Shona, with Special Reference to their Religion.* Gweru: Mambo Press.

Chavunduka, Gordon, 1994, *Traditional Medicine in Modern Zimbabwe.* Harare: University of Zimbabwe Publications.

Chitando, Ezra, 2000, "The Image of God Among Destitute Women in Harare: Implications for Religious Studies in Africa", *Bulletin for Contextual Theology in Africa,* Vol. 7, No. 2, pp. 40–45.

—, 2001, "'Stop Suffering': An Examination of the Concepts of Knowledge and Power with Special Reference to Sacred Practitioners in Harare", *Religion and Theology,* Vol. 7, No. 1, pp. 56–68.

—, 2002, *Singing Culture: A Study of Gospel Music in Zimbabwe.* Research Report No. 121. Uppsala: Nordiska Afrikainstitutet.

Cox, Harvey, 1996, *Fire From Heaven: The Rise of Pentecostal Spirituality and the Reshaping of Religion in the Twenty-First Century.* London: Cassell.

Dahlin, Olov, 2001, *Zvinorwadza: Being a Patient in the Religious and Medical Plurality of the Mberengwa District, Zimbabwe.* Uppsala: Department of Theology, Uppsala University.

Daneel, Marthinus L., 1971, *Old and New in Southern Shona Independent Churches.* Volume 1. The Hague: Mouton.

Gaidzanwa, Rudo, 1999, *Voting with their Feet: Migrant Zimbabwean Nurses and Doctors in the Era of Structural Adjustment.* Research Report No. 111. Uppsala: Nordiska Afrikainstitutet.

Gibbon, Peter (ed.), 1995, *Structural Adjustment and the Working Poor in Zimbabwe.* Uppsala: Nordiska Afrikainstitutet.

Gundani, Paul, 2001, "Church, Media and Healing: A Case Study from Zimbabwe", *Word and World,* Vol. 21, No. 2, pp. 135–143.

Kamete, Amin Y., 2002, "The Rebels Within: Urban Zimbabwe in the Post-Election Period", in H. Melber, *Zimbabwe's Presidential Elections 2002: Evidence, Lessons and Implications.* Uppsala: Nordiska Afrikainstitutet.

King, Ursula (ed.), 1995, *Religion and Gender.* Oxford: Blackwell.

Marechera, Dambudzo, 1978, *The House of Hunger.* London: Heinemann.

Mashiri, Pedzisai, 2000, "Street Remarks, Address Rights and the Urban Female: Sociolinguistic Politics of Gender in Harare", *Zambezia*, Vol. 27, No. 1, pp. 55–70.

Mukonyora, Isabel, 2000, "Marginality and Protest in the Sacred Wilderness: The Role of Women in Shaping Masowe Thought", *Southern African Feminist Review*, Vol. 4, No. 2 and Vol. 5, No. 1, pp. 1–21.

Prozesky, Martin, 1984, *Religion and Ultimate Well-Being*. London: Macmillan.

Ter Haar, Gerrie, 1998, *Halfway to Paradise: African Christians in Europe*. Cardiff: Cardiff Academic Press.

The Revised Standard Version of the Bible, 1952. New York: Thomas Nielson.

Trudell, Barbara, 2002, "Introduction: Vulnerability and Opportunity Among Africa's Youth", in B. Trudell, K. King, S. McGrath, and P. Nugent, *Africa's Young Majority*. Edinburgh: Centre of African Studies, University of Edinburgh.

Van Dijk, Rijk, 2000, "Christian Fundamentalism in Sub-Saharan Africa: The Case of Pentecostalism", Occasional Paper, Centre of African Studies, University of Copenhagen.

Zinyama, L.M., D.S. Tevera and S.D. Cumming (eds), 1993, *Harare: The Growth and Problems of the City*. Harare: University of Zimbabwe Publications.

CHAPTER 2

Conditional Certainty:
Ugandan Charismatic Christians Striving
for Health and Harmony

Catrine Christiansen

Introduction

When travelling in any larger town in eastern Africa, one's attention is constantly drawn to the many colourful signs with their messages of "In God we trust", "Jesus saves", and "Jesus Paves the Way". In the swarm of cars, people and hens, and the noisy beeping and yelling, these bright signs on nearly every bus stand out as religious expressions in the public sphere. Taking into account the sorry state of many of these busses, the message "In God we trust" may promptly become relevant even to the most atheist traveller. These lucid Christian messages are repeated in the crusades that take place in city parks and at crossroads, often organised by Christians belonging to churches such as Divine Harvesters, Miracle Centre Church, Prayer Palace Christian Centre and Victory Christian Church. Within these fellowships, pastors and believers claim to heal any kind of illness, sorrow or pain one might be going through. As "pipelines" for Almighty God, they heal with the powers of the Lord. Whether it is physical, psychological or social hardship, individual or social, they guarantee that any kind of misfortune is healed.

The claims to certainty expressed in this kind of Christian religiosity are characteristic of the global wave of Charismatic Christianity, which during the past three decades has become extremely popular across Africa (see, for instance, Gifford 1998, 1994; Meyer 2004, 1999; van Dijk 2000; Maxwell 1998; Marshall 1993). The movement's attractiveness is often attributed to its North American origin and its spread from this epicentre of global culture with the processes of globalisation and modernisation (Marshall 1993; Meyer 1999; van Dijk 2000). Yet the appeal to African Christians is also ascribed to the correspondence between ideas concerning causes and remedies of affliction in local aetiologies and Charismatic Christianity (Meyer 1999; van Dijk 2000).[1] Based on research among Charismatic Christians

---

1. For a similar explanation of the popularity of Charismatic Christianity in India, see Caplan 1995.

in Ghana, Birgit Meyer argues that the recognition of local spirits and the ritual capability to deal with spiritual intrusion are crucial for understanding Christians' impetus to turn away from mainline to Charismatic Christianity (Meyer 1999:100–4, 174–5). Meyer follows the general critique that mission-based Christianity tends either to disregard local aetiologies of spiritual intrusion or to deal with such spiritual interference (Meyer 1999; van Dijk 2000; Kassimir 1999). In the African Christian context, the popularity of this recent version of Christianity is thus often closely related with the spiritual needs of African Christians to deal actively with affliction. Furthermore, in comparison with traditional ways of dealing with misfortune, as described for instance in Susan Whyte's ethnography on the Nyole in Uganda, it is striking that whereas traditional healing practices are performed in a mode of questioning and uncertainty, similar actions within Charismatic Christianity are performed in a mode dominated by clarity and certainty (Christiansen 2001).

This chapter explores the local constructions of certainty within the Charismatic Christian religiosity in Uganda and how adherents can live with certitude during prolonged insecurity. The analysis focuses on the objectified claims to assurance as well as on the practice of dealing with adversity in a mode dominated by certainty.

I argue that the relationship between the individual and God forms a key for understanding Charismatic claims to and experiences of certainty. This argument takes its point of departure in Michael Jackson's (1998) conceptualisation of intersubjectivity and Cecilie Rubow's (2000) analysis of how particular intersubjective relationships shape social worlds and structure people's ways of believing.[2] Jackson regards intersubjectivity as a dynamic field where the relation between self and other can be presumed as a balancing between the world within which one has a sense of control, or of navigation, and the world within which one experiences being an object of others' control (1998:8, 17–8; 1996:23–9). The constant efforts to strike such a balance are a condition of social existence, a condition between "being" – in the sense of the ability to act, influence and manoeuvre – and "nothingness", where an absence of options leaves the human being passive, speechless and unable to act (Jackson 1998:16–8). It is the "struggle for control that is the driving force of intersubjective life" (Jackson 1998:18).

---

2. Cecilie Rubow's analysis is based on ethnographic research into religiosity in the Danish National Church. For a discussion on the use of Rubow's findings in an African context, see Christiansen 2001.

Following this conceptualisation, certainty may be understood as personal beliefs and experience in being able to manage the relations between self and others. This perspective seems particularly relevant in an African context where individuals are commonly believed to be open and susceptible to forces from outside (Meyer 1999:205).

The notion of intersubjectivity as personal experience of manoeuvring relations is also the focal point in Rubow's analysis of religiosity among Danish Christians (Rubow 2000). In her research, Rubow approaches faith as attention to what is beyond the materiality and knowledge of everyday phenomena (Rubow 2000:10–11). In this sense, faith is part of people's imaginations, trust, assumptions, desires and hopes, all of which influence relations between human beings, and between humans and their social world. The ways in which people imagine and experience their social world create patterns, where certain understandings of phenomena, such as sickness and suffering, become more plausible than others (see also Mitchell 1997:86–9). Ways of believing are consequently interrelated with particular worldviews. In her analysis of Christian ways of believing, Rubow identifies three types of relationships between human and transcendent beings that Christians constantly move between when they seek to understand vital occurrences as well as their everyday life. The three relations are characterised by various degrees of human ability to influence the transcendent beings and will be introduced below.

In the first kind of relationship God is perceived as "the radical other", the Father and Creator who has withdrawn from the human world and whose ways are beyond human influence and comprehension (Rubow 2000:90–2). The second kind of relationship is characterised by an understanding of God as someone who has momentarily united with human beings – that is, God has become part of the social world of the living people. Jesus Christ is recognised as the most remarkable instrument of divine union with the world (Rubow 2000:92–4), but appearances of the Holy Spirit in, for instance, rituals, individual dreams and prayers can also be interpreted as signs of divine union. In the Ugandan Christian context, ancestral and other local spirits may also fuse with living people.[3] While the presence of these spirits is perceived with ambiguity both traditionally and among nominal Christians (being seen, for example, as messengers of advice and as causes of illness and hardship), within Charismatic Christianity the spirits are reduced to

---

3. For a detailed description of diverse categories of spirits see Whyte (1997:87–155).

unequivocal demons (Meyer 1999:40–47). Furthermore, it is characteristic for Charismatic Christians to assign more power to the (evil) spirits and to interpret any kind of misfortune as a demonic manifestation (Meyer 1999; Asamoah–Gyadu 2005:180–87). These manifestations do not leave converts in a world ruled by evil, since Charismatic Christians believe that God is interested in rescuing His people from evil influence. In the ritual settings of faith healing, converts can demand the presence of God to empower them to cast out demons. The ability to make such demands refers to a third type of relationship, which rests on notions of reciprocity and mutual influence between human beings and God (Rubow 2000:94–96). I argue that the Ugandan Charismatic Christians seek a reciprocal relationship with God, a relationship in which the individual through thoughts and actions can invoke God's grace, and through the Almighty's power feel assured about his or her own wellbeing. I argue, thus, that the Charismatic way of believing is oriented towards the certainty implied in the third type of relationship with God. This relationship is, however, only one out of three simultaneous relations between human beings and God – and the two other relations are characterised by God being either the "radical other" or being immanent in the world of human beings but difficult to affect – so this Christian way of believing consists of certainties as well as uncertainties.

The argument will be illustrated by drawing upon ethnographic research on connections between faith, health, and social networks among Christians in Busia district since 1999. Busia district is situated in the south-eastern corner of Uganda, bordering with Kenya on the eastern side and the shores of Lake Victoria on the southern side. Busia town is located in the northern part of the district along the highway connecting Central Africa with the ports of Mombasa and is a place with a constant flux of goods and people. Until the late 1980s most goods never reached the clearance points since local inhabitants took advantage of the country's instability to enrich themselves through smuggling goods such as petrol, sugar, coffee and paraffin. When Museveni became president, smuggling decreased quite rapidly, affecting household economies to the extent that women who had become second, third or fourth wives to men engaged in this profitable business had to be "sent home" (Katahoire 1998:26-7). Ugandan soldiers are permanently stationed in the area to control smuggling activities, although this trade no longer engages the common man who instead bases his living on subsistence cultivation and, to a lesser degree, fishing. Means of employment are sparse although small industries such as a fish factory and a beach resort have recently been established. In addition to economic poverty, the district is marked by the consequences of the AIDS epidemic. While the country as a whole has succeeded in reducing HIV prevalence to about 6%, prevalence in the Busia district is sustained at about 13% (UNAIDS 2004), the mobility within the border town (Obbo 1993) and the fishing villages probably being important factors in this. Apart from the border town, Busia district consists of rural areas, inhabited by roughly 230,000 people, primarily the Samia ethnic group (Christiansen 2001).[4] Kinship among the Samia is patrilineal and virilocal, meaning that children are born into their father's clan and remain members of this clan throughout their lives. Although clan membership is an important marker of identity and engages bonds of affection, the former stronghold of clans as the means of access to resources is declining.

Catholic and Anglican missionaries began evangelising in the beginning of the 20th century and dominated the religious landscape until the late 1980s when Charismatic preachers started evangelising. Situated on the border with Kenya, the area soon witnessed a spillover of preachers moving across to set up Charismatic churches in Uganda. In 1999, the district hosted 45 churches with evocative names such as Divine Harvesters and Miracle Palace and regularlopen-air crusades with hundreds of people gathering in the afternoon to listen, praise, pray and be healed by the power of God. At these services, preachers often predicted that God would appear at a particular time and place to heal people from any kind of suffering. In the initial months of my research in 1999, I attributed Charismatic expressions such as "The Holy Spirit will descend at 2 am" to inaccurate translation from Lusamia into English. Gradually, however, I became aware of the significance of this certainty for understanding a central characteristic of Samia Charismatic religiosity: namely, its ability to invoke God's spirit in healing rituals.

This chapter will draw on the beliefs of a Charismatic pastor, Martin Ouma, who has experienced a prolonged period of domestic insecurity.[5] Martin's case illustrates a personal striving to maintain a sense of certainty, which I argue is characteristic of Charismatic religiosity, that God will provide for those who follow Him.[6]

---

4. The Samia belong to the larger *Abaluya* group and they speak a language classified as Bantu and related to the Luyia languages (Katahoire 1998; Cattell 1992).
5. All names are pseudonyms.
6. The example of this pastor is particularly illustrative because the pastor clearly articulates the ideas that make up the Charismatic Christian worldview and, in his long struggle to resolve personal problems, he must manoeuvre between the extremes of this enchanted world.

Before attending to the case of how a person can sustain certainty while experiencing immense uncertainty, the chapter will describe the constructions of certainty within Charismatic Christianity by looking into the transformative processes of conversion and the importance of adherence to a particular lifestyle. First, however, I will introduce the reader to the Christian landscape in Uganda.

Charismatic christianity in Uganda

The Christian landscape in Uganda has changed markedly since the National Resistance Movement (NRM) came to power in 1986 as this political context created the space for an influx of Charismatic churches and popular expressions of Christianity within the mission-based churches (Kassimir 1999:248–49). During colonial times, the Roman Catholic Church and the Anglican Church of Uganda shared a virtual monopoly among the approximately 85% Ugandans who were Christians. This Christian dualism was sustained during the period of national insecurity under the regimes of Amin and Obote after independence in 1962 (Kassimir 1999; Sundkler and Steed 2000:1006–11; Gifford 1998:151–2). With the reopening of the borders, a new socio-political context provided space for a range of Christian movements, the most profound one being the global wave of Charismatic Christianity (Gifford 1998:153).[7] This recent version of Christianity has led to the founding of numerous denominations and to revival movements within the mainline churches such as the Charismatic Renewal within the Catholic Church (Gifford 1998:150–68; for Ghana see Meyer 1999; for Kenya see Cattell 1992; for Zambia see Ter Haar 1992; for India see Caplan 1995).[8] It is important to note that since the 1930s, the Church of Uganda has been influenced by a revival movement, namely the East African Revival, with many characteristics similar to Pentecostalism,. This movement had its roots in the Anglican Church in neighbouring Rwanda and spread throughout East Africa (Ward 1989; Garrard 2002:273; Gifford 1998:152). The revival essentially consisted in a lay community emphasising the personal commitment of faith, high moral standards, and an

---

7. The most dramatic development was the Holy Spirit Movement of Alice Lakwena, which later led to the Lord's Resistance Army that is still causing major security problems in the northern region of the country (see Behrend 1999).

8. Due to lack of systematic, comparative research on Charismatic Christianity in Africa, it is not possible to explain why this strand of Christianity arose earlier and on a more massive scale in the former British colonies (Meyer 2004:453).

unbending rejection of any assimilation between the church and the world (Gifford 1998:152). Adherents call themselves *Balokole*, which in Luganda[9] literally means "the saved people". During two decades of influence from Charismatic Christianity, a fraction of the *Balokole* has attempted to accommodate healing practices within the movement, based on the rationale that failure to include healing practices is a main reason for members shifting to Charismatic churches (Christiansen 2001). Paradoxically, the revival movement may have provided space for the general acceptance of Charismatic Christianity in Uganda where, as David Maxwell notes, adherents are so numerous and their leaders so prominent that Charismatic Christianity has become as mainstreamed as the established Anglicanism and Catholicism (2006). Due to their focus on salvation, Protestant converts are also called *Balokole,* whereas adherents belonging to the Charismatic revival in the Catholic Church are called *Ohwekaluhania buyaha*, which translates as "the revived people".[10] In order to include both the *Balokole* and the Catholic "revived people" in one term, I will use the local jargon of "Savedees".

Choosing God: Conversion and cosmology

The central tenet of Charismatic Christianity is that each individual must accept Jesus as his or her personal saviour (Caplan 1995:103), or, as it is also phrased, every individual must become "born again" (Maxwell 1998:353; Meyer 1998:318). To proclaim salvation is considered an assertion of faith that transforms the individual person's life and his/her relationship with God. Samia converts expressed the turning point as an inner transformation of the individual; as they put it, "the double-hearted person becomes one-hearted". Among the Samia, the notion prevails that a human being is born with *emyoyo chibiri,* which means "two spirits resting in the heart". By nature humans are hence connected with spiritual beings that fill up the "spiritual vacuum" in the individual's physical heart. In the local culture, these spirits are understood as ambiguous beings, a duplicity that predisposes people to think and act for the benefit as well as for the harm and destruction of others. Savedees, however, reduce this ambiguity of spirits

9.   Luganda is the language of the Baganda, the largest ethnic group who live in the heartland of Uganda.
10. The main difference between the local Protestant and the Catholic versions of Charismatic Christianity is the question of whether a living human being can be certain of salvation in the hereafter. For futher distinctions, see Christiansen (2001:36–42).

and talk instead of two types of spirits: good spirits that are Christian spirits guided by the Holy Spirit, and referred to as *emyoyo omuhulundu,* literally meaning "the Almighty spirit", and bad spirits that are agents of the most powerful evil spirit called Satan (*Sitani*). According to Savedees, the Holy Spirit, which resides as a potential in everybody's heart, wakes up when a person proclaims salvation. This awakening leads the person to be guided only by the Holy Spirit, hence the metaphor that the person *"becomes one-hearted".* The awakening strengthens the personal relationship with God, and simultaneously the person's relations with other living people and the deceased are significantly reduced. Savedees speak of this transformation as an emancipation from kinship ties with the living and the deceased, and maintain that this freeing makes it impossible for others to interfere with their life through witchcraft or other evil actions. For converts, life before and life after conversion are therefore clearly distinguished from each other, and converts underline this turning point in their personal conversion stories by giving the year, date and situation in which they chose salvation.

The discursive emphasis on salvation as a rupture from the individual's prior way of living and the person's freeing from kinship ties reflects, according to Meyer, "the construction of a modern individual realizing a new independent life" (1999:337). The transformative process of conversion does, however, not imply a complete break with the person's past. On the contrary, Savedees, similarly to other African Charismatic Christians (see, for instance, Meyer 1999; Gifford 2004, 1998; Maxwell 1998), continue to live with kinship interferences. Neither does the transformation make the individual autonomous, freed from any vital relations with others. The transformation into becoming "one-hearted" seems, however, to give a sense of increased closeness to God. This is symbolised, for instance, in the notion that the convert becomes part of God's lineage, with Moses, Abraham and Jesus as ancestors. In the social context, the new family is made up of other Savedees with whom the convert is expected to strive to maintain a state of inner purity necessary to maintain relations with the Holy Spirit. Following the concept of intersubjectivity, the transformative dimensions of conversion consist, on the one hand, of a strengthening of the person's relationship with God and, on the other, of a weakening of the relations between the convert and potentially harmful people and evil ancestral spirits in his/her social world. These alterations lead to a notion that the relationship with God becomes superior to all other relations and the convert becomes accountable to God alone. Resting on a belief that God is unequivocally good and wants to dealing with any issues that make His people suffer, conversion can be understood as empowerment of the individual convert to control his/her life trajectory. In this sense, conversion entails an enlarged space within which the convert gains a sense of control over negative interferences (cf. Jackson 1998).

It is significant to note that this individual empowerment takes place in a cosmology clearly divided into a dualism between God and Satan. Whereas other Samia Christians believe spirits to be ambiguous beings, Savedees tend to demonise spirits, to say that spirits can only be evil. The reduced ambiguity of the cosmology contributes to the construction of a world within which one knows who to relate with and who to detach oneself from: a simplified world that one can manoeuvre in with more aptitude and certainty (cf. Jackson 1998). However, as Meyer has illustrated comprehensively in her book *Translating the Devil*, the demonisation of local spirits has within Charismatic churches led to a detailed discourse on the Devil and to perceptions of spirits as beings who pose a constant danger to people, threatening to make them objects of their evil (1999:40–7, 83–5, 103–10, 171–4). This idea about lasting evil pressure on the lives of human beings is interrelated with the understanding of any kind of antisocial behaviour, psychological troubles and illness as spiritual interference (Meyer 1998:323).[11] A basic difference between Savedees and other Samia Christians is exactly this combination of demonising local spirits and interpreting any kind of misfortune and behaviour disruptive of social concord as demonic intrusion. These changed notions do not leave Savedees in a re-enchanted world where evil rules. On the contrary, Savedees believe that Almighty God is willing to partake in every human encounter with evil. But the goodness of God is not given arbitrarily to anyone. The transformative process of conversion is an essential first step, but – equally essential – the convert must unceasingly confirm the personal bond with God.

Holy guidance and demonic temptations

After a person has proclaimed salvation, the convert is re-socialised into a fellowship of Savedees, as Maxwell describes:

11. In Ghanian Charismatic churches acute poverty is also included in the catalogue of behaviour and conditions that are regarded as a result of sin or spiritual interference. The inclusion of poverty can be understood in the context of widespread preaching according to a theology where faithfulness is supposed to materialise in prosperity (Meyer 1998:323). In Uganda, the predominant theology is based on the faith gospel, with a focus on healing rather than prosperity in a material sense (Gifford 1998:161–7).

> The new believer is captured and remade in two ways: first, through the continuous involvement in religious, social and welfare activities centred upon the church; secondly through abstinence from what are popularly described as "traditional" rituals and practices and by means of participation in Christian alternatives (Maxwell 1998:353).

Prayer meetings, bible studies, crusades, trans-night prayers, and home visits provide an array of scenes for fellowship with other Savedees and for new converts to accommodate the key Charismatic teachings on faith, behaviour, prayer, healing and spiritual warfare. Assisted by modern electronic instruments, such as keyboards, and/or local drums, the praising and worshipping are expressed in a lively liturgy and in an egalitarian manner, making room for anyone in the congregation to lead the singing prayers such as "Put your burdens on to Jesus for he cares for you". It is through participation in these activities that converts may accommodate the truth-claims of Charismatic Christianity such as the urge to convert and to follow the prescribed behaviour. In addition to the importance paid to learning from the Holy Scripture, Savedees often tell about being influenced by listening to personal testimonies of divine intervention. Towards the end of a prayer session or any other event, members of the congregation testify recent experiences in the spiritual realm. One example is from a Sunday service, in mid-1999, in a village-based gospel church where an adult man testified the following:

> Praise the Lord. I have been disturbed by the demons of alcohol, they disturbed me so much before I became a man of God. Two weeks ago, the demons showed up in my brother (demons guided the brother's behaviour) and convinced me to drink *amalwa* (local brew). Oh, I drank so much, and the next day I just wanted to continue. Then God showed Himself in our pastor [as] he came to my house and we discussed my problem. We prayed to God for forgiveness, and I can say now that God has forgiven me that sin, and with the Holy Spirit I will remain firm and never let those evil spirits disturb me again – hallelujah – that is why I stand [here now] to praise our great Lord.[12]

In the testimonies, Savedees express the numerous ways God intervenes in their own suffering and they assert that strong faith and a close personal relationship with the divine enables them to overcome any hardship. In conjunction with this notion of divine intervention is an understanding that

---

12. The numerous "halleluja", "amen" and pauses have been omitted in this and other quotations.

evil spirits entice a person who is not constantly alert and strong in faith. It is common that evil spirits influence Savedees to commit the very sins they want to leave behind, as illustrated in the above testimony by a man who could not control his alcohol habits. As Meyer notes, past sinful behaviour is "represented as autonomous entities still able to haunt a person even after he or she underwent a profound change" (Meyer 1998:323). This image is notably different from non-saved Samia Christians, who would most probably read excessive intake of alcohol as a bad habit without necessarily linking this behaviour to a spiritual influence. For Savedees, on the other hand, every thought and every act reflects whether the person follows the guidance of God or Satan. As a female pastor in the Elim Church explained:

> The spirits are in your heart, the good ones and the bad ones, and they guide your thoughts and everything you do with your body. Before a saved person does anything you must think twice, so you are aware of what you are about to do. Is it the way of God? [Or] is it the way of the demons? Then you decide what to do. We Samia don't think with our head only, we think with both our head and our heart. In fact, you cannot separate the two, our thoughts and our deeds are one.

A consequence of the notion that thoughts and actions are indicative of either divine or demonic guidance is the constant strengthening of ties between the person and the spiritual being. When a Savedee acts according to *"the way of God"* this reinforces the relationship or, as the above testimony illustrates, when a person gives in to the *"demons of alcohol"* his/her desires increase for more of this allegedly sinful behaviour. Interestingly, while the interlacing of thoughts and deeds with human-spiritual relations reflects a re-enchanted worldview, the individual responsibility to *"think twice"* – to consider which spiritual guidance to follow – underlines human detachment from spiritual influence. On the one hand, Savedees consider human beings to be born with relations to spiritual beings which have considerable influence on human lives and, on the other hand, they maintain a cultural recognition of a self, an autonomous capacity and willpower that enables humans to make choices independently of spiritual beings. Although Samia Savedees can be seen to re-enchant the cultural worldview and attribute virtually any failure or success to spiritual power, this re-enchantment does not diminish the identification of the individual self. The emphasis on, rather than diminution of, the individual capacity to make decisions and maintain a sense of self in a world with powerful spiritual entities can, according to Meyer, be associated with the individualisation of Charismatic Christianity

(Meyer 1999). From the perspective of intersubjectivity, the prominence of the individual self is crucial for the converts in order for them to sustain a sense of being a partner in the relations with the powerful spiritual beings. Without a sense of a solid self, converts would be left powerless, in the control of spiritual beings (cf. Jackson 1998). Thus my point is that the notion of a human self, able to make decisions about ways of living, is crucial for understanding the Charismatic claims of certainties through the relationship between the individual person and God. It is the individual person who decides to commit her/himself to the unequivocal God (proclaim conversion), and with the transformative power of *"becoming one-hearted"* the convert must strive to maintain this closer tie with God.

With references to Paul's 'First Letter to the Corinthians' (The Bible I Cor. XII:4–11), conversion is assumed to provide the converts with one or more of the powers or gifts (charisms) of the Holy Spirit. As explained by Martin, a pastor in the Divine Church and whose story I will later describe in more detail:

> We call the fruits and the gifts of the Holy Spirit the graces of God, and they come out in so many ways. There are the gifts of prophecy, preaching, and speaking in tongues. The greatest gift is the one of healing. God gives us these gifts to make us know that even though Jesus is no longer here, actually, He is here with us all the time. We just don't see His body like you see mine.

According to Savedees, the fruits of conversion are as much material as they are spiritual: apart from a guaranteed place in Heaven, Savedees are promised health, success, happy family lives and pleasing conditions in which to enjoy them. Such gifts can enable Savedees to improve their own life as well as the livelihood of others. Yet these gifts are of a temporary nature, and God can withdraw them if the convert does not follow His guidance as spelled out in the Bible and by the Charismatic pastors. The most important gift of all is healing, since it provides the Savedees with the ability to deal with hardship – it is through healing powers that Savedees can ultimately combat evil interference.

Before turning to the divine gifts in rituals of deliverance, it is important to note the assurance expressed for instance by the pastor quoted above *"even though Jesus is no longer here, in fact, He is here with us all the time"*. All the facets of the Charismatic liturgy – the songs, prayers, worship, preaching and testimonies – are oriented towards human experiences of God's presence. The experiences are structured according to a narrative about human misery stemming from failure to defeat evil influence, and then God unites with "His people" (that is, He empowers Savedees with gifts of the Holy Spirit) to emancipate the person. This liturgical emphasis on personal experiences of the union with God does not negate the importance of doctrinal formalities, but rather relates to the tendency among African Charismatic Christians to "centre their Christianity on the experience of God the Holy Spirit, seeing this experience as the heartbeat of their faith" (Asamoah-Gyadu 2005:7; see also Marshall-Fratani 1998). It is a liturgical practice oriented towards enduring and empowering relationships with a present God, who engages in reciprocity with those who follow Him. Following the described reasoning when a Savedee adheres to the prescribed lifestyle, God empowers the person with divine gifts to improve his/her life.

Regulating relations: Health rituals

Relationships between human and transcendent beings may, as noted above, take various forms characterised by different degrees of human ability to influence the transcendent beings. Inspired by Rubow's (2000) identification of three types of relationship, this section gives an in-depth analysis of the relationships between a Savedee (person) and God, arguing that these relationships form a key for understanding the Charismatic claims to certainty. A detailed description of a ritual of faith healing will form an apt basis for analysis, partly because the ritual process dramatises different relations between human and spiritual beings. Since this dramatisation of relations is intertwined with the ritual construction of certainty, the description will furthermore contribute to the argument that these rituals are performed in a mode dominated by certainty.

Rituals of faith healing are basically prayer sessions that follow a certain structure, but vary considerably in expression. The setting can be a prayer meeting, a crusade, a seminar, a all-night prayer session, or a visit to a patient at home or in hospital – in other words it can be just about any place where Savedees gather. As Savedees are supposedly under constant exposure to powerful evil influence, healing rituals are a central part of the pastoral care, which, as Asamoah-Gyadu writes from research among Charismatic Christians in Ghana, aims at bringing converts' lives "*fully* under the control of the Spirit" (Asamoah-Gyadu 2005:168, original emphasis). Before turning to the ritual performance, it is necessary to provide some background information on the persons involved.

Martin, the previously quoted pastor from the Divine Church, and his wife, Justine, had been married for 10 years and brought four children into the world but the disharmony in their marriage was threatening to become permanent. They had both been saved for about five years and Martin had worked hard to establish a small church and a reputation as a strong healer. During their evening prayers, the couple had prayed for the restoration of domestic harmony. Their faith and prayers did not, however, solve their marital disputes. During a Sunday service in Martin's congregation, joined by several other Savedee pastors, the couple required the gathering to assist in restoring their marital harmony. Martin narrated:

> It was during the time where any person can come forward with a problem to be prayed for. Together with the other pastors I had prayed hard for the demons to leave these other people [other Savedees]. Then Justine and I kneeled down, the pastors and some very strong people [members of the congregation who are strong in faith] made a circle around us, each [of them] touching Justine or myself. Pastor Okello [a locally respected healer] led the prayers, but we all prayed hard. We praised the Almighty Lord for His wonders, the Creator of the earth and the sky, the ruler of the universe, the omnipresent Lord who binds evil, made His son suffer for the sinfulness of all human beings, defeated death and paved the way for salvation, and makes us people see just how powerful He is. Oh, we praised God and we praised our salvation. Hallelujah! The demons started speaking in Justine. Oh, she was shaking and speaking very fast. It was the demons of fornication and lust that spoke. Pastor Okello commanded the Holy Spirit to fill him. To fill the strong believers so they together could cast out the demons. I was overwhelmed by the Spirit, filled completely. In the name of Jesus Christ, our Lord and saviour, we sent those spirits out of her body. We commanded them never to come back to this home. Then we praised God. Hallelujah!

Thus, in the social situation of a church service, the couple asks fellow Savedees to join them in their prayers for divine intervention to restore the marriage. The ritual follows a structure in which participants begin by praising the Almighty God who is distinctively different from sinful human beings and who made His son suffer for the sake of humankind's salvation. "We praised our salvation" indicates a shift in focus to the people gathered at the service, each of whom has made the choice of salvation and strives to live in faithfulness to God. In the initial phase of the ritual, the relationship between human beings and God thus moves from one in which God is considered as a "radical other" – in the sense of God being a distant Creator withdrawn from the human world – to a relationship in which God is taking part in the human world through His incarnation in Jesus Christ and appearances of the Holy Spirit. While referring to to the distant omnipotent God is essential to the belief in divine ability to combat evil powers – and as I will discuss below, to explain short-term effects of a healing ritual – it is significant that the praise quickly shifts to a focus on divine manifestations in the lives of human beings. The praise often consists of references to biblical stories about the apostles' experiences with Christ, their faith and doubts. The act of praising the God who suffered so as to reunite with human beings, followed by an appreciation of the people who have chosen God's direction, can be understood as an expressive performance of a this-worldly union between Savedees and God.

When "the demons started speaking" the ritual becomes, as Meyer phrases it, "an arena of spiritual warfare" (Meyer 1998:321) between Satan and God, manifested respectively in the inflicted person and the group of healers. According to Savedees, it is the divine presence that evokes demons to announce their sway over the inflicted person. Demons "speak out" through the voice of the inflicted or through signs like screaming, heavy sweating, trembling or vomiting. In the above case, *"demons of fornication, demons of lust"* explicitly announce their sway over Justine as she is physically shaking and speaking abnormally. Extramarital relations are regarded as a sin, so the demonic manifestations are interpreted as a diagnosis of the cause of marital plight.

The demonic presence takes the ritual process to a phase of deliverance, and the leading pastor *"commanded the Holy Spirit to fill him, fill the strong believers so they together could cast out the demons"*. The pastor and the gathered group of Savedees thus demand the Holy Spirit to use them as *"pipelines of the divine powers"* since this empowers them to bind the demons. Such human anticipation reflects a marked weakening in the transcendence of God. This weakening is based on notions of a reciprocal relationship between human beings and God: provided the individual adheres to God's conditions (faith expressed in conversion and lifestyle), he or she will experience God's grace (gifts of the Holy Spirit). For Savedees, this reciprocity entails notions of God as someone who can be merciful and loving as well as fiercely angry and rebuking, hence He is someone with whom humans can engage in a relationship. A significant feature of this relationship with God is that one can be certain that He, being unambiguous, will realise His promises. The calls on Him to fill them with the Holy Spirit are thus made in the certainty that God provides for those who follow Him.

With loud commanding words of authority, demons are then cast out "in the name of Jesus Christ". This process may take form of shattering discussions between God, manifested in the leading pastor, and the demons, manifested in the inflicted person. The discussions are believed to reflect the power of Satan and the anointing of the gathered people. At no time does the battle point to weaknesses in God's power. Although the deliverance may take time – and occasionally require additional firm healers – God's power always casts out the demons, and the ritual thus ends with the congregation praising Almighty God for His intervention.

The ritual construction of certainty can be understood as a dramatisation of relations between human beings and God. The dramatisation follows a structure that moves from human praise of God's radical otherness, to the praise of God for taking part in the human world, and, finally, to the anticipation that God will unite with the particular people at that very moment. This ritual process provides space for Savedees to experience the certainty so profoundly expressed among Charismatic Christians that a firm personal relationship with the unequivocal God entails a guarantee of healing.

It is crucial to recognise the importance of the personal experience "that proves the reality of doctrine through practical expression" in coming to believe in the certainties claimed (Asamoah-Gyadu 2005:8). As William James argued in his philosophical analysis of religious experiences, the most profound moments of certainty may occur when embodied and objectified knowledge are mutually enhancing (James 1902/1994:116–20). Among the Samia, the truth of the Bible is unquestionable and so is the presence of spirits. In the healing rituals, the truth of the Bible and the presence of spirits are mutually enhanced through the possession of, respectively, Justine – by local spirits – and the preachers – by God. As Lambek argues on the basis of Muslim rituals in the Indian Ocean, it is the simultaneous spiritual presence, referring to two different forms of knowledge (textual and embodied), that produces a persuasive ritual power based on "an embodiment of the text and a textualization of the body" (Lambek 1995:264). Ritual participation renders the experience that demonic presence precedes the more powerful divine authority, and while spirits are not Christian, the gathered people truly are.

A brief comparison of Charismatic practice with traditional ways of dealing with misfortunes further illustrates how Charismatic healing rituals are performed in a mode of certainty. Among the Nyole of eastern Uganda, the traditional ways of dealing with misfortunes such as prolonged illness and domestic dissonance are marked by "questioning, doubting, and trying out" (Whyte 1997:3). The Nyole generally try out medicines, rituals and the skills of various experts in their attempts to alleviate a problem and thus reduce uncertainty. Diviners play a key role in the processes of understanding the cause of the problem and the required actions. Divinations take the form of dialogues between the diviner and the client who negotiate which agents – spirits or human – could be the cause of the matter at hand. In this non-saved context, spirits are considered ambiguous, and to have the capacity to mislead the diviner, so clients may approach several experts before taking further action. Ambiguities and uncertainty are, according to Whyte, "acknowledged as a characteristic of both the experience of misfortune and the process of dealing with it" (Whyte 1997:19). This stands in stark contrast to the Samia Savedee healing rituals which identify one cause (demonic influence), one solution (divine intervention) and one ritual means (faith healing). In fact, it is not necessary for the individual to determine the cause of the hardship as the divine powers are all-pervading and, provided the healing group consists of converts living appropriate lives, the unequivocal God will combat the demons. Whereas diviners and clients negotiate the cause and the remedy, in the healing rituals demons speak out before divine powers deliver the afflicted person. Compared to the negotiations, doubts and hesitations that mark the traditional ways of dealing with affliction, the Charismatic ritual processes are performed in a mode of certainty, following a straightforward structure and with authoritative powers.

Demonic doorways and divine uncertainties

Although healing rituals are performed in a mode of certainty, alleviating suffering through casting out evil spirits, ritual deliverance does not guarantee that the demonic influence will not return. The ritual power is grounded in the anointing of daily life and so it depends on the person's everyday living to preserve the attained healing. It is, in other words, the responsibility of the individual person to sustain a strong relationship with God by living a faithful lifestyle. According to Savedees, this is difficult because demons are powerful spirits and part of a person's immediate past (before conversion), ancestral past (lives of parents, grandparents, and great-grandparents), and local practices of the non-saved (such as intake of alcohol in daily life and at rituals such as funeral rites). A complete turning-away from demons is therefore regarded as a long-term process during which a Savedee must continually be delivered from evil disturbances (see also Meyer 1998:318–25). This section will discuss how Martin, like other Savedees, during prolonged hardship attempts to maintain the certainty that he will be relieved from suffering through his personal relationship with God.

In the aftermath of the healing ritual where Justine was delivered from the "demons of fornication and demons of lust", the marital relation was once again relatively harmonious. Martin and Justine associated the demons with the behaviour of Justine's deceased mother, not with Justine. The mother was a nominal Christian who died from poisoning after some female neighbours discovered that she engaged sexually with their husbands. The spirits now tried to induce the daughter to continue this sexual behaviour. Together they prayed for continual harmony, but the domestic harmony was fragile and Martin soon discovered that Justine had a sexual relationship with a man in the church. According to Martin:

> She invited those spirits of her mother to guide her. They overwhelmed her and she became stubborn, in fact I might say that she was very quarrelsome. When I prayed over her, demons spoke out. Oh, they fear Jesus for they know He is stronger. Jesus chased them away but she invited them back. If you drive out one spirit and then invite it to come back that one brings many friends, they will come in big numbers.

Morally wrong attitudes and behaviour such as being stubborn and quarrelsome, even fornicating, are typical signs of someone who is under demonic influence. In order to relieve his wife of this evil, Martin *"prayed over her"*, and thus carried out rituals of faith healing where he chased away the demons in the name of Jesus Christ. As such these rituals were successful. However, the wife *"invited them to come back"*. This was not only a set-back in Martin's plans of relieving her from demonic sway and re-establishing the harmony at home, her "invitation" also worsened the situation as even more evil spirits came to guide her. When explaining the long process of making a rupture with practices and social relations before conversion, it is common for Savedees to underline that a demon previously cast out may return with *"many friends, they come in big numbers"*. Demons find "doorways" (Asamoah-Gyadu 2005:181) or areas of moral vulnerability to influence a converted person. Such doorways are often related to a person's previous indulgence in sinful practices such as drinking alcohol, having extramarital sexual relations, or having evil dreams about or feelings towards others. The continual deliverance of evil spirits related to a person's behaviour and social relations before conversion is, as Meyer (1998) argues from the Ghanaian Pentecostal setting, a way of engaging in a dialectics of remembering and forgetting. In the case of Justine, it is by attending to the relations with her mother and other non-saved relatives, that she, as a Savedee, can put herself at a distance from them – and possibly also from the sexual relationship she had with another man. Although there is a general acceptance of the need for continual deliverance, the individual is expected to work hard to stop "sliding back" to previous sinful practices. Justine's inability to break away from the extramarital affair and her relatives frustrated Martin, as he explains: "I have been furious with my wife. For a long time I requested her to repent all her sins to God, pray for forgiveness and stay firm, but she wouldn't listen."

The self-reflective individual person must re-establish the relationship with God by repenting of sin, praying for forgiveness, and then changing his/her lifestyle. Healers can deliver demons in ritual settings, but only the individual can maintain a strong personal bond with God. In this case, Justine did not consent to Martin's requests and eventually she eloped with her lover. Throughout the following seven years, the spouses have fought over custody of the children, Justine's well-off brother has threatened Martin with physical violence, and Martin has taken legal action. Justine has had a child with her new husband, while Martin has not (yet) succeeded in finding a new wife. Parallel to this, Martin has also been going through a process of disintegration with the church since members are sceptical of his abilities to lead the church when he is not even able to lead his own home. Despite these longlasting and ongoing problems in his marital life, home and church, Martin maintains his certainty that his personal relationship with God will relieve him from misery:

> All the evil that my wife brought into the home never put any shade on my strong relations with God. Ever since we had that very first dispute, I have continued to be God's servant, and moved in the villages to heal patients. I have chased away demons in these people. Oh, God has chosen me to be the servant. Many times He has spoken words that have calmed my burdened heart. The Lord has confirmed that I am not to blame for the deeds of my wife. I have no fears for God will provide. We must be patient and not always [try to] understand the ways of the Almighty. God is with those who follow His guidance.

Throughout the domestic disputes and after his wife eloped, Martin experienced that God continued communicating with him when he prayed and made him able to deliver evil spirits from patients. Since healing gifts are considered the most important anointing – because they are the ultimate divine empowerment to combat evil spirits – Martin interprets his deliverance of evil spirits as strong evidence of his innocence in the domestic dispute.

The sentence *"we must be patient and not always [try to] understand the plans of the Almighty"* can be interpreted as an expression of not understanding why the domestic dispute turned into a disintegration of the home and uncertainty about his failed attempts to begin a new home. Savedees often resorted to such expressions about God as the the "radical other", when they were in situations in which no other explanations within their cosmology made sense, i.e. when the person was certain to adhere to God's conditions but did not experience improvement. This recognition of uncertainty in Charismatic religiosity is important to note although it is constantly overshadowed by the prospect of certainty. As illustrated in the above quote, instead of dwelling on his experience of prolonged suffering, Martin resorts to the general certainty that "God is with those who follow His guidance". By doing so, Martin moves from relating to God as the "radical other", the Creator who is beyond human comprehension and influence, to relating to God as someone who will alleviate the suffering of His people. As Martin further narrated:

> Last week God told me some time at night to go into the church. I went and God told me to look up several scriptures, I read, I prayed very hard, and I could feel that God wanted to tell me something very important. For hours I was reading scriptures, praying hard and the Holy Spirit was so clear, but still I couldn't understand what the message was. At last I fell asleep and in my dreams I had a vision. God will not allow that child to live, that child of my [previous] wife must die. My wife and her new husband will not be able to produce [children who will live]. When God has spoken that child will die automatically.

According to Martin, his vision revealed that God has stepped in to make Martin's wife and her new husband aware of their immoral actions.[13] Martin's certainty that God will "automatically" let the child die, that "the child of my wife must die", should be understood in the context of God being unambiguous, "one-hearted", and never under the sway of evil. This trustworthiness is in stark contrast to notions about human beings' "double hearts" and their predisposed ambiguous intentions as well as general notions about

---

13. The reasoning is that when God prevents this new couple from establishing a home, He gives them a chance to realise their immoral actions behind their relationship and choose once again to follow His guidance. For this reason, the death of their first-born child is for their own good.

the uncertainty of whether local spirits are speaking the truth or just playing around. Martin has no doubt as to the reliability of the vision, and he is sure that God will bring about this pledge, as he is confident that God is interested in rewarding those who follow Him. Yet, this contractual relationship between a person and God is complemented by the recognition that since God is distinctively different from human beings, they cannot always understand His ways. Such moving between different types of relationship between humans and God is constantly taking place, be it in situations of talking, preaching or healing. This means that the various relationships should be understood as simultaneous (Rubow 2000). As a whole, the different relations make up a version of the world in which these Christians live and which guides their way of believing. It is a world in which Savedees navigate certainties and uncertainties through their relations with the divine.

Conditional certainty

In this chapter, I have illustrated how Samia Savedees construct certainties and how they live with their experiences of certainties in times of prolonged uncertainty. Based on cultural notions of uncertainty located in human nature, in interpersonal relations as well as with local spirits, I have argued that Savedees construct certainty through their personal relationship with God. The certainties so profoundly expressed among Charismatic Christians centre on their personal relations with the unambiguous God who, through signs in their material live, shows His grace to those who follow Him. Any kind of misfortune or uncertainty can be interpreted as caused by evil spirits, and ritual healing by the powers of God is the one solution to whatever issue arises – from concerns for passing an exam to being mortally ill. The construction of certainty involves a reduction of the cosmology's ambiguity, dividing it into good and evil and eliminating grey zones that may cause doubt or hesitations about how to interpret a troublesome issue. Whereas other devoted Christians in Samia society perceive localised spiritual beings as ambiguous, Samia Savedees see these spirits as unmistakably evil. Since Savedees perceive the spirits as powerful beings that persistently seek to influence living human beings, any misfortune can be interpreted as a demonic manifestation. The social world of Samia Savedees may thus be understood as a re-enchanted arena in which the individual person is situated in an ongoing battle between the powers of God and Satan. To live in this world might seem frightening and very uncertain to many people, but to most Savedees, their everyday life is quite certain because they believe that when one fulfils His plain conditions, God has guaranteed grace to change one's livelihood.

It is in the very moment that Samia Savedees proclaim salvation, and hence instigate the personal transformation of the conversion process, that they sense they move to a closer relation with the Almighty and unambiguous God. God is, however, not one but rather a threesome with whom human beings form different types of relations. The relations may be identified according to the human ability to understand and influence God. At the one extreme, Savedees relate to God as the "radical other", a God beyond human comprehension and influence, and as such, this is a relationship that entails a human experience of uncertainty. At the other extreme, Savedees engage in a rather certain reciprocal relationship with the divine, a relationship in which the individual – for instance in a ritual setting – can demand God to provide them with the power to relieve a suffering person. Most Savedees, like Martin, moved between these two extremes of certainty and uncertainty in a mode dominated by certainty, and without giving up on the objectified certainties claimed within the Charismatic churches. Thus, even though certainty is conditional and a person may fulfil conditions without being relieved of his/her hardship, this rarely calls into question the certainties as such. Rather, uncertainties about the immediate alleviation do not transform into to uncertainties about how to comprehend the adversity or how to deal with it. To uphold a view of a certain world partly founded on in-built uncertainty, is truly an art, perhaps characteristic of "the art of believing" (Rubow 2000: 161). For Samia Savedees faith entails daily striving to steerclear of temptation and, with the power of God, to restore health and harmonious living.

Acknowledgement

The research was funded by Danida, Nordic Africa Institute and the Institute of Anthropology at the University of Copenhagen, Denmark. It formed a part of an interdisciplinary research programme between Ugandan and Danish universities engaged with community health in Tororo and Busia districts in Uganda. The author would like to thank the affiliated institute, the Child Health and Development Centre at Makerere University in Kampala, and the informants in Busia district.

References

Allen, Tim, 2006, *Tribal Justice. The International Criminal Court and the Lord's Resistance Army.* London: Zed books, p. 77.

Asamoah-Gyadu, J. Kwabena, 2005, *African Charismatics. Current Developments within Independent Indigenous Pentecostalim in Ghana.* Leiden: Brill.

Behrend, Heike, 1999, *Alice Lakwena & the Holy Spirits. War in Northern Uganda 1986–97.* Oxford: James Currey.

Cattell, Maria, 1992, "Praise the Lord and say no to men: Older Women empowering themselves in Samia, Kenya", *Journal of cross-Cultural Gerontology, 7*, pp. 307–330.

Caplan, Lionel, 1995, "Certain Knowledge. The encounter of global fundamentalism and local Christianity in urban south India", in Wendy James (ed.), *The Pursuits of Certainty. Religious and Cultural Formulations.* London: Routledge, pp. 92–111.

Christiansen, Catrine, 2001, "Frelst til forandring. Et studie af konversion, sygdom og person blandt basamia kristne i Uganda" [Changed by Salvation. A study about conversion, health and personhood among Samia Christians in Uganda], Master thesis no. 214, Institute of Anthropology, University of Copenhagen, Denmark.

Garrard, David J, 2002, "Uganda" in S.M. Burgress and E.M. van der Maas (eds), *The New International Dictionary of Pentecostal and Charismatic Movements.* Michigan: Zondervan, pp. 273–276.

Gifford, Paul, 1998, *African Christianity. Its Public Role.* London: Hurst & Company.

Jackson, Michael, 1998, *Minima Etnographica. Intersubjectivity and the Anthropological Project.* Chicago: University of Chicago Press.

James, William, 1902/1994, *The Varieties of Religious Experience.* New York: The Modern Library.

Katahoire, Ann, 1998, "Education for Life: Mothers' Schooling and Children's Survival in Eastern Uganda". PhD diss., Institute of Anthropology, University of Copenhagen, Denmark.

Kassimir, Ronald, 1999, "The Politics of Popular Catholicism in Uganda", in Thomas Spear and I.N. Kimambo (eds), *East African Expressions of Christianity.* Oxford: James Currey, pp. 248–275.

Lambek, Michael, 1995, "Choking on the Quran. And other consuming parables from the western Indian Ocean front", in Wendy James (ed.), *The Pursuits of Certainty. Religious and Cultural Formulations.* London: Routledge, pp. 258–281.

Marshall-Fratani, Ruth, 1998, "Mediating the Global and the Local in Nigerian Pentecostalism", *Journal of Religion in Africa,* Vol. 28, No. 3, pp. 278–315.

Marshall, Ruth, 1993, "Power in the Name of Jesus': Social Transformation and Pentecostalism in Western Nigeria 'Revisited'" in T. Ranger and O. Vaughan (eds), *Legitimacy and the State in the 20ᵗʰ Century Africa*. Oxford: St Anthony's MacMillan Series, pp. 213–246.

Maxwell, David, 2006, "Post-colonial Christianity in Africa", in Hugh McLeod (ed.), *The Cambridge History of Christianity, World Christianities c. 1914– c. 2000*, Volume 9. Cambridge: Cambridge University Press

—, 1998, "'Delivered from the spirit of poverty?' Pentecostalism, prosperity and modernity in Zimbabwe", *Journal of Religion in Africa*, Vol. 28, No. 3, pp. 351–371.

Meyer, Birgit, 2004, "Christianity in Africa: From African Independent to Pentecostal-Charismatic Churches", *Annual Review of Anthropology*, Vol. 33, pp. 447–474.

—, 1999, *Translating the Devil. Religion and Modernity among the Ewe in Ghana*. Edinburgh: Edinburgh University Press.

—, 1998, "Make a Complete Break with the past: Memory and Post-colonial Modernity in Ghanaian Pentecostalist Discourse", *Journal of Religion in Africa*, Vol. 27, No. 3, pp. 316–49.

Mitchell, Jon P, 1997, "A Moment with Christ: the importance of feelings in the analysis of belief", *Journal of the Royal Anthropological Institute*, 3, 1, pp. 79–94.

Obbo, Christine, 1993, "HIV Transmission through Social and Geographical Networks in Uganda", *Social Science & Medicine*, Vol. 36, No. 7, pp. 949–955.

Rubow, Cecilie, 2000, *Hverdagens Teologi. Folkereligiösitet i danske verdener*. Copenhagen: Anis.

Sundkler, Bengt and Christopher Steed, 2000, *A History of the Church in Africa*. Cambridge: Cambridge University Press.

Ter Haar, Gerrie, 1992, *Spirit of Africa: The Healing Ministry of Archbishop Milingo of Zambia*. London: Hurst & Company.

van Dijk, Rijk, 2000, "Christian Fundamentalism in Sub-Saharan Africa: The case of Pentecostalism", Occasional Paper, Centre for African Studies, University of Copenhagen, Denmark

Ward, Kevin, 1989, "Obedient rebels – the Relationship between the early "Balokole" and the Church of Uganda: The Mukono Crisis", *Journal of Religion in Africa*, Vol. 19, No. 3, pp. 194–226.

Whyte, Susan Reynolds, 1997, *Questioning misfortune. The pragmatics of uncertainty in eastern Uganda*. Cambridge: Cambridge University Press.

Publications by institutions:

Det Danske Bibelselskab, 1998, *Bibelen*, Viborg: Nörhaven A/S.
UNAIDS, 2004, *Report of the global HIV/AIDS epidemic*, UNAIDS.

CHAPTER 3

The Tragedy of Ageing: Witch Killings and Poor Governance among the Sukuma

Simeon Mesaki

Introduction

Witch killing among the Sukuma people in the area south of Lake Victoria has been called "Tanzania's silent holocaust" (Mfumbusa 1999). In spite of several attempts by the government to come to grips with the problem, the witchcraft-associated murders of older people, and women in particular, continues relentlessly. The murders continue to threaten social stability throughout Sukumaland, an area south of Lake Victoria, creating a climate of fear and uncertainty among its people. Even in cases when victims escape death, they are forced to run away from their homes to save their lives. The problem has become so serious that old women in the Sukuma countryside are "becoming an endangered species", as expressed by the Tanzania Media Women Association (TAMWA), a non-governmental organisation (NGO) advocating human rights. A survey conducted in 1999 by the same NGO found about 100 old women begging in the streets of Shinyanga, the hometown of the Sukuma. These old women had run away from their villages for fear of being killed (Nkya 2000).

The iniquitous practice of killing suspected witches in Sukumaland became gradually noticeable in the early 1960s (Tanner 1970). By the mid-1970s these murders had become so notorious and high in number that the government embarked on what came to be known as the "Operation against killings" (*Operesheni Mauaji* in Swahili, the national language of Tanzania), aiming to catch the suspected perpetrators of these dreadful crimes. The operation turned out to be an embarrassing episode for the government when a number of apprehended suspects died while in police custody. As a result some police and security officers were convicted and jailed for mishandling the operation, and even some cabinet ministers took political responsibility for the mishap and ultimately had to resign). Consequently, the operation was abandoned, whereupon the killings resumed and continued to such an extent that, by the late 1980s, the situation seemed to be getting out of hand. This led to the formation of the Mongela Commission (on witchcraft), in 1988, appointed by the ruling party, Chama Cha Mapinduzi (CCM), to investigate this disturbing phenomenon. The commission came out with some startling results. For example, between 1970 and 1984, 3,693 people – 1,407 men and 2,286 women – were killed in witchcraft-related incidents in the whole of Tanzania. Out of these, 2,347 deaths (63.5% of the total) occurred in the regions of Mwanza, Shinyanga and Tabora, which are all areas inhabited predominantly by the Sukuma people. There are no reliable figures on the killings from 1984 to 1993, but in recent years the two regions of Mwanza and Shinnying have continued to hold the unenviable position of leading in witch-related murders, which appear to be on the increase (*Nipashe*, December 19, 1998). Thus a front-page story in the *Daily Mail*, reads as follows: "20 women murdered monthly in grisly Shinyanga witch hunt" (September 30, 1998). In another story it is claimed that in Shinyanga region as many as 100 elderly women were being killed each year due to witchcraft practices (*Mtanzania*, June 1, 1999). Another newspaper, *Mzalendo*, reports that between 1996 and 1998, a total of 325 people were killed in Shinyanga region, providing figures for each of those years: 133 in 1996, 102 in 1997, and 90 between January and October 1998 (*Mzalendo*, October 4, 1998:5). A survey conducted by TAMWA revealed that between 1993 and 1998, 318 elderly people were killed in Mwanza region alone (*Daily News*, March 11, 1999). It is to be noted that these figures are hardly exhaustive; they represent only the cases brought to the attention of the police. Many other innocent people are murdered each year in remote villages of the Sukuma countryside and according to an official of the police department in Shinyanga region, the killings had become very common, occurring virtually on a daily basis in the regions of Shinyanga and Mwanza.

In this chapter, based on many years of intermittent anthropological fieldwork (Mesaki 1993, 1994) I explore this phenomenon of witch killing, seek to assess its salient features, as well as its possible causes, and examine why this practice has not only persisted, but might even be on the increase. The chapter also discusses the apparent failure of the government, in spite of the many attempts, to control the situation. Before we proceed, I will provide an introduction to the Sukuma, the area and the people, and describe their witchcraft belief and practices.

Changing livelihood in "Sukumaland"

The land of the Sukuma (Usukumani), called "Sukumaland" by the British colonisers, refers to the area south of Lake Victoria covering the whole of what is today Mwanza and Shinyanga regions and parts of Mara, Kagera and Tabora regions. It is part of the treeless expanse of land commonly called the "cultivation steppe". Now, with a population close to 8 million people, the Sukuma are the largest ethnic group in Tanzania, which has a total population of 35 million.[1]

At the beginning of German colonial rule (1890–1919), the Sukuma had already started agricultural intensification in response to population pressure. During the early period of British rule (1919–1961), an ambitious tsetse fly eradication campaign was implemented by clearing away the natural habitat of the deadly flies. This campaign opened up more land for agriculture and created new tsetse-free outlets for grazing purposes. Moreover, the Sukumaland Development Scheme (SDS), carried out between 1947 and 1956, was instrumental in population redistribution and extensive migrations, which are still ongoing. In essence, the SDS was designed to maximise the possibilities for productive use of the land by redistribution of what appeared to be surplus populations of people and livestock. After the implementation of the Sukumaland Development Scheme an overall increase in population and livestock density took place in all parts of Sukumaland, not least because possibilities for migration to nearby areas had been exhausted.

Today many of the Sukuma occupy large areas of land in the regions of Kagera, Tabora, Rukwa and Mbeya, and they have even ventured into Zambia. The Sukuma are basically cultivators, but livestock and, particularly, cattle constitute an important asset economically, socially and culturally. Their most important food crops are maize, millet, sorghum, cassava, paddy, sweet potatoes, various types of legumes and vegetable crops such as beans and cowpeas. Nowadays the Sukuma are engaged in cotton production, which is one of Tanzania's major export crops. The main environmental problems experienced in Sukumaland in general are water shortages, scarcity of pasture, deforestation, soil erosion and loss of soil fertility. The people have implemented dramatic changes in farming practices. For example, whereas in the past sorghum and millet were the main staples today the Sukuma rely more on maize, rice and cassava. Overall, there has been pressure on land due to the increase in the livestock and human populations and the success of cotton production.

---

1. The Sukuma belong to the Bantu-speaking people who migrated from south of Lake Chad some 400 to 500 years ago through the Congo River Basin and across Lake Tanganyika before they settled south of Lake Victoria (Malcolm 1953:4).

The Sukuma have endured many "top-down" development programmes, ranging from the soil conservation and de-stocking measures of the colonial government to the "villagisation programme" of the 1970s. Villagisation was a countrywide operation spearheaded by the first president of Tanzania, Julius Nyerere. It aimed at relocating people into nucleated villages in order to provide them with the basic services of water, education and health care. The villagisation exercise was particularly traumatic for the Sukuma because of their cultural and environmental setting. Despite its good intentions, villagisation disrupted the original setup of rural settlements. Traditionally, Sukuma settlements were characterised by mobility and a high degree of adaptation to local ecological conditions, but the new village patterns made adaptation to local conditions difficult (Brandström 1985:6). The radical departure from the more fluid pre-villagisation patterns were replaced by a more or less permanent or closed community. Varkevisser (1969:42) states that, "… concentrated settlement is alien to traditional Sukuma society". Also Madulu (1998:6) argues that there has been a continuing process of disintegration of the Sukuma's generational family structure which began during the villagisation campaign in the 1970s. In addition, increasing numbers of family members began to work alone in non-agricultural activities compared with the past when communal labour in the fields was prominent. In particular the villagisation resettlement programme is blamed for having imposed monocentric village structures upon the agro-pastoral farmers. In the past, the mutual traversing of space between homesteads also constituted, in effect, an expression of solidarity between people (Stroeken 2001:305). This kind of solidarity ceased to exist with the new settlement patterns.

Many traditional institutions such as communal reciprocal working groups, age-grade systems and "secret societies" have been replaced by the government's top-down system of governance. At the same time there are concerted efforts to convert the tradition-bound Sukuma to Christianity. Shinyanga region leaders, in particular, have invited Christian evangelists to make an impact through missionary work, which might deter people from practising witchcraft (*Sunday News*, March 8, 1992:7). Also, the Catholic Church in Tanzania has designed a radio programme to combat the Sukuma witch killings. According to the coordinator of the campaign the aim is to "… broadcast religious programmes to the predominantly pagan population, especially in Shinyanga region in northern Tanzania where more witchcraft-related killings are reported."[2] In spite of such efforts, the prac-

---

2. Personal communication.

tice is still going on and, seemingly, increasing. In the coming sections I shall describe the phenomenon in more detail.

Belief in witchcraft

Research conducted in various parts of Africa shows a widespread fear of and preoccupation with witchcraft in both rural and urban settings. Contrary to earlier assumptions by colonial officials, their postcolonial successors and social scientists, modernisation and urbanisation have not eliminated belief in witchcraft (Geschiere 1997; Kohnert 1996; Moore and Sanders 2001; Ashforth 2001, to mention but a few). Indeed, recent research in Africa shows that such belief can and does co-exist with modernity (see also Comaroff and Comaroff 1993).

According to popular beliefs among the Sukuma, witches fly at night and consume children. They transform themselves into animals, and they frequently gather in organised company with other witches. They are believed to conjure storms and wreak havoc on crops. Illnesses and accidents, it is believed, can often be traced to the older witches of a neighbourhood, and, as will become clear in this chapter, such belief has resulted in the death of a large number of women allegedly practising witchcraft.

Witches in Sukumaland are perceived to possess some common characteristics. The witch is hardly ever a stranger; on the contrary, he or she is someone familiar, someone close to you, someone who knows you well but who, allegedly, wishes you ill. Often, people accused of witchcraft are poor; they may be deformed; they may make others feel guilty and therefore incur the anger of such people, as well. But the supposed witch can also be someone very beautiful, clever, or wealthy and prosperous in life. Thus, there is usually a great fear of displaying one's ability to build a remarkable house, dress smartly, or do well in school. Among the Sukuma witches are often females and men are rarely accused of witchcraft.

The Sukuma also commonly believe that witches prey upon non-witches and "consume" the body and mind of their victim in some physical or mental fashion; one physical manifestation of a bewitched person might be, for example, any lingering and chronic illness. As with the Azande, Sukuma witches are believed also to derive their power from some innate witchcraft substance (cf. Evans-Pritchard 1937).

Witchcraft beliefs are strong among the Sukuma, intrinsic to their way of life and embedded in their systems of knowledge and morality. The Sukuma accept that there are various types of witchcraft practices, but regard all forms as deliberately planned and directed towards some intended victim(s). The most prevalent and most feared form involves the insertion of poison – that is, harmful medicine (*bulisiwa*) – into food and drink. *Bupandya* is another notorious variety, which involves placing harmful substances at particular places where an intended victim will come into contact with it – often at crossroads. It is held that the poison will affect only the intended victim. In a third form, *nhamanhama,* it is believed that the witch makes himself or herself invisible and beats the victim with a stick dipped in poison or the witch blows poison through a straw into the victim's face. Some witches are also said to keep animals, such as hyenas, snakes and swarms of flies, and purposely send them as couriers of evil to harm an enemy. Others are held to be capable of transforming their victims into zombies (*ng'witunga*) who, in turn, are brought out to work for the witch at night. Witchcraft in Sukumaland may be presumed to be responsible for almost any calamity or misfortune, such as sudden storms on the lake, the failure of rain, the sudden death of a healthy person, infertility and miscarriages, or even getting lost, as when one is unable to find one's way to a particular destination (Mesaki 1994:49).

Ralph Tanner (1970:39), who did research among the Sukuma in the 1960s, writes that witchcraft beliefs constitute a lived experience among people rather than an abstract notion. Varkevisser (1973) also attests that despite a century of missionary activity and widespread formal education in Sukumaland, "…very few individuals, if any, ever achieved perfect freedom from fear of the potency of black magic" (1973:18). Referring to the situation in the late 1990s, Kibuga (1999:33) asserts that witchcraft "…is a belief which many people in the rural areas of Sukumaland hold whether they are educated or not, whether they are rich or poor, young or old, and whether they are members of a modern religion or not". According to Hans Cory (1954:53), traditionally, the Sukuma had three main ways of dealing with witchcraft and those accused of practising witchcraft. First, there was the neighbourhood council of elders (*banamhala*) who castigated, chastised and warned alleged witches. Second, witches were ostracised and denied access to essential services in the village, such as water and grazing. Third, the more serious cases were referred to the court of the *ntemi* (chief) and his assessors (*banang'oma*), a court powerful enough to sentence a witch to death if the evidence was believed to be conclusive. Tanner (1956:437), however, notes that cases leading to capital punishment were very rare. Iliffe (1979) describes how the first colonialists, the Germans (1885–1914) are remembered for their ruthless actions against those who claimed to identify witches, in some cases hanging the accusers. The British, who ruled Tanganyika between 1919 and 1961, were less drastic, choosing instead to enact legislation to control witchcraft for the whole territory.[3]

With regard to the Sukuma, Tanner (1970) states that their customary law was formally recorded by a government sociologist and translated into Swahili, whereupon copies were deposited with every court in the area. But strangely, it made no mention at all of witchcraft (Tanner 1970:23). Soon after independence in 1963, the new government transformed traditional leadership in the country, replacing traditional chiefs with a hierarchical system of appointed functionaries in charge of administration. According to Tanner, this process left something of a vacuum with regard to witchcraft beliefs and anxieties. He argues that "…in the postcolonial era the ordinary man in trouble was bound to consider using self-help if he possibly could rather than depending on the agencies of government" (1970:39). A situation was then created whereby the individual was compelled to deal with his or her own problem as there were no formal structures to deal with them. Witch killings began to be resorted to, as the next section demonstrates.

Older women as victims of witch killing

The following case provides a typical scenario of how a witch-related killing drama unfolds.

> On the evening of January 1ˢᵗ, 1970, in Mwamazenge village, in Kwimba district of Mwanza region, two peasant women were warming themselves as usual in front of the family fire, *chikome*. One of them, Njile, aged 53, was an inhabitant of the village who was being visited by her sister-in-law, Bugumba. Suddenly a gang of assailants pounced on them and hacked the defenceless women to death with machetes (*mapanga*). The perpetrators disappeared as quickly as they had come, taking advantage of the darkness to conceal their identity.
>
> Investigations by the police led to the arrest of three people. Their statements during the preliminary investigation disclosed that four years prior to this tragic event, Njile's husband and his brother were involved in quarrel over agricultural fields with their neighbour, a man named Washa. The conflict was brought before the village elders but no solution was found. The animosity continued to the extent that the protagonists no longer even greeted each other. Sometime later Njile's husband died and Njile continued with her life as usual. When Washa's children died of unspecified causes, things got worse. The situation was further worsened when a snake bit another of Washa's children. These events, in addition to the old conflict over

3. The Witchcraft Ordinance was first introduced in 1922.

the *shamba* (farming land) were still unsolved, to Washa, who, predictably, suspected Njile of bewitching his children. Whereas the conflict over the land had been referred to village authorities, the accusation of witchcraft was never brought to any hearing. Instead, Washa had gone to a diviner who, according to Washa, had confirmed that Njile was responsible for the misfortunes he was experiencing. The only solution was to get rid of Njile.

The story about Njile and her female friend is not unique. It was apparent that Washa and another person were responsible for the killing of the two women (for more details, see Mesaki 1993:201). Usually older women, often widowed, are the most likely to be accused of witchcraft, and as responsible for other people's misfortune, as a result of which they are killed. My own research shows that there is a clear preponderance of women being killed. Out of the 2,347 "witches" killed in Mwanza, Shinyanga and Tabora regions between 1970 and 1984, 2004 (85.3%) were women (Mesaki 1993:202). Of the 185 witch suspects killed in Shinyanga region between 1997 and 1999, 168 (90.8%) were older women.

Traditionally, older Sukuma women had important and respected roles in society. Older women used to participate in the councils of elders and had a strong say in such tasks as organising marriage, mediating family disputes, and maintaining customary practices. They instructed male youths in appropriate traditional practices and were advisors and mentors to young girls. Older women would also be responsible for the "ceremonial cry" (*lupundu*), which informs the social environment about an important event, such as when the herd of cattle leaves the groom's homestead as part of the bridewealth practice. A similar *lupundu*-cry was made by the oldest women in the bride's community to mark the approach or arrival of the livestock. Many older women also had a central role in performance of customary rites of passage. They would perform rituals at the graves of stillborn twins, the locations of which would be known only to the older women of certain clans. Such rituals involved the offering of foodstuffs or livestock (milk, bananas, white goats and black hens) at ceremonies on sacred hilltops or under revered ancient trees. Some women were traditional birth attendants and healers, others looked after their grandchildren during *chikome*– the evening fire chats – and told them stories with strong socialising features. Ironically, the *chikome* has now turned into a common site for witch killings.

The advisory and ceremonial role of older women is now diminishing as Sukuma society undergoes enormous changes. Many older women can no longer rely on their own families to assist them economically. Family support is dwindling as young people migrate to towns and families face difficulties meeting basic needs in the harsh economic climate of modern times. Consequently, many younger people have not had the opportunity to absorb the wisdom of their elders, partly as a result of the aforementioned factors. Some young people even fail to grasp the importance of helping older people – an unquestioned value from the past. During my fieldwork in Magu district of Mwanza (1989–1992) region older people complained that these days they feared young people, and some women had even been beaten by the young (Mesaki 2001). Many older people were deliberately provoked and harassed, and whenever they complained, they were told that they were "behind the times" (*wamepitwa na wakati*) or "old-fashioned". Older women said they were treated with scorn and contempt. They also felt that they sometimes were considered a burden by their own families. Some older people consequently had to beg their relatives for their basic needs to survive. Many women expressed fear that if they became a nuisance to their closest relatives, they would be accused of being witches so as to get rid of them.

This situation is especially common for widows, and divorced women. It is also held to be true for barren women who allegedly are indifferent to other peoples' children. Grandchildren provide companionship and household help. However, looking after grandchildren can also be dangerous: if anything apparently malevolent happens to them, their grandmother is likely to be suspected, as illustrated in the story about Shoma below. Often lonely, poor, weak and vulnerable, such older women cannot fight off suspicions. They have no influence or voice in the community to defend themselves. Moreover, many of them have some of the physical signs, which are regarded by those who believe in witchcraft as indicative of witchcraft and thus labelling them *nogi* (witches). Kate Forrester Kibuga, who did a study of the witchcraft in Magu district on behalf of the Help Age International (HAI), notes that some older women are suspected of witchcraft simply because of their appearance: witches are believed to have bloodshot eyes, wrinkles, bags under the eyes, grey hair, twisted limbs and gnarled hands (Kibuga 1999a:66) all of which are, of course, common characteristics of old age. Older women become easy targets for those who need a scapegoat to explain their troubles.

Another common feature of Sukuma witch killings is that the whole idea of implicating a suspect begins within the family. I will further illustrate this point in the case of Shoma, a widow that Kibuga (1999a:20) writes about.

> Shoma lived comfortably with her sons and daughters-in-law in the home
> where she had moved to when she got married in the 1950s. Her husband

died many years previously, but had ensured that his wife would be provided for in her old age by leaving much of the property in her care. She was devoted to her grandchildren and spent much time with them when the other adults were out working in the fields. Then one day the two of the smaller grandchildren became sick. As the days turned into weeks, there seemed to be nothing the local traditional healer could do for the children who, instead, became weaker and weaker. In the end, the family suspected witchcraft and went to the village diviner. According to Shoma's eldest son, the diviner pointed a finger at Shoma, suggesting that she was casting an evil spell on the children. Horrified by this news, her oldest son contacted a group of thugs who were prepared to do anything for a price. Shoma herself, informed of the suspicions, fled to a distant house. Not long afterwards, two hooded youths broke into the house during the night and hacked her to death with machetes.

I myself I recorded a similar case in 1991. Nyanzobe (not her real name), was a 70-year-old woman who had run away from home because she suspected that some members of her own family were planning to kill her, as they believed she was causing harm by using witchcraft. Nyanzobe had found refuge in a government welfare facility, where she told me her story (Mesaki 1993:226):

> I ran away from the village after being suspected of being a witch. ... There were many deaths [of young children] in the family ... then rumour began to spread in the village that I was the one who killed them ... My own children started to hate me ... some of them started taunting me as a witch. I tried to explain but they did not give me the chance to vindicate myself. Considering what had happened to others – they had all been brutally killed – I knew what would befall me. Thus, when one of my grandchildren whispered to me that they (her own children) were about to kill me, I left the same evening. ... They had discussed the issue in front of my grandchildren and this saved my life... Although I love my family, there is no way of going back to face death.

The above stories are typical of many witchcraft-related killings, which have been going on in Sukumaland for more than four decades now. The murders tend to follow a certain pattern, in which the assailants break down the door of the victim's house at night, go straight to the victim's bedroom and kill her, using either an axe or a sharp machete (*panga*). They usually do not harm anybody else in the house. Nor do they steal anything.

Among the Sukuma these killings are treated by the majority of the people as appropriate and deserved. Once the alleged witches are killed, and social tension is replaced by a sense of relief in the community, the assailants are thus regarded more as heroes than as criminals. The killing is viewed as retribution on a dangerous person whose lethal witchcraft is thereby expunged. Thus, as a district councillor from Pandagichiza in Shinyanga rural district testified, such deaths are not mourned, as custom otherwise would dictate. Instead, it is reported that if a person were to be seen to be mourning a witch, he or she would be ostracised (for more details, see Mesaki 1994). As the director of one of the NGOs now operating in the research area said: "In the Sukuma community, if you kill a witch it is not really considered a crime but rather that you are doing something good for the community. It's a culturally acceptable thing to do." The perception is that an evildoer has been wiped out with the ferocity he or she deserves.

It is assumed that once these suspects are eliminated, misfortunes will cease. Such drastic steps are expected to deter other witches from practising; therefore the killing is perceived as deterrant as well as revenge. But even the former Tanzanian President, Ali Hassan Mwinyi, commented on the fate of the alleged witches in the following manner:

> You are killing innocent women, some of them your own mothers, grand-mothers, or old people who have all along taken good care of you: how come they have suddenly become witches? Do you pay back by killing them? (*Sunday News*, August 23, 1987).

Witch finding and divination

The killings of alleged witches are often set in motion through the traditional practice of divining among the Sukuma. The Sukuma may consult a diviner (Kisukuma *nfumu*; pl. *bafumu*) for anything of importance to their livelihood and existence. The *nfumu*, (from *kufumbula, meaning* to discover or diagnose) provides answers to a host of problems in the community. People would consult a diviner before undertaking any uncertain enterprises of various kinds. These might include propitious times for going on a journey, when to expect rainfall, as well as seeking causal explanations for afflictions and misfortunes. Historically the *bafumu* have had enormous influence over Sukuma life because of their ability to convince their clients that they can understand the unknown and unseen. They are a source of what might be termed psychological security in society; through their power they are able to instil peace of mind by actively combating the forces of witchcraft. It must also be noted that, though the profession of divining was once the honoured occupation of a few experts, the *nfumu* has always been an unpredictable figure, who commands an ambiguous set of powers, to harm and heal. It is clear that the benevolence of the diviners is increasingly being doubted, since most of them are now held responsible for the witch killings afflicting Sukumaland. According to the then (1991) Regional Commissioner for Mwanza region, the Sukuma still have great trust in diviners. However, he notes that many people do not realise that some of these diviners are more interested in making money than solving social conflicts.

Thus, divination, which used to be considered an honourable profession, has now been been invaded by a plethora of dubious people, some of whom are most likely charlatans. The irony is that even the charlatans are able to operate with the tacit acknowledgement of the government. The Department of Culture at the district level issues "permits" (*vibali*) to traditional *waganga* (healers). However some of these healers misuse their permits by embarking on more lucrative activities, such as identifying witches for money. This has resulted in the emergence of a new set of characters in Sukumaland, the *bapembeji* (plural, con man) who exploit people's fears and anxiety; a common trajectory of this relation being the hiring of unscrupulous thugs to kill supposed witches.

The following summary from Kibuga's fieldwork in Magu district of Mwanza region is a vivid illustration of the collusion between *wapiga ramli*, the diviner, and the *bapembeji* (con men) in the operation.

> The case involved a brother and a sister. One day the sister went to her brother and said that she is going to cultivate one of the family *shambas* (fields). The brother refused, pointing out that the sister was now married into another clan and should therefore go and farm on a plot belonging to her husband. The sister was angry. She asserted that that her clan (represented by her brother) had received dowry from her marriage, and consequently she felt she still had a right to her original clan lands. She then decided to cultivate the *shamba* anyway. The brother with members of his family chased the "intruders" (represented by his sister and her people) from the *shamba*, beating them with sticks in the course of the eviction. Observing what transpired was a man associated with the local diviner (*mpiga ramli*), who usually reported any local dispute or trouble brewing to the diviner. The brother then went to calm his temper at a local beer club, ranting about the appalling behaviour of his sister. Soon afterwards he received a message that his daughter had fallen seriously ill and he rushed home to find his wife weeping. The wife wanted the child to be sent to a hospital immediately. The husband, convinced that there was a "human hand" (*mkono wa mtu*) involved in the incident, decided that the only way to find out who has caused the series of unfortunate events was to consult a diviner. He proceeded to

the local diviner. The diviner shook, rattled and cut up the chicken they had been asked to bring with them. The brother was then informed by the diviner that his misfortunes were caused by the evil intentions of the sister. The diviner gave the brother a concoction of sorts to administer to the sick daughter. Amazed by the diviner's power, the brother, paid him a large sum of money.

The brother returned to the beer club where he continued to complain about his sister. Lurking in the background, listening to the conversation, was a thuggish character who happened to belong to a gang of witch kill-ers. After hearing that transpired he approached, the brother, saying, "Why should you put up with this sort of trouble? Do you think it will end here? There is a simple solution to this, which my boys and me can sort out for you". The brother handed yet more money to the thug, agreeing to show the gang leader his sister's house the following day.

The following night, the sister and some of her family members went to sleep. The gangsters broke into the house, went straight to the sister's bed, and hacked her to death with machetes, after which they ran off into the night. The rest of the family was distraught and ran to the Village Executive Officer (VEO), who said, it is the middle of the night, what can we do now? Go back home to sleep and we'll work on it tomorrow morning" (Kibuga 1999a:35).

Corruption and witchcraft

The above description by Kibuga fairly illustrates how underlying conflict within the family, coinciding with the onset of illness, can lead to the need to find out the causes of the situation, and how this might lead a person to consult a diviner of dubious standing, resulting in a tragedy for all those involved. Even though this case did not involve the killing of witch it closely parallels the kind of the sequence of events that often result in the killing of older women alleged to be bewitching proximate relatives.

The story also raises a number of issues. I will dwell on two of them. Firstly, witchcraft may be used as a tactic to attain certain ends, for exam-ple, the resolution of misunderstandings, quarrels and conflicts over matters such as land, property or inheritance. "Con men" not only often operate in such situations, but also, sometimes actively incite disputes. As such, resort-ing to witchcraft may be just a ploy used to legitimise the settling of scores or getting rid of difficult relatives, all of which benefit such characters, as the diviners who identify the alleged witches, and the con men who carry out the actual task of getting rid of the accused for money. The older women who are the victims of these heinous crimes have to live a life of pressing anxiety and fear. Secondly, Kibuga's story raises questions about avenues for conflict resolution in the communities. According to her, the most important institution to deal with witchcraft accusations should be the village government. But alas, as she writes,

> [V]illage governments do not actually seem to take an active role in the issue of *uchawi* (witchcraft). This does not mean that they have nothing to do with it – on the contrary, their role appears to be passive, to stand by in silence ... although their mandate is to guarantee peace and security within the community (Kibuga 1999a:33).

In my own study, ordinary people claimed that the increasing prevalence and acceptance of bribery plays an important role in the witch killings. Many people claimed even that the system encourages conflict because justice or rights are up for sale. Money is demanded for cases to be heard even by the official local authorities; as one villager observed: "Village governments do not help the needy, they favour the rich and the old are disregarded." Regarding the role of the various organs of the government in the villages, the informants said, "It is useless to go to the Village Executive Officer (VEO), the Magistrate, and the Ward Executive Officer (WEO) because one has to have money. In the old days, cases were judged to restore peace and harmony; nowadays money decides".

It is those with money who have rights: "One with no money is not listened to, that is why even witchcraft thrives", added a woman resident of Salong'we. Informants claim that traditional methods of governance were more just because the accused were able to defend themselves and fines were fair. Today corruption is rampant and morals are ignored. According to the Regional Police Commander in this region, "it is virtually impossible to investigate such cases because relatives, friends and neighbours of the victim stick together and put up a wall of silence towards the investigators". It would seem that the various parties resort to blaming each other.

Police and court action against the killings leaves much to be desired. The police, faced with shortages of competent staff and equipment, have had little success in dealing with the problem, while the prosecution of cases in the courts has rarely been successful. Thus, out of 1,622 persons (1,447 men and 175 women) according to the ruling party's commission of 1988, who were arrested in connection with the killings of up to 1988, only seven cases were successfully prosecuted and ended in convictions. In the same vein, whereas 90 suspects were arrested in Shinyanga region between 1993 and 1998, 180 cases were still pending to be heard as of May 1999. The

Mwanza Deputy Regional Police Commander is quoted as saying that one of the problems in curbing the crime is the lack of evidence when the suspects are taken to courts of law. According to him, 215 suspects had been arrested since 1990, but due to lack of evidence none of them had been prosecuted. He attributed this to the fact that the murderers are usually hired from distant places and, although close relatives of the victim guide them, the community would not dare to reveal their identities for fear of reprisals (see *Majira*, May 22, 1999).

The Mongela Commission

The Mongela Commission on witchcraft, set up by the ruling party (CCM) in 1988, made many recommendations on how to tackle the problem of witchcraft killings (*Mzalendo*, June 25, 1989:3). For example, the Commission recommended that cases should be heard more quickly, and that the courts should be reformed to deliver justice in a way that was more democratic. More specifically, it was recommended that the functioning of Ward Courts, established since 1985, and the creation of Elders Councils should deal with witchcraft cases. The Commission also underscored the importance of special education programmes to combat superstitions in areas where witchcraft killings were most common. "Traditional doctors" (*waganga*) were to operate from permanent locations instead of roving from place to place. Professionalism was to be encouraged and their expertise made more relevant and beneficial to the nation. A law regulating their conduct was to be enacted specifying the rights of the patients or clients visiting such doctors. The Witchcraft Ordinance, the Criminal Procedure Code of 1985, and the Law of Evidence of 1967, were viewed as obstacles to the elimination of witch killings, because they failed to deal with complaints and conflicts, which in the end led to accusations of witchcraft. The Mongela Commission recommended the repeal of existing laws on witchcraft and the creation of new legislation in order to streamline the various means of dealing with witchcraft suspicions and accusations at the village level. It also sought to address the question of how accusations could be authenticated, and evidence accepted by incorporating acceptable village standards. The Commission argued that the root cause of the problem was inadequate social services, and it recommended concerted and deliberate efforts to bring socio-economic progress to the area, which would, hopefully, relieve the inhabitants of these "superstitions" (*ushirikina*) and "false beliefs" (*imani potofu*).

Apparently these recommendations were not implemented, and witch killings have continued. An upsetting element related to the killings, according to the then Tabora Regional Commissioner, has been the fact that the problem is compounded by corrupt practices within the police force and the judiciary (*Uhuru,* March 10, 1999:7). He admitted that the government was not doing enough to end the killing of old people (*Majira,* March 8, 1999:1):

> ... these killings could be done away with easily if the government was serious in doing so .... the government knows the killers but nothing is done due to embedded corrupt practices in law enforcement agencies of the country, being a project within the police force and judiciary in the Lake [Victoria] Regions.

Explaining how Tabora region had managed to deal with the problem, the Regional Commissioner said that in his region a lot had been achieved in the war against the problem by arresting all the grown-up children and other relatives of the killed suspects. Unfortunately, this procedure encountered "hue and cry" by the human rights organisations. This has been the stumbling block towards their "success". The police, on the other hand, complain that it is not fair for the public to pass a negative judgement on their performance, arguing that they are facing a very complex situation with a lot of factors at play, including ignorance, religion, poverty, and culture. The Regional Police Commander in Mwanza region, in particular, has argued that the killings are due to such factors as quarrels over boundaries of agricultural land inheritance, care of grandchildren, and also the elders' interference in marriages of their siblings (see *Uhuru,* March 10, 1999:4).

Conclusion

This chapter has endeavoured to explain the complexity and severity of the phenomenon of witch killings among the most populous ethnic group in Tanzania, the Sukuma. Whereas in the past, witchcraft practices were handled by traditional institutions and the killings of suspected witches were rare, today, however, they have become common and the Tanzanian state seems incapable of coming to grips with the problem. For one thing, witch-finding and the killing of witch suspects has become a lucrative business. Whereas in the past divination was a respected and genuine occupation of a few traditional "doctors" (*waganga*) it has, more recently, become a sinister preoccupation in which older women become scapegoats for some of the ills of society.

Although this phenomenon of witch killing is very complex and difficult to treat exhaustively in such a short space, this chapter has attempted to illuminate some of the underlying causes of this phenomenon as it is practised among the Sukuma. Certain interrelated factors must be highlighted as producing and causing the witch killing. The first is the commercialisation of the *waganga*. Many persons who have been officially licensed to practise traditional medicine become involved in the business of identifying witches and joining ranks with murderous thugs for money. This is a sad transformation of a group whose traditional role was to help people cope with risk and uncertainty as well as avert contingent disasters.

Secondly, the recent changes in post colonial governance have both resulted in a lack of trust in local institutions and increased the perception of local people that they have to attend to their own problems. This is an attitude that has been further reinforced by a lack of trust in the police and the courts, which, it is believed, can be bought and would only mete out justice to those who are able to pay. The third factor might be regarded as constituting a conjunction of these previous two, deriving from a rise in anxiety, fear and distrust. All these factors have a role to play in the killing of older women which still occurs in Sukumaland today.

Sadly, it must be must be concluded that the performance of the government, in terms of apprehending the culprits, is deplorable.

Traditional organisational groups such as *dagashida*[4] as well as *sungusungu*[5] have not lived up to the expectations. A number of NGOs such as Concern for the Elderly (COEL) and the Sukumaland Older Women's Programme (SOWP) have been addressing the problem. The Sukumaland Older Women's Project is attempting to stem the growing incidence of abuse and witchcraft accusations against older people through projects that link the generations and help raise awareness of and respect for older people's contributions to the community. These aim to improve awareness among older people about their rights and sources of relevant legal support and information.

Varkevisser (1969:55) concluded over 40 years ago that "the only remedy lies in fighting the symptoms of witchcraft by improving public health,

4. The *dagashida* is a traditional Sukuma community assembly led by a council of elders which decides what sanctions to impose on individuals caught in breaking community rules.
5. The *sungusungu* are village (youth) vigilante groups established by the Sukuma and Nyamwezi people in 1981 to handle disputes in their communities (see Heald 2006).

agriculture and education". A similar view might seem to be held by the Mongela Commission. Both views would seem to simplify a rather complex situation. Increased education, the availability of health care, and improved agricultural conditions, do not necessarily eradicate belief in witchcraft. However, one cannot help but agree that these would be important first steps to the elimination of the underlying causes of the killings of older women in Sukumaland.

References

Ashforth, A., 2001, "An Epidemic of Witchcraft? The Implications of AIDS for the Post-Apartheid State", *African Studies*, 61(1), 121–143.

Brandström, P., 1985, "The Agro-Patoral Dilemma: Underutilisation or Overexploitation of Land among the Sukuma of Tanzania", African Studies Programme, Department of Anthropology, Uppsala, Working Papers in African Studies Number 8.

Chama cha Mapinduzi, 1988, Ripoti ya Tume ya Kamati Kuu ya Halmashauri ya Chama Cha Mapinduzi Kuhusu Mauaji ya Kikatili Katika Mikoa ya Tabora, Mwanza na Shinyanga CCM HQs Dodoma.

Comaroff, Jean and John L. Comaroff, 1993 (eds), *Modernity and Its Malcontents: Ritual and Power in Postcolonial Africa*. Chicago: Chicago University Press.

Cory, H., 1954, *The indigenous political system of the Sukuma and proposals for political reform*. Nairobi: The Eagle Press.

Evans-Pritchard E.E., 1937, *Witchcraft Oracles and Magic Among the Azande*. Oxford: Clarendon Press.

Geschiere, P., 1997, *The Modernity of Witchcraft: Politics and the Occult in Postcolonial Africa*. Charlottesville: University Press of Virginia.

ICRALearningMaterials–SukumalandCaseStudy–http://www.icra-edu.org/objects/anglolearn/Sukuma3_Scenarios1.pdf+sukumaland+development+scheme&hl

Heald, Suzette, 2006, "State, law and vigilantism in northern Tanzania", *African Affairs*, 2006,105, 265–283

Iliffe, J., 1979, *A modern history of Tanganyika*. Cambridge: Cambridge University Press.

Kohnert, Dirk, 1996, "Magic and Witchcraft: Implications for Democratisation and Poverty-Alleviating Aid in Africa", *World Development,* Vol. 24, No. 8, pp. 1347–1355

Kibuga, K., 1999a, "Wisdom and Witchery", *The Courier*, No.176:66–67.

—, 1999b, "Older People in Magu-Tanzania: The Killings and Victimisation of Older Women". Research Report. Help Age International, Dar es Salaam.

Madulu, N., 1998, "Changing Lifestyles in Farming Societies of Sukumaland: Kwimba District, Tanzania", *De-Agrarianisation and Rural Employment Network Working Paper* No. 27. Leiden: Afrika-Studiecentrum.

Malcolm, D., 1953, *Sukumaland: an African People and their Country.* Oxford: Oxford University Press.

Mesaki, S., 1993, "Witchcraft and Witch killings in Tanzania: Paradox and Dilemma". Unpublished Ph.D. thesis, Department of Anthropology, University of Minnesota.

Mesaki, S., 1994, "Witch killing in Sukumaland Tanzania", in R. Abrahams (ed.), *Witchcraft in Contemporary Tanzania.* Cambridge: Cambridge African Monographs, pp. 47–60.

—2001, "Baseline Survey of Magu District Villages". Consultancy Report for Sukumaland Older Women's Programme (SOWP)/Help Age International, Dar es Salaam.

Mfumbusa, F.B., 1999, "Witch Killings: Tanzania's Silent Holocaust", *Africanews,* 29:7–8.

Moore, H. and S. Todd, 2001, *Magical Interpretations, Material Realities: Modernity, Witchcraft and the Occult in Postcolonial Africa.* London: Routledge.

Nkya, A., 2000, "Witchcraft murders target elderly women in Tanzania", *The Artemis Arrow: Articles, Observations, Poems and Opinions,* October/November Issue.

Stroeken, K., 2001, "Defying the Gaze: Exodelics for the Bewitched in Sukumaland and Beyond", *Dialectical Anthropology,* Vol. 26, No. 3–4, pp. 285–309.

Tamric Agency, 2000, "Gender and witchcraft killings in Tanzania", March 27, Dar es Salaam.

Tanner R., 1956, "The Sorcerer in Northern Sukumaland, Tanganyika", *South-Western Journal of Anthropology,* Vol. 12, pp. 437–443.

—, 1970, *The Witch-murders in Sukumaland: A Sociological Commentary.* Uppsala: Scandinavian Institute of African Studies.

The Indigenous of Mwanza: The Sukuma People! http://www.mwanzacommunity.org/sukumaenglish.html

TOMRIC Agency, 2000, *Africa News Online,* March 27, Dar es Salaam.

URT (United Republic of Tanzania), 1997, *Socio Economic Profile of Mwanza Region.*

Varkevisser, C., 1969, "Growing Up in Sukumaland", in *Primary Education in Sukumaland.* Groningen: CESO Walters-Noorrhoft.

—, 1973, "Socialisation in a Changing Society: Sukuma Childhood in Rural and Urban Mwanza, Tanzania." Den Haag: Centre for the Study of Education in Changing Societies.

CHAPTER 4

Invisible Hands and Visible Goods: Revealed and Concealed Economies in Millennial Tanzania

Todd Sanders

[African] leaders must become more accountable to their peoples. Transactions must become more transparent, and funds must be seen to be properly administered, with audit reports made public and procurement procedures overhauled (World Bank 1989:15).

The capacity to govern well in Africa is developing but still limited. Technical capacity is weak. Accountability and transparency are lacking (World Bank 1994:183).

"Transparency" is a major watchword – if not *the* major watchword – for policymakers, politicians and other proponents of "modernity" at this *début de siècle*.[1] In the US today this observation is as patent as it is pedestrian. Discourses of transparency permeate an array of American political arenas ranging from the Freedom of Information Act to the periodic unfolding of various Presidential "Gates": Nixon's Watergate, Reagan's Irangate, Clinton's Zippergate. "We have the right to know," or so the public and media often proclaim. From this vantage point, openness is desirable while things hidden from view are morally untenable. For only when political doings (and naturally, their *un*doings) are revealed in full can people be held accountable for their actions.[2]

---

1. This chapter first appeared in *Transparency and Conspiracy: Ethnographies Suspicion in the New World Order*, eds, H. West and T. Sanders (Duke 2003), and is reprinted (with minor changes) by permission of the publishers.
2. The fact that modernisation theory was largely an American creation (e.g., Rostow 1960), and that its advent coincided with post-war tensions on the international political scene, is not coincidental. At least according to official discourses, modernity meant freedom to choose, whether political parties or economic goods. It meant, above all, an open society, the workings of which were transparent and readily obvious to all. In this sense, to be modern was to be American. Naturally, this model made most sense when anchored firmly in its Cold War context, contrasted as it was with the "closed" and "unfree" Soviet Union.

Nor is this solely an American preoccupation. All across the globe, modernity's mouthpieces place a heavy emphasis on, for instance, "transparency" in democratic processes, free elections in which all dealings are open to scrutiny, and the importance of such public visibility for legitimating those processes (e.g., Dundas 1994; Koffi 1993; Scholte 1998; Shukla 1998). The notion of "transparency" similarly lies central to the everyday operation of myriad transnational institutions like the United Nations, European Union, World Bank, World Trade Organization, International Monetary Fund and various non-governmental organisations (Clamers 1997; Kopits and Craig 1998; Kratz 1999; Marceau and Pedersen 1999). Whether uncovering covert weapons of mass destruction, monitoring electoral processes in far-flung locales, or revealing hidden (and sometimes hideous) realities through Truth and Reconciliation Commissions or war tribunals, such institutions frequently operate on the assumption that obscurity and the New World Order are fundamentally at odds. A modern world must be a transparent world.

This desire to unveil the hidden, to disclose the closed, to reveal the concealed – in short, to make transparent that which is out of sight – is as central to economic processes as it is to political ones (Larsson and Lundberg 1998). Hardly surprising, really, given the popular Western view that political and economic liberalisation are mutually intertwined (see Callaghy 1993). To provide but one example, the IMF, in the interests of promoting democracy, has continually insisted on radical economic restructuring across the globe, calling for the decentralisation and privatisation of state-run enterprises. In persistently asking probing questions about who controls what economic resources, to what ends and for whose benefit, developers aim to make visible an underlying market-run rationality, to make "transparent" the everyday workings of local and global economies.

This is as true for Africa as elsewhere, as the above epigrams from the World Bank suggest: there can be no "development", no "modernisation", until economic transactions are laid bare, until they are rendered "transparent" for all to see. To be truly modern, so the reasoning goes, our world simply *must* be transparent. Where it is not, we must make it so. In this respect transparency is both a process and an outcome – it is modernity's moral compulsion as well as its characteristic feature; at once its motor and its message.

Yet if modernity is characterised by "intensive reflexivity" (Eisenstadt 2000:3; Giddens 1990:36ff), as Max Weber long ago assured us it was (see Faubion 1993:113–15), it is somewhat surprising that "transparency", one of modernity's most conspicuous current tropes, has received so little sustained analytic attention. All the more so when we notice that, in the real world, modernity and transparency rarely march hand in hand.

Take Tanzania. Many Tanzanians are today skeptical that modernity, in any form, necessarily coincides with transparency and accountability as many Western proponents claim it should. This skepticism is multifaceted, but results in part from their historical experiences with their northern neighbours of Kenya.

On the face of it, postcolonial Kenya has been one of the most enthusiastic supporters of the ideology of transparent political and economic processes. They have held elections. They have encouraged free enterprise. And they have fostered private ownership of land. Perhaps unremarkably, given the Kenyan government's seeming modern line, Western developers have believed and encouraged their efforts in the form of massive amounts of economic capital that have flowed, and continue to flow, into the country.

Yet what seems to capture many Tanzanians' imaginations is not these lofty ideals of "transparency", but rather the "politics of the belly" (Bayart 1993) evident in the workings of the modern Kenyan system. For simmering beneath the surface of claims to transparency and rationality lurks the seedy underside of modern African governmentality: obscure but determining political intrigues from the lowest to the highest levels; élites who publicly espouse openness and fair competition, but who, off stage, accumulate staggering amounts of personal wealth – houses and automobiles, livestock and land – often through shadowy dealings with fellow "tribesmen", friends and colleagues. As a result many Tanzanians see the Kenyan model of modernity *not* as a model of clarity or rationality, but as the very epitome of obscurity and ill-understood processes.[3] Modernity, from this perspective, breeds ambiguity not transparency.

This is certainly the view held by the Ihanzu of northern Tanzania with

---

3. Of course Tanzania, with its postcolonial history of socialist ujamaa policies, was for many years seen by Kenyans and Westerners as the epitome of the closed society. And yet, ironically, ujamaa aimed to promote the very transparency it was criticised for ignoring, and which was seen to be lacking in Kenya. In theory, all Tanzanians were meant to participate in clearly identifiable chains of command that linked the most distant villager with the highest government official in Dar es Salaam. The economy, similarly, would operate as an open book, being collectively owned and run by the people for the people. Whether any of this happened in practice is a topic for another time.

whom I have lived and carried out fieldwork since the early 1990s.[4] For these people – and the Ihanzu are scarcely alone here – modernity as locally envisaged and experienced is not about revealing but concealing the powers that animate their world. As the Ihanzu are increasingly drawn into broader regional, national and international markets and political structures, a process that has been ongoing for well over a century, the operation of powers in their world has been made not more rational, clear or comprehensible but less so. This is an obfuscating process: a movement from relative understanding to virtual incomprehension, a subtle but certain undoing of all that is done. The irony, of course, is that Ihanzu experiences with modernity have proved precisely the opposite to what Western liberal visions would predict.

Today, we find one of the clearest Ihanzu statement on modernity, somewhat unexpectedly, in local discourses on witchcraft. But why witchcraft? As people modernise, shouldn't witchcraft and other "traditions" fade into oblivion, as Marx, Durkheim and Weber, each in his own way, assured us they would? Hardly. African witchcraft, it turns out, has proved engagingly flexible and inflexibly engaged with novel postcolonial realities (Ashforth 1996; Auslander 1993; Comaroff and Comaroff 1993; 2002; Geschiere 1997). Witchcraft is a discourse of the moment, speaking, in so many ways, to the conundrums of our contemporary world. It provides a particular sort of social diagnostics (Moore and Sanders 2001). How, exactly, this is so for the Ihanzu is the principle focus of this essay.

My argument runs as follows. In the Ihanzu cultural imagination modernity is, above all, a world of modern material goods. Such modern goods circulate differently than what they call traditional goods. While both modern and traditional goods are reputedly moved through the economy by the unseen powers of witchcraft, the powers that animate traditional transactions can be *seen* – by diviners and by the zero-sum logic made manifest in such processes. And because they are seen they are also understood. The powers that ensure the circulation of modern goods, in contrast, remain

---

4. This chapter is based on fieldwork carried out in Ihanzu, Tanzania, from August 1993 to May 1995 and from June to September 1999. I acknowledge the generous support of the UK Economic and Social Research Council, the US National Institute of Health, the Royal Anthropological Institute and the London School of Economics for funding different portions of this research; and the Tanzania Commission for Science and Technology (COSTECH) for granting me research clearances. I am grateful to Jean Comaroff, Harry West and an anonymous reviewer for their constructive comments, and especially to the men and women of Ihanzu who have graciously allowed me to trespass in their lives.

entirely hidden from view. The circulation, accumulation and destruction of modern goods do not betray the powers of the hidden logic that drive such processes. Nor can such obscure logics be uncovered through divination. It therefore remains unclear whether accumulating modern goods necessarily implies, as it does with traditional goods, destroying the wealth of others. This has ensured that Ihanzu encounters with modernity remain, above all, deeply ambivalent.

To begin, we need to paint, with broad brushstrokes, a picture of Tanzania today and situate Ihanzu on this canvas. Only then can we begin to appreciate the extent to which Ihanzu witchcraft singlemindedly seeks out the sense – and the senselessness – of a rapidly changing postcolonial world.

Millennial moments in the Tanzanian postcolony

In recent years, the contours of Tanzania's postcolonial landscape have changed in remarkable ways. So much so, in fact, that the term "postcolonial" itself has little meaning, given the homogenising demands the term makes on a nation that has continually transformed itself since independence in 1961. The advent of these changes, changes that would forever alter the nascent nation's cultural, political and economic landscapes, can be traced to President Julius Nyerere's renowned programme of African Socialism. *Ujamaa*, as it was known, was arguably the grandest social experiment ever attempted in Tanzania. Its avowed aim was to transform Tanzania into a modern nation state, its populace into modern citizens. Crucially, this would be a "meaningful modernity", a modernity on their own terms, the parameters of which would not be dictated by the West.

Ujamaa had broad philosophical underpinnings. In theory, *ujamaa* was a "non-Marxist socialism"(Tripp 1997:62) that many saw as uniquely African, at least insofar as it was informed by notions of unity (*umoja*) and self-reliance (*kujitegemea*) within the world system (see Nyerere 1968). In practice *ujamaa* followed a Chinese model of state centralisation, whereby administrative powers were highly concentrated in the central government and delegated to local-level authorities in diminishing amounts. Following the famous 1967 Arusha Declaration, in particular, the state's involvement in the economy grew dramatically, leading to the nationalisation of major commercial, financial and manufacturing institutions.[5] Borders with neigh-

---

5. Writings on the *ujamaa* period are voluminous. See Hyden (1980); Shivji (1995); Stoger-Eising (2000); and on the *ujamaa* villagisation programme, Ergas (1980); Scott (1998: Ch. 7).

bouring countries were closed; severe import restrictions on foreign goods and currencies were imposed; emphasis was placed on production within the nation, for the nation – a nation of citizens toiling for the good of all Tanzanians. For a number of complex reasons, *ujamaa* did not survive over the long run.

By the time I arrived in Tanzania in the early 1990s, the draconian socialist edifice called *ujamaa* was on its last legs. The gradual yet irreversible withering of the omnipresent state had been underway for some years. And now, in the 1990s, a number of factors coalesced that would transform Tanzania's political and economic landscapes forever.

Central to these changes was the Zanzibar Declaration of 1991, as it later came to be known, which boldly challenged the 1967 Arusha Declaration and led to a number of consequential "amendments" to it; amendments that, in reality, radically undermined rather than updated the Arusha Declaration's original vision. "The symbolic importance of these changes," notes Tripp, "cannot be emphasized strongly enough, for the Arusha Declaration was the central document in establishing the egalitarian, self-reliant, and socialist orientation that Tanzania adopted" (Tripp 1997:171). A new "open" Tanzania now sat tantalizingly on the horizon. And this novel vision permeated every imaginable domain.

By 1992, Tanzania's ruling Revolutionary Party, the *Chama Cha Mapinduzi* (CCM), had allowed independent political parties to register. Within a few years, Tanzania's first ever multiparty elections were held. The Party has since surrendered its stranglehold over the media. The three officially sanctioned, government-owned newspapers now circulate alongside a multitude of locally produced newspapers, tabloids and magazines, not to mention any number of international news sources. The single state radio station has, of late, been joined by manifold others from near and far and listeners tune in to listen to news, football matches and other items of interest. Additionally, mainland Tanzania saw its first ever television broadcast in 1994. Today, urban and some rural citizens can watch the private network ITV which broadcasts local and foreign serials and newscasts, as well as many American sitcoms and action movies. Furthermore, many urbanites in Dar es Salaam, Arusha and other bustling centres now have regular access to cable and satellite systems that offer programming from across the globe.

Coinciding with these far-reaching political changes has come economic liberalisation. In the early 1990s, the second President of the United Republic of Tanzania, Ali Hassan Mwinyi, opted publicly and categorically for the wholesale adoption of the IMF's structural adjustment programme in a bid to transform Tanzania into a viable post-socialist state. Several international banks like Standard Charter and Barclay's, following their post-independence expulsions, have since re-established themselves or are actively taking steps to do so. No longer do foreign exchange restrictions apply; US dollars and other foreign currencies can now be readily – and legally – exchanged at any number of Bureaux de Change. Formerly tightly-controlled or closed terrestrial borders with neighbouring countries have all been re-opened, and everyday and luxury consumer goods (formerly controlled by the state) today flow *en masse* across them.

It is in the cities that these dramatic changes have most radically reconfigured people's life-worlds. Privately owned shops are filled with consumer goods of every type imaginable. The informal economy is booming (Tripp 1997). Street markets bustle with urbanites, young and old, buying imported radios and CD players, Levi's and Calvin Klein clothing. Following decades of shortages under *ujamaa*, enterprising Tanzanians have today filled their country with a plethora of new consumer goods – and dreams for a better future. "*Ujamaa* is dead," one Dar es Salaam street vendor enthusiastically told me in 1999. "Today, if we try, we can have anything we want!"

But such dreams are not always good ones, and can just as easily become nightmares. For as wealth in the shops and amongst an élite class of individuals increases, so, too, across a much broader segment of the population do relative poverty, envy and untenable and unobtainable dreams of a vastly better future. On this score, ordinary Tanzanians recognise full well that economic liberalisation has come with devastating costs (Kaiser 1996; Lugalla 1995; 1997; Ponte 1998).

As this suggests, there is a certain "millennial capitalism"(Comaroff and Comaroff 1999) in the air that appears to have affected – or, more correctly, *infected* – many Tanzanians. By this term, I do not simply mean "capitalism at the millennium", but, more fundamentally, "capitalism invested with salvific force; with intense faith in its capacity, if rightly harnessed, wholly to transform the universe of the marginalised and disempowered" (Comaroff and Comaroff 2002). Indeed, while such millennial capitalism has recently reared its head across the globe, it has done so most spectacularly in post-revolutionary places like Eastern Europe, the former Soviet Union and Tanzania, "where there has been an abrupt conversion to laissez-faire capitalism from tightly regulated material and moral economies; where evocative calls for entrepreneurialism confront the realities of marginalisation in the planetary distribution of resources; where totalising ideologies have suddenly given way to a spirit of deregulation, with its taunting mix of desire and disappointment, liberation and limitation" (Comaroff and Comaroff 2002). In such overdetermined circumstances, many Tanzanians feel, paradoxically, that they can do anything, and nothing at all, to better their situation.

No Tanzanian is unaware today of the country's recent, monumental transformations. The extent to which they have participated in them, however, is quite another matter. For even as new idioms of *demokrasia* and "the free market" (*soko huria*) have taken hold and blazed, like wildfires, across the land, they have done so in a jerky and irregular manner. Economic liberalisation, on the whole, has been an uneven process. The people of Ihanzu, like Tanzanians everywhere, are eager to come to terms with the sweeping changes that have recently arrived – if only piecemeal – on their doorstep.

The Ihanzu live over some 600 square miles in north-central Tanzania, in the northernmost part of Iramba district.[6] This semi-arid, relatively remote region is poorly connected to Tanzania's major urban centres: it is a ten-hour drive from Arusha, most of this on irregular, unpaved roads; it is even further from Dar es Salaam. The Ihanzu are predominantly agriculturalists, and subsist in their precarious environment on sorghum, millet and maize. These grains are used to make *ugali*, a stiff porridge that forms the basis of all meals. Sorghum also forms an important source of cash income when made into beer. Grain is rarely sold, since there are no local markets for the sale of foodstuffs. Nor, given the often unforgiving climate, is there ever much excess grain that could be sold anyway. Rainfall in this region is far from certain. Droughts and famines are common.

These harsh realities notwithstanding, of late, at this particular millennial moment, Ihanzu has experienced a veritable flood of modern consumer wares – or at least this is true for the better-connected parts of Ihanzu. One such place is the village of Ibaga.

Ibaga is located in western Ihanzu. While the village first appeared on the map in the early 1960s, it was only with the demise of *ujamaa* policies and the increased opening-up of the economy through the 1990s that business interests sky-rocketed. Today Ibaga is home to five guesthouses, a small restaurant, a high proportion of zinc-roofed homes, eight reasonably large, well-stocked shops, two petrol-powered grinding machines and three fairly regular bus services that connect what has now become a regional economic trading centre with the larger town of Singida and the city of Arusha. One particularly enterprising shopkeeper even has a generator that powers the only

---

6. The people refer to themselves as Anyîhanzu – "the people of Ihanzu". The land they call "Ihanzu".

television and video player for hundreds of miles. It is here, too, in Ibaga, that people from all over Ihanzu come to purchase Tanzanian-made and imported products at a thriving monthly market. In comparison with the rest of Ihanzu, Ibaga has an abundance of modern material goods and goodies, all of which have provided fodder for imagining what a "modern" Ihanzu might look like, and the powers that might make such a possibility into a reality.

One of the most intractable problems villagers face has been coming to terms with the production, circulation and consumption of these newly-arrived "modern" goods; in establishing, in other words, a meaningful relationship between distant sites of production and local sites of consumption. How, exactly, do local shopkeepers, business persons and others attract and amass "modern" wealth? It is at this juncture that witchcraft enters the picture. To see how and why, we must first consider Ihanzu notions of "modernity" and "tradition" and the colonial context from which they sprang.

"Modernity", "tradition" and the Ihanzu historical experience

The aim of this section is to outline the role German and British colonial powers played in Ihanzu, first, in reifying the categories of "tradition" and "modernity" and, second, in filling these categories with meaning. There are three principle points I wish to make. First, colonial and postcolonial administrators envisage(d) a world sharply divided between "tradition" and "modernity". Second, in these imaginings, tradition is about "things local" while modernity is about "things distant". And finally, the Ihanzu today largely subscribe to this historically prevailing discourse on tradition and modernity, both in terms of the categories and contents (Sanders 2003). In the sections that follow we turn more directly to the role witchcraft plays in imagining "modernity" today.

German and British colonial officials never found Ihanzu an easy place to deal with. In fact, from the first – and bloody – colonial encounter with the Ihanzu in 1893, European colonial powers considered the Ihanzu "primitive", "superstitious" and "tradition-bound".[7] Of course these views were

---

7. Such terms appear time and again in early written sources. The Germans were the first to enter the area. For some of their views on this point see Werther (1894; 1898), Kohl-Larsen (1939; 1943). For later British perspectives: 'Kondoa-Irangi Annual Report, 14 April 1920', p. 13, Tanzania National Archives (hereafter *TNA*), File 1733/1; 'Singida District Annual Report 1927', p. 8, *TNA*, File 967:823. 'Kondoa-Irangi Annual Report 1920-1921', p. 16, *TNA*, File 1733:5; 'Mkalama: the back of beyond,' (c.1928) Rhodes House (hereafter *RH*), File MSS Afr. s. 272.

commonly held by colonials almost everywhere they landed, given the prevailing social evolutionary paradigm through which they viewed the world at the time. Yet Ihanzu's distant location and harsh climate nurtured these images to a greater degree than might have otherwise been possible.

As far as colonial power centres were concerned, Ihanzu remained well off the beaten track. The German-built fort at the Ihanzu village of Mkalama was one of the most remote and undesirable postings in the whole of German East Africa. At least one German officer died and was buried there. When British forces took over the fort following the First World War, they fared little better. By 1919, only a year or so later, no fewer than nine British political officers had come and gone due to the "notoriously unhealthy climate".[8] In most British administrators' minds, Ihanzu truly was "the back of beyond".[9]

Given the ever-present uncertainties of the climate and Ihanzu's relatively distant location, German and British administrators alike considered Ihanzu an improbable site for large-scale, intensive cash-cropping.[10] Accordingly, throughout the colonial era, comparatively few efforts were made to improve local infrastructures. The "primitive" people of Ihanzu were instead looked upon more as a labour reserve for other, more fertile parts of the country. If these people were to be "developed" or "modernised", they would have to enter the modern sphere not at home as producers but in distant locations as migrant labourers. The Ihanzu, like their neighbours, have thus been forced to trek long distances in search of labour – to urban centres like Singida and Arusha – since the Germans first imposed taxes in the area around the turn of the century (Adam 1963a; Iliffe 1979: 161).[11]

British administrators posted in Ihanzu never entirely abandoned hope that these "tradition-bound" people might one day become "modern", however, even in the villages. Consider one District Commissioner's comments in the 1920s concerning a recently inaugurated Ihanzu chief:

---

8. 'Mkalama Annual Report 1919-1920', pp. 2, 22; *TNA*, File 1733/1.
9. Acting District Officer, A. W. Wyatt (c. 1928) 'Mkalama: the back of beyond,' *RH*, File MSS Afr. s. 272.
10. The one and only early attempt of which I am aware – a rubber plantation set up by Herr Bell near Mkalama village – failed miserably immediately after the First World War. See 'Mkalama Annual Report 1919-1920', p. 21, *TNA*, File 1733/1.
11. Administrative Officer in Charge, J. F. Kenny-Dillon, 'Mkalama Annual Report, 1924', p. 2, *TNA*, File 1733/14: 91; Assistant Probation Officer, 'Local Courts, Iramba Division', 1957, *TNA*, File 68/L4/2.

The authority, Asmani, comes of a line of rainmakers, but having spent the last seven years in the K[ings] A[frican] R[ifles] [in Dar es Salaam] prior to succeeding to the chiefship this year on the death of his uncle, Kali, it is more than probable that he does not know much about the art which was always jealously guarded by old Kali [the previous "chief"]. As far as can be ascertained, Asmani has not been initiated in accordance with tribal custom. It is anticipated therefore that rainmaking will not play such a prominent part in the tribal life as hitherto.

Asmani is a self-confident, large moustached, pushing native, addicted to European silk suiting and Panama hats. The Assistant District Officer informs me that he feels quite ashamed of his own poor khaki when Asmani strolls in to give him good-day.

[...] When he has become used to the change from private in the K.A.R. to leader of a tribe he will probably be quite a useful man.[12]

Among other things, these remarks show how some colonial administrators serving in Ihanzu, first, sharply differentiated between "traditional" things like rainmaking and more "modern" things like European silk suits and Panama hats; and, second, how the former would eventually, it was hoped, be overcome by the latter. Additionally, they point up a particular colonial spatial imagining: distant is to modern as local is to traditional. The fact that Chief Asmani had lived far away from Ihanzu during his military service, and donned European garments, made him more progressive and modern in colonial eyes. It was thus thought he would prove "quite a useful man", as chief, in wrenching the Ihanzu people from the traditional, locally focused world they reputedly inhabited.

Colonial administrators' beliefs that the Ihanzu were traditional, combined with their policies on migrant labour and local (non-)development, largely account for the situation in Ihanzu today. The few roads are unsealed and rarely graded. There is no electricity; no telephone access; and there are few working water pumps. The few government dispensaries are poorly stocked, and often have no medicines at all. Even though Ihanzu has long been enmeshed in the modern world system, it bears few material markers that might underscore this point.

Today, postcolonial administrators continue to discuss the people of Ihanzu – if they discuss them at all – as an archetypal tradition-minded people. In a decidedly uncomfortable encounter with the District Commissioner (DC) in 1995, he told me this:

12. 'Singida District Annual Report 1927', p. 12, *TNA*, File 967:823.

Well, you know, the chiefs here in Tanzania for a long time stopped modernity (*maendeleo*). They kept people from becoming modern (*watu wa kisasa*). They were against education, against good roads, against business and against change. They only wanted old customs (*mila za zamani*), not modernity. Perhaps it's better that the chief stays there in Kirumi with his rainshrine. He had many years to send modernity backwards (*kurudisha nyuma maendeleo*). Now they're gone and the government's here. We will develop these people! Eh, I have yet to receive any of your reports from your work here. [...] I'd be very interested to read them. I think there might even be some cultural factors that are stopping these people from becoming modern, something I don't know about.

Anthropologists are not the only ones subjected to such unfortunate views. Worse still, the men and women of Ihanzu are regularly chastised for their alleged offence, as I discovered at many public, government meetings in the 1990s. "You should build modern houses with large windows, cement floors and tin roofs, not miserable *matembe* like your grandparents built," demanded the DC on one such occasion. The implication of such patronising harangues, both today as in the past, is that the Ihanzu and the things they do are traditional and backward while things modern are found elsewhere, usually in distant, urban places.[13] These discourses, their origins far from innocent, have given definitive shape to villagers' own conceptions of the categories "tradition" and "modernity".

In Ihanzu eyes, the categories of tradition (*jadi* or *mila*) and modernity (*maendeleo*) are conceptually and practically distinct. Everything in their cultural universe, so I was told, may be fitted into one of these two diametrically opposed categories. When Ihanzu men and women discuss tradition they often imply that it is made up of timeless, unchanging artifacts and behaviors. This is the expressed ideal. Nevertheless, practices can and do belie these ideals since what counts as tradition – take annual rainmaking rites (cf. Adam 1963b; and Sanders 1998; 2008a) – has sometimes changed dramatically over the years. Moreover, some things that are today considered "traditional" have been outright invented in recent years. For instance, in a 1986 battle over cattle between the Ihanzu, Iramba and Sukuma on the one hand, and the pastoral Datooga and Maasai on the other, a Sukuma vigilante organisation known as *Sungusungu* was used to great effect against

13. Due to the spottiness of historical documentation, the extent to which notions of "modernity" and "tradition" have changed from the colonial to the contemporary period remains an open question, but is no doubt a question that merits further investigation.

the pastoralists.[14] The Ihanzu created their own version of this organisation which they call *Nkili*. It has since been expanded to deal not only with cases of cattle theft, but theft of all sorts as well as some witchcraft cases. *Nkili*, people say, deals with things traditional and is therefore itself "traditional". Other things are considered appropriate for their inclusion in the category of tradition for their apparent longevity.

Starting fires with sticks, for example, rather than with matches, is said to be traditional since "this is how the ancestors did it". Other activities are similarly said to be traditional and, in theory, unchanging: all rainmaking rites; building mud and stick houses; cultivating sorghum and millet; brewing beer; hunting with bows and arrows; and herding. By extension, certain things are considered "traditional wealth": royal rainstones, rainmaking medicines, grain crops, livestock, mud and stick homes and children, among other things. Note that all "things traditional" are thought to come from home. It is here, in the villages, that such traditional things are normally produced, exchanged and consumed.

"Things modern" (*mambo a kisasa*), to the contrary, are invariably produced in and linked to faraway places: the cities of Arusha and Singida or, better still, Europe, America and (given their post-independence *ujamaa* polices) China.

Although modernity means many things to many people – Christianity, sealed roads, street lamps and well-stocked hospitals – modernity's overriding feature for most Ihanzu is its blatant and unrelenting materiality. More than anything else, the Ihanzu imagine modernity as a "world of goods", to borrow Douglas and Isherwood's (1979) phrase. But not any goods will do. More precisely, it is manufactured material goods that are not – and cannot – be produced at home in the villages. Bicycles, radios, plastic pitchers, tinned food, motorised transport, zinc-roofed houses are the stuff of modernity for most Ihanzu today. The origins, movements and frequently consumption of such modern goods are translocal in nature.

In light of Ihanzu's colonial and postcolonial experiences, and their current understandings of modernity and tradition, it is wholly unremarkable that they see modernity as something possessed by other peoples in other places; something experienced briefly in the cities during wage labour, and left behind when returning home. For this reason modernity is something that by definition lies beyond their grasp, almost. This is also why Ibaga vil-

---

14. For more on Sukuma *Sungusungu* vigilante groups see Bukurura (1994), Abrahams (1987), Mwaikusa (1994), Fleisher (2000).

lage – the only plausible local example of modernity-in-the-making – has recently proved the site of such avid speculation.

"Traditional" and "modern" wealth are thought to move differently through the economy (see also Sanders 1999). What I hope to show in what follows – and this is the crux of my argument – is that the powers that ensure the circulation of traditional wealth can be rendered visible and thus comprehensible while those concerning the circulation of modern wealth cannot and thus remain, all told, mystified and mystifying.

Seen and unseen realms, witchcraft and "traditional" wealth

The Ihanzu divide their world into two distinct realms. The first is the manifest world, the world that is visible and "obvious" to all. Herein lies the stuff of people's everyday existence: farming, herding, political dealings, economic exchanges and so on.

The second world is unseen and runs parallel to the first. This is the realm of witches (*alogi*), ancestral spirits (*alüngü*) and god (*itunda*). There is nothing particularly "wondrous" or "awe-inspiring" (Murphy 1998) about this invisible realm or the powers that operate within it. I would for this reason be reluctant to label it "supernatural", since such labels risk exoticisation. Rather, this realm and its powers are very much a part of the Ihanzu lived-in world – albeit an invisible part of that world – and can more accurately be understood as "public secrets" (Ashforth 1996:1194) that are both everyday and commonplace. People sometimes talk about the inner workings of this second realm as a "true secret" (*sili tai*), since such processes are, given their invisibility, poorly understood. Be that as it may, as we shall see shortly, seers, as well as the visible effects of at least some types of witchcraft, provide enough clues for people to have a fairly good idea of how these hidden powers operate.

These visible and invisible realms are thought to be causally linked in that power originates in the unseen realm and has visible effects in the everyday world. That is, the world Ihanzu inhabit in their day-to-day lives is animated by unseen forces from another realm, the ultimate source of all cosmic power.[15] Hidden powers determine public outcomes. Thus, as with the logical of conspiracy theories, most everyday activities in Ihanzu – be

---

15 In this respect Simmel was surely correct in noting that "[t]he secret offers, so to speak, the possibility of a second world alongside the manifest world; and the latter is decisively influenced by the former" (Simmel 1950 [1906]:330).

they politics, economic transactions or whatever – are thought to be guided and shaped in fundamental ways by invisible powers. Our everyday world is simply a façade that masks a deeper, more important and "real reality", one that lies beyond our immediate comprehension (Ashforth 1996:1220; Douglas 1970:xvi).

Obscure though this second realm may be, not everyone is excluded from it. Ihanzu seers (*aganga*; sing. *mûganga*), in particular, are precariously poised between visible and invisible worlds. And they allegedly move freely between them. The term "seer" I use intentionally rather than, say, diviner, healer or anything else, to emphasise the visual nature of their perceptual powers. Seers allegedly experience the unseen realm of power first-hand, usually at night, by smearing special medicines (*makota*) just above their eyes. This enables them "to see" (*tûona*) witches in action (cf. Goody 1970:227). Witches, for their part, are said to use similar medicines smeared above their eyes to make themselves invisible to mere mortals.

If seers participate in and thus understand the invisible realm of power, they can also access that world through divination sessions. Seers see clearly the determining powers of events-in-this-world, past, present and future as inscribed on their chicken oracles. Seers and others sometimes described such oracles (*nzelya*) to me as a "traditional X-rays" (*X-ray za kinyeji*), once again underscoring the visual nature of such perceptual powers. During divination sessions seers are said "to see" witches, spirits, problems and answers while reading (*kûsoma*) their X-ray chickens' entrails. With their insights into the invisible realm of witches, seers can reputedly understand the truth (*tai*) about witches – who they are, what they do, and how they do it.

Traditionally, one of witches' favourite ploys has been to destroy other people's wealth in order to amass it for themselves. Grain in particular, usually sorghum, seems to be the type of wealth most coveted by witches. Sometimes they are said to use their powers to amass livestock too. When it comes to accumulating so-called traditional wealth through witchcraft, all methods imply an economy of limited good or a zero-sum game economy. In other words, traditional wealth, in Ihanzu eyes, exists "in finite quantity and is always in short supply" (Foster 1965:296). What the witch takes, others lose. Seers see this only too well – in the invisible realm and in their chickens' entrails. They can see clearly, so I was told, which witch has stolen what from whom. The operation of so-called traditional power is transparent not only to the seer, but to ordinary villagers too. This is due to the visible traces such hidden powers leave in the everyday world including, as we shall see, wealth differentials generated between haves and have-nots.

There are a few methods witches reputedly use to accumulate so-called traditional goods. The first is to suck the sorghum from fellow villagers' plots and onto their own with the aid of certain medicines. Men and women commonly claim that a witch often farms a small parcel of land but reaps an unusually large harvest. For this reason many of those who regularly obtain large harvests are rumoured to have dabbled in the diabolical to acquire their goods, implying that other villagers have been robbed. When it comes to traditional wealth like grain, Ihanzu witches can therefore rightly be considered mystical thieves (cf. Heald 1986). I know of several villagers who, having rapidly acquired unusual amounts of grain, are rumoured to have done so at other villagers' immediate expense. As one woman told me, "You go out to your field and find that your sorghum has ripened, but that it is all rubbish. There's nothing (no grain) there. It has been sucked to some witch's plot." It may not be obvious who, exactly, got what from whom. Or at least not obvious to ordinary villagers. But there is no doubt that one farmer's gain is another's loss.

A second method witches allegedly use to amass traditional wealth is to attack medicinally and kill people in order to appropriate their labour. The following story, one that virtually anyone in Ihanzu could provide, tells of how this is supposedly done:

> Witches ride their hyenas through the night to find people and bewitch them. They are invisible, you know, because they put medicines on like this (*indicating smearing just above the eyes*) [...]. That person dies later, maybe in a week or a year. The witch then goes to the grave and pulls the corpse from the ground with medicines like this (*indicating touching a medicinally-covered index finger on the ground*). The witch takes this corpse home, puts medicine on its eyes so you can't see it, and makes it work on his fields at night. Sometimes these zombies (*atumbúka*) brew beer too and cook for the witch.

In this particular vision the ever-consuming witch does nothing whatsoever except eat – quite literally – the fruits of the exploited zombie labour force in the form of stiff porridge, beer and human labour.[16] In a similar but less extreme vein, witches sometimes steal people's souls at night, but return them by morning, so these souls can assist the witch in farming and other

---

16. Other Tanzanian groups like the Sukuma (Mesaki 1994:49), Iramba (Lindström 1988:183, n7), Fipa (Willis 1968: 4) and Kaguru (Beidelman 1963: 66, 93) appear to hold similar beliefs about nocturnal zombie labourers. None of the information I collected on Ihanzu zombie labourers suggests any link with the slave trade which probably tangentially affected Ihanzu in the late 1800s (cf. Shaw 1997), nor with local imaginings of migrant labour (Comaroff and Comaroff 2002).

domestic duties. The hapless victim is said to wake with an aching and exhausted body. As with stolen grain from a neighbour's field, both these nefarious methods of obtaining labour imply an economy of limited good. In terms of traditional wealth like sorghum, a witch only gains what others lose, something all villagers are ruefully aware of.

Another means witches reputedly use to gain traditional wealth is to make a "pact with a seer" (*ndagŭ*). A witch-to-be may visit a seer with the aim of accumulating extraordinary amounts of traditional wealth. This wealth may be in the form of children, livestock or grain, though the latter two are more common.[17] The seer, who knows about such matters from his participation in the invisible world, is said to provide the necessary medicine to make it happen. But accumulating wealth in this way comes only at a cost, and a high one: the party in question must forego one form of wealth – frequently child-bearing capabilities – to amass another like grain or livestock. Consider the following case, itself iconic of many others.

There is a well-known middle-aged couple that lives in the village of Matongo. This couple, it is rumoured, are witches. Msa, as I will call him, is a reasonably well-to-do Christian man. He and his wife Maria, also a Christian, own and farm unusually large tracts of land: three acres near their home, one acre in Maria's father's village and another 13 acres in a third village. In their house they have three large grain stores which provide ample grain for them and their two adopted children even in the worst famine years. This, together with 19 cows, 26 goats, five sheep and some 30 chickens, makes them one of the wealthiest families in the area, at least in terms of "traditional" measures of wealth.

The fact that their children are adopted is not, villagers claim, incidental. Maria is infertile. Their children are in reality those of Msa's sister, a fact everyone (except Msa and Maria) was eager to make apparent to me. But most are unsympathetic, for Msa has allegedly made a pact with a seer in which he willingly exchanged his wife's child-bearing capabilities for a guarantee of copious quantities of livestock and grain. As such, it is said that the couple will be wealthy for life in terms of livestock and grain, though decidedly and irrevocably impoverished when it comes to children.

---

17. Other types of pact are theoretically possible but less likely. For example, a couple may choose to forego large harvests and all livestock in order to bear many children. However many suggest that such choices are uncommon and probably foolish, since too many children without the means to care properly for them is a sure recipe – and in this case, an everlasting recipe – for personal disaster.

There are additional factors in this case worth noting. First, several villagers told me that Maria's breasts fluctuate in size inversely with the amount of grain in their grain stores. Thus, before the harvest, when grain stores are at their lowest levels, Maria's breasts are said to swell to considerable proportions. Conversely, when grain stores are filled to the hilt, just after the harvest, her breasts are virtually non-existent.[18] This seasonal waxing and waning of breasts and crops points up in a somewhat conspicuous manner the direct trade-off imagined between different types of wealth and fertility, in this case, crops versus child-bearing capabilities.

The foregoing should make it abundantly clear that those goods considered "traditional" – namely, grain, livestock and progeny – are thought to circulate, one against the other, in what amounts to a zero-sum economy (cf. Meyer 1995; Gable 1997). Witches benefit only by depriving other villagers (or with the *ndagú* pact, themselves) of their wealth. Whether sorghum is sucked directly from one plot to another, or acquired less directly by killing and then appropriating the deceased's labour power, the witch's gain is the moral man's loss. Within this discourse, the traditional Ihanzu witch is simultaneously the prime accumulator *and* consumer of material wealth. Witches' powers over the circulation of traditional wealth operate within a conceptually and geographically closed universe. For traditional wealth, the sites of production and consumption are virtually the same.

Seers know this. They can "see" the operation of invisible powers in their X-ray chickens. And they can even enter the invisible world of witches, if and when necessary, to get a better look. All other villagers know that traditional goods circulate in this way too. Such goods are locally produced and are always in limited supply. They cannot be created from thin air. Thus, although the invisible realm of power is not open to inspection by ordinary villagers under ordinary circumstances, the *modus operandi* of those powers is plain enough. Witches must destroy to accumulate. The everyday effects of witchcraft involving traditional goods render its operational logic transparent – or at least transparent enough for people to make sense of the relationship between occult power and traditional wealth. This is manifestly *not* the case when it comes to so-called modern economic processes.

Witchcraft and the circulation of "modern" wealth

If witchcraft is often evoked in Ihanzu to understand the circulation of traditional goods, this is also the case with modern goods. Not unexpect-

---

18. For the record, she reputedly makes up for the difference in the off season by stuffing old clothes in her blouse.

edly, the powers of this (im)moral economy operate in roughly the same way. Invisible powers continue to determine the visible world. And witches, so people claim, continue doggedly to accumulate and destroy things. Yet there is at least one crucial difference between economies of traditional and modern goods that should give us pause: the workings of witches' powers in "modern" contexts are no longer obvious. Diviners claim not to be able to see them. Ordinary people claim no longer to understand them. These invisible powers thus remain deeply ambivalent. To see why, I must provide further details.

On witches destroying modern wealth, the Ihanzu Lutheran preacher had this to say:

> If a witch were clever perhaps they would use hyenas to carry sorghum home from their fields! But that would be progress/modernity (*maendeleo*) and the witch is against that. Instead they ride aimlessly through the night [...] to bewitch their own clanmates and children. This is the work of the witch in Ihanzu, stupidity taken to an extreme. Witches destroy – that's their job – people and progress.

In Ihanzu such views are common. Witches, all seem to agree, intensely dislike development, modernity or progress, all terms glossed as *maendeleo*. In this sense Ihanzu witches, ever envious of their better-off neighbours, reinforce the familiar ethos of "keeping behind the Joneses" or "nightmare egalitarianism" (Gable 1997) commonly found across Africa (Gluckman 1956:96; Winter 1956:147; Ardener 1970:147–48; Fisiy and Geschiere 1991:253). One shopkeeper in Ibaga village put it like this: "Most Ihanzu don't do business because they're afraid of their neighbours (i.e. witches) who won't allow them to get ahead (*kuendelea*)."

Another Ibaga shop owner I knew well, a Sukuma man by birth, told me the following:

> There is something you must understand. Sukuma witches are ruthless, their medicines more powerful than those of the Ihanzu [witches]. The difference, though, is that Sukuma witches are not jealous (*wivu*) and so don't care if individuals prosper. [...] Ihanzu witches are different; they don't want people to modernise (*kuendelea*); if they see someone is getting ahead, he gets bewitched.

Over the course of my fieldwork I recorded many cases where unspecified witches allegedly destroyed modern goods in Ihanzu: ripping zinc roofs from people's homes with their medicines; compelling buses to crash into rocks, trees and ditches or simply to stop dead in their tracks; stealing and joy-riding buses on nocturnal forays at ridiculous speeds through the bush; ruining petrol-powered grinding machines by causing snakes, hyraxes and other small animals to enter and jam their inner gears. All such stories suggest that the Ihanzu witch and modernity cannot peacefully coexist. It comes as no surprise, then, to discover that men and women regularly evoke witchcraft to explain what they see as the failure of modernity in Ihanzu. Witches have always destroyed wealth. They continue to do so in its more modern forms (see Sanders 2008b).

But this is not the whole story. For, tellingly, people are not certain that witches attack modern wealth in order to accumulate it for themselves, as they supposedly do with traditional wealth. Their stories instead suggest that anti-modern witches are more ridiculous than scheming, and may gain nothing themselves for their dubious destructive efforts. Accumulation and destruction of so-called modern wealth appear *not* to be directly linked, a fact evident in what people say about local shopkeepers, their wealth and the occult powers they supposedly deploy to acquire it.

It was noted that today, in the wake of Tanzania's recent liberalisation of the economy, Ibaga village provides many Ihanzu with a convenient local example of modernity-in-the-making. This village, and more specifically those who do business there, are often the subject of intense speculation and suspicion of witchcraft. No one else in Ihanzu has so much and does, so it seems, so little to get it. Shop shelves are piled high with seemingly endless supplies of modern consumer goods – pots and pans in all imaginable and unimaginable shapes and sizes, cloth, oil, mosquito nets, nail polish with sparkles, plastic jewelry, tennis balls, thread, combs with pictures of Rambo on them, knives, clothes pins, candies and candles, transistor radios and even Pepsi. It would be strange if villagers did not speculate about the sources of such goods. And speculate they do. From whence come these wares?

Many I spoke with in private voiced their concerns that such business persons used witchcraft to acquire their wares, since it is common knowledge that no one gets rich by accident. Rather, accumulation of any sort requires determined efforts and frequently demands the exploitation of unseen powers of witchcraft. Yet, particularly with modern wealth, one central conceptual dilemma remains: since ordinary villagers in Ihanzu do not themselves possess many modern material goods, it is not conceivable that Ibaga shopkeepers acquire their wealth by depriving nearby residents. When it comes to modern wealth, there can be no locally-based finite economy.

It would be quite impossible, after all, to steal in a mystical manner goods from locals who do not possess such goods to begin with. As one elderly women succinctly noted:

> All those shopkeepers [in Ibaga village] are witches. How else do you think they fill their shops with those things they sell? Witchcraft, of course. [...] I don't know how they do it – who really knows the work of witches but witches? – but I do know one thing: they didn't get all those things from me!

And here, at last, we come to the heart of the matter. When it comes to modern material goods it is no longer reasonable to assume that Ihanzu witchcraft works in a zero-sum fashion as it does with more traditional forms of wealth (Foster 1964). Of course it might. It is just conceivable that the global movement of goods – translocal transactions between Ibaga shop-keepers, Arusha, Dar es Salaam, Kenya, Europe and America – might be a conceptually closed, if vastly expanded, economy of goods. If so, then local shopkeepers are depriving others in far-flung locations, but not local villagers, of their modern wares. If not, these business witches are simply amass-ing modern material wealth from a distant and unlimited store of goods. In either case, modern economic processes, by spanning vast distances, have become virtually unintelligible. Unlike the powers that drive traditional goods through local economies, the movements of modern goods cannot be monitored – they cannot be "seen" through divination and through their transactional zero-sum logics. The logic of translocal transactions thus remains elusive. Myriad questions remain for the Ihanzu concerning the movements of modern wealth through the economy. Do modern witches really accumulate without depriving others? Are the distant economies of goods in which some locals now participate limited or limitless in supply? Furthermore, why do some witches continue to destroy modern wealth if not to benefit themselves? Or do they benefit but in ways we have yet to understand? The distances between modern sites of production and local sites of consumption are simply too great, the paths between them too Byz-antine, to know for certain the mechanism at work. In short, the driving mechanism of modernity, its *motor spiritus*, remains a topic of ongoing, anx-ious deliberation. And a good deal of such deliberation is done through an idiom of witchcraft (also Sanders 2001; 2008b). Drawing meaningful links between distant "modern" sites of production and local "traditional" sites of consumption is, and will no doubt remain, an unfinished project.

Conclusion

I have argued that Ihanzu witchcraft involving what locals see as traditional wealth operates within a conceptually closed universe: it requires mystical predation where witches gain only at the expense of others. Thus, although the precise workings of "traditional" witchcraft are hidden from view, the operating logic can be inferred from its visible manifestations and from what diviners say. In contrast, where notions of witchcraft meet more "modern" forms of wealth, the nature of the links between wealth and invisible powers becomes much less obvious. Somewhat inexplicably, witches destroy wealth with seemingly no desire to appropriate it for themselves. Still other witches gain wealth, but apparently at no one's immediate expense, or at least no local's expense. The fact that these two discourses on modern witchcraft remain distinct suggests that Ihanzu experiences with "modernity" at home have been, at the very least, ambivalent. While encounters with modern materiality seem, on the surface, to offer the promise of amassing wealth at no one's expense, everyone suspects, on another level, that wealth must come from somewhere and someone. No one gets something for nothing. These competing notions of modern witchcraft appear to express people's hopes of actively participating in a world of material plenty, while at the same time acknowledging their apprehensions about the vast inequalities – and thus grave moral quandaries – that such material accumulation implies.

But allow me to be entirely clear, lest my argument be misunderstood. By no means do I wish to impute to the Ihanzu some pre-logical *mentalité primitive* that, muddled in a mystical fog, is incapable of grasping let alone coping with the ambivalences of our contemporary world. Quite the contrary. The Ihanzu may in fact possess better not worse insights into the conceptual quagmires of modernity. They may be better situated than many in the West to engage with the vagaries and incertitudes that frequently if not always accompany modern markets and novel regimes of production and consumption.

Recall, from the outset, that Western discourses of "modernity" and "transparency" go hand-in-hand, stressing, as they do, clarity, openness and rationality of process. What is more, Western economics has guns and butter graphs, supply and demand curves that flaunt, in a most visible way, this apparent rationality. But we also have our "invisible hands" that move economies in mysterious and inexplicable ways. And when our models of *homo oeconomicus* fail us altogether, in an effort to rescue them, we cry "market failure!" to indicate that our market-model oracle has itself been bewitched. Rather than downplaying or ignoring such magicalities of modernity (Comaroff and Comaroff 1993) – the patently odd fact that hidden hands and other enigmatic economic processes drive, in some unspecified manner, our everyday world – the Ihanzu dwell on such absurdities. Indeed for the Ihanzu, quite unlike many Western champions of modernity, these ambivalences are integral to modernity's make-up. Seen in this light the Ihanzu hold what is perhaps a more nuanced view of "the modern". They recognise and confront head-on its deep-seated ambivalences. Not for a moment do they pretend, for convenience's sake, that our world can ever be rendered entirely "transparent". From their perspective, it cannot. The world just doesn't work that way. The point, rather, is to try to make sense of modernity's seeming insensibilities, however fleeting that sense may be.

References

Abrahams, Ray G., 1987, "*Sungusungu*: Village Vigilante Groups in Tanzania", *African Affairs,* 86:179–96.

Adam, Virginia, 1963a, "Migrant Labour from Ihanzu". Conference Proceedings from the East African Institute of Social Research, Makerere College.

—, 1963b, "Rain Making Rites in Ihanzu". Conference Proceedings from the East African Institute of Social Research, Makerere College.

Ardener, Edwin, 1970, "Witchcraft, Economics and the Continuity of Belief" in Mary Douglas (ed.), *Witchcraft Confessions and Accusations.* London: Tavistock, pp. 141–60.

Ashforth, Adam, 1996, "Of Secrecy and the Commonplace: Witchcraft and Power in Soweto", *Social Research,* 63(4):1183–234.

Auslander, Mark, 1993, "'Open the Wombs!': The Symbolic Politics of Modern Ngoni Witchfinding", in Jean and John Comaroff (eds), *Modernity and Its Malcontents: Ritual and Power in Postcolonial Africa.* Chicago: University of Chicago Press, pp. 167–92.

Bayart, J-F., 1993, *The State in Africa: Politics of the Belly.* New York: Longman.

Beidelman, Thomas O., 1963, "Witchcraft in Ukaguru", in John Middleton and E. Winter (eds), *Witchcraft and Sorcery in East Africa.* London: Routledge and Kegan Paul, pp. 57–98.

Bukurura, Sufian H., 1994, "*Sungusungu*: Vigilantes in West-Central Tanzania". PhD thesis, Department of Anthropology, University of Cambridge.

Callaghy, Thomas M., 1993, "Vision and Politics in the Transformation of the Global Political Economy: Lessons from the Second and Third Worlds" in R.O. Slater, B.M. Schutz and S.R. Dorr (eds), *Global Transformation and the Third World.* Boulder: Lynne Rienner Publishers, pp. 161–257.

Clamers, Malcolm (ed.), 1997, *Developing Arms Transparency*. Bradford: Bradford University Press.

Comaroff, Jean and John Comaroff, 1993, "Introduction", in Jean and John Comaroff (eds), *Modernity and Its Malcontents: Ritual and Power in Postcolonial Africa*. Chicago: University of Chicago Press, pp. xi–xxxvii.

—, 1999, "Occult Economies and the Violence of Abstraction: Notes from the South African Postcolony", *American Ethnologist*, 26(2):279–303.

—, 2002, "Alien-Nation: Zombies, Immigrants, and Millennial Capitalism", *The South Atlantic Quarterly*, 101.4(2002):779–805.

Douglas, Mary, 1970, "Thirty Years after 'Witchcraft, Oracles and Magic'", in Mary Douglas (ed.), *Witchcraft Confessions and Accusations*. London: Tavistock, pp. xiii–xxxviii.

— and Brian Isherwood, 1979, *The World of Goods: Towards an Anthropology of Consumption*. New York: W.W. Norton and Company.

Dundas, C.W., 1994, "Transparency in Organizing Elections", *Round Table*, 329:61–76.

Eisenstadt, S.N., 2000, "Multiple Modernities", *Dædalus (special issue: Multiple modernities*, 129(1):1–29.

Ergas, Z., 1980, "Why Did the *Ujamaa* Village Policy Fail? Towards a Global Analysis", *Journal of Modern African Studies*, 18(3):387–410.

Faubion, James D., 1993, *Modern Greek Lessons: A Primer in Historical Constructivism*. Princeton: Princeton University Press.

Fisiy, Cyprian F. and Peter Geschiere, 1991, "Sorcery, Witchcraft and Accumulation: Regional Variations in South and West Cameroon", *Critique of Anthropology*, 11(3):251–78.

Fleisher, Michael L., 2000, "Sungusungu: State-Sponsored Village Vigilante Groups among the Kuria of Tanzania", *Africa*, 70(2):209–28.

Foster, George M., 1964, "Treasure Tales, and the Image of the Static Economy in a Mexican Peasant Community", *Journal of American Folklore*, 77:39–44.

—, 1965, "Peasant Society and the Image of Limited Good", *American Anthropologist*, 67:293–315.

Gable, Eric, 1997, "A Secret Shared: Fieldwork and the Sinister in a West African Village", *Cultural Anthropology*, 12(2):213–33.

Geschiere, Peter, 1997, *The Modernity of Witchcraft: Politics and the Occult in Postcolonial Africa*. Charlottesville: University Press of Virginia.

Giddens, Anthony, 1990, *The Consequences of Modernity*. Stanford: Stanford University Press.

Gluckman, Max, 1956, *Custom and Conflict in Africa*. Oxford: Basil Blackwell.

Goody, Esther, 1970, "Legitimate and Illegitimate Aggression in a West African State", in Mary Douglas (ed.), *Witchcraft Confessions and Accusations*. London: Tavistock, pp. 207–44.

Heald, Suzette, 1986, "Witches and Thieves: Deviant Motivations in Gisu Society", *Man*, 21:65–78.

Hyden, Goran, 1980, *Beyond Ujamaa in Tanzania: Underdevelopment and an Uncaptured Peasantry*. London: Heinemann.

Iliffe, John, 1979, *A Modern History of Tanganyika*. Cambridge: Cambridge University Press.

Kaiser, Paul J., 1996, "Structural Adjustment and the Fragile Nation: The Demise of Social Unity in Tanzania", *The Journal of Modern African Studies*, 34(2):227–37.

Koffi, N., 1993, "L'ideologie De La Transparence Et La Democratie Contempraire", *Quest*, 12(1):289–92.

Kohl-Larsen, Ludwig, 1939, *Simbo Janira: Kleiner Grosser Schwarzer Mann*. Kassel: Im Erich Röth.

—, 1943, *Auf Den Spuren Des Vormenschen (Deutsche Afrika-Expedition 1934–1936 und 1937–1939)*. Stuttgart: Strecher und Schröder.

Kopits, George and Jon Craig, 1998, *Transparency in Government Operations*. Utgort? International Monetary Fund.

Kratz, Catherine, 1999, "Transparency and the European Union", *Cultural Values*, 3(4):387–92.

Larsson, Mats and David Lundberg, 1998, *The Transparent Market*. London: Macmillan Press Ltd.

Lindström, Jan, 1988, "The Monopolization of a Spirit: Livestock Prestations During an Iramba Funeral", in S. Cederroth, C. Corlin and J. Lindström (eds), *On the Meaning of Death: Essays on Mortuary Rituals and Eschatological Beliefs*. Uppsala: Acta Universitatis Upsaliensis, pp. 169–83.

Lugalla, Joe L.P., 1995, "The Impact of Structural Adjustment Policies on Women's and Children's Health in Tanzania", *Review of African Political Economy*, 63:43–53.

—, 1997, "Development, Change, and Poverty in the Informal Sector During the Era of Structural Adjustment in Tanzania", *Canadian Journal of African Studies*, 31(3):424–51.

Marceau, Gabrielle and Peter N. Pedersen, 1999, "Is the Wto Open and Transparent? A Discussion of the Relationship of the Wto with Non-Governmental Organisations and Civil Society's Claims for More Transparency and Public Participation", *Journal of World Trade*, 33(1):5–49.

Mesaki, Simeon, 1994, "Witch-Killing in Sukumaland", in R. Abrahams (ed.), *Witchcraft in Contemporary Tanzania*. Cambridge: African Studies Centre, pp. 47–60.

Meyer, Birgit, 1995, "'Delivered from the Power of Darkness': Confessions of Satanic Riches in Christian Ghana", *Africa*, 65(2):236–55.

Moore, Henrietta L. and Todd Sanders, 2001, "Magical Interpretations and Material Realities: An Introduction", in Henrietta L. Moore and Todd Sanders (eds), *Magical Interpretations, Material Realities: Modernity, Witchcraft and the Occult in Postcolonial Africa*. London: Routledge, pp. 1–27.

Murphy, William P., 1998, "The Sublime Dance of Mende Politics: An African Aesthetic of Charismatic Power", *American Ethnologist*, 25(4):563–82.

Mwaikusa, J.T., 1994, "Maintaining Law and Order in Tanzania: The Role of *Sungusungu* Defence Groups", in J. Semboja and O. Therkildsen (eds), *State, Ngos and People's Organizations in the Provision of Services in East Africa*, Copenhagen: Centre for Development Research.

Nyerere, Julius K., 1968, *Ujamaa: Essays on Socialism*. Dar es Salaam: Oxford University Press.

Ponte, Stefano, 1998, "Fast Crops, Fast Cash: Market Liberalization and Rural Livelihoods in Songea and Morogoro Districts, Tanzania", *Canadian Journal of African Studies*, 32(2):316–48.

Rostow, W.W., 1960, *The Stages of Economic Growth*. Cambridge: Cambridge University Press.

Sanders, Todd, 1998, "Making Children, Making Chiefs: Gender, Power and Ritual Legitimacy", *Africa*, 68(2):238–62.

—, 1999, "Modernity, Wealth and Witchcraft in Tanzania", *Research in Economic Anthropology*, 20:117–31.

—, 2001, "Save Our Skins: Structural Adjustment, Morality and the Occult in Tanzania", in Henrietta L. Moore and Todd Sanders (eds), *Magical Interpretations, Material Realities: Modernity, Witchcraft and the Occult in Postcolonial Africa*. London: Routledge, pp. 160–83.

—, 2003, "Reconsidering Witchcraft: Postcolonial Africa and Analytic (Un)Certainties", *American Anthropologist*, Vol. 105, No. 2, pp. 326–340.

—, 2008a, *Beyond Bodies: Rainmaking and Sense Making in Tanzania*. Toronto: University of Toronto Press.

—, 2008b, "Buses in Bongoland: Seductive Analytics and the Occult", *Anthropological Theory*, Vol. 8, No. 2, pp. 107–132.

Scholte, Jan Aart, 1998, "Globalization, Governance and Democracy in Post-Communist Romania", *Democratization*, 5(4):52–77.

Scott, James C., 1998, *Seeing Like the State: How Certain Schemes to Improve the Human Condition Have Failed*. New Haven: Yale University Press.

Shaw, Rosiland, 1997, "The Production of Witchcraft/Witchcraft as Production: Memory, Modernity, and the Slave Trade in Sierra Leone", *American Ethnologist*, 24(4):856–76.

Shivji, Issa G., 1995, "The Rule of Law and *Ujamaa* in the Ideological Formation of Tanzania", *Social and Legal Studies*, 4(2):147–74.

Shukla, S.N., 1998, "Good Governance: Need for Openness and Transparency", *Indian Journal of Public Administration*, XLIV(3):398–406.

Simmel, Georg, 1950 [1906], "The Secret and the Secret Society", in Kurt H. Wolff (ed.), *The Sociology of Georg Simmel.* Glencoe, Illinois: Free Press, pp. 307–76.

Stoger-Eising, V., 2000, "*Ujamaa* Revisited: Indigenous and European Influences in Nyerere's Social and Political Thought", *Africa,* 70(1):118–43.

Tripp, Aili Mari, 1997, *Changing the Rules: The Politics of Liberalization and the Urban Informal Economy in Tanzania.* Berkeley: University of California Press.

Werther, C.W., 1894, *Zum Victoria Nyanza: Eine Antisklaverei-Expedition und Forschungsreise.* Berlin: Gergonne Verlag.

—1898, *Die Mittleren Hochländer Des Nördlichen Deutsch-Ost-Afrika.* Berlin: Hermann Paetel.

Willis, Roy G., 1968, "Kamcape: An Anti-Sorcery Movement in South-West Tanzania", *Africa,* 38:1–15.

Winter, E.H., 1956, *Bwamba: A Structural-Functional Analysis of a Patrilineal Society.* Cambridge: W. Heffer and Sons Limited.

World Bank, 1989, *Sub-Saharan Africa: From Crisis to Sustainable Growth.* Washington DC: World Bank.

—, 1994, *Adjustment in Africa: Reforms, Results, and the Road Ahead.* New York: Oxford University Press (for the World Bank).

CHAPTER 5

Disease and Disruption:
Chagga Witchcraft and Relational Fragility

Knut Christian Myhre

Prelude

"He should cut her ear off and tell her: 'Stop bewitching my children!'".
MaSway, my elderly female host, was visibly angry.[1] We were sitting in the
shade in her homestead's courtyard when I told her of my visit to a local
healer, *mwaanga*, with my friend and assistant Herman, his wife, and their
two-year-old daughter. MaSway knew Herman and his family well, as he
worked for her every morning, helping her cut fodder for her livestock. Herman, in his early 30s, lived nearby with his young family, and his daughter
had been ill for some time. She was first admitted and treated for malaria
at the local government health station. A month later, she contracted an
unidentified illness, which her parents called "fever", *homa*. Instead of going
back to the health station, Herman and his wife decided to take their child
to a female healer in a village several kilometres away. When we arrived
on foot that day, the healer diagnosed the child, using a medicated horn,
which she applied to the girl's body and sniffed repeatedly. She made small
incisions and washed *isinga*, small objects, out of the girl's groin and abdo-
men, using a certain kind of leaves and medicated water. All involved were
adamant that these objects had been inserted into the child's body by means
of witchcraft, *usavi*.

It was hearing of these events that caused MaSway's outburst. She con-
fided to me her conviction that the witch, *musavi*, was Herman's brother's
wife, who lives in the homestead neighbouring his. MaSway claimed that
his brother's wife is envious of Herman's "development", *maendeleo*, and
the fact that he works and earns money. By making his child ill, she ensures
that Herman has no time for work, and spends his money trying to get his

---

1. Fieldwork in Rombo district, Kilimanjaro region, Tanzania, was carried out between April 2000 and September 2001. Preliminary and follow-up visits were
   made in November 1998, April 2002 and April 2003. Subsequent fieldwork was
   undertaken between October 2006 and February 2007, and between August
   and November 2008, after the drafting of this text.

daughter cured. The witch thus "sets him back" and destroys his development.

African witchcraft and modernity

MaSway's reference to "development" suggests that witchcraft in Rombo is linked to relatively recent social changes. *Maendeleo* was a central concept in Nyerere's projects of national independence and African Socialism, but many of the phenomena that constitute "development" in present-day Rombo – such as education, employment, and access to cash – have their origin in colonial times. Since Richards's (1935:460) claim that witchcraft and magic had "actually increased by contact with the white civilization, and the resultant economic and social changes in Northern Rhodesia", it has been a commonplace assertion in anthropology that African witchcraft is a "modern" phenomenon. After Evans-Pritchard (1937) discovered that accusations and suspicions of witchcraft only occur among Zande commoners, anthropologists have interpreted witchcraft in terms of strained social relationships, which are often seen as the result of the disruptive consequences of colonial rule and the incorporation in a cash economy.[2] Initially, witchcraft accusations were described as releasing and relieving pent-up social tension, ultimately serving as a conservative force upholding the social structure.[3] More recently, however, accusations and the resort to healers have been interpreted as attempts to redress the imbalances and alienations that arise from modern social changes. Thus, although witchcraft was at first seen in terms of its integrative social functions within a colonial context, it has since been understood as a critique of, and resistance to, a globalised and globalising "modernity" within a postcolonial setting.[4]

2. For excellent summaries of anthropological approaches to African witchcraft since Evans-Pritchard (1937), see for instance Douglas (1970), Ellis (2002), Kapferer (2002), and Moore and Sanders (2001).
3. Marwick (1950; 1952; 1965) is probably the best known exponent of witchcraft as a social safety valve.
4. The Comaroffs (1993) are credited with giving rise to the conception of witchcraft as a critique and a form of resistance to "modernity". However, in a similar fashion, Willis (1968) argues that the "ritual drama" of witchcraft eradication is a temporary "quasi-revolution", which ultimately serves a conservative purpose. Green (1997) and Yamba (1997) argue that the anthropological claim that witchcraft is a vernacular critique of, and resistance to, "modernity" must be firmly placed in a context of local power relations.

In different ways, these conceptions skilfully expose the relationships between African witchcraft and broader, even global, social processes. As Moore and Sanders (2001:8) point out, they even represent historical approaches, in spite of the functionalist insistence on ahistoricism. However, eagerness to prove the strong connection between witchcraft and modernity means that these histories are painted in broad brushstrokes. Even recent accounts that aim to demonstrate the plural and diverse nature of African "modernities" – explicitly to undermine the idea that they constitute a monolithic phenomenon – tacitly presuppose that these processes have a destructive impact on local social relationships, which results in increased notions and actions pertaining to witchcraft.[5] Despite their heightened sophistication, anthropological approaches continue to conceive of African witchcraft in terms of a uniform trajectory, where concepts and practices are reactive phenomena that represent and respond to externally imposed events. Interpreted as what Sanders (2003:327) calls "metanarratives", vernacular discourses on witchcraft are thereby transmogrified into a verbal, voluntary and intentional communication about something that originates outside of the local context. Such conceptions not only sin against the avowed plurality of "modernities", but, more importantly, they neglect the fact that witchcraft primarily concerns living persons who are entangled in localised social relationships. As Favret-Saada (1990:192) argues from France, witchcraft constitutes a "peculiar network of human communication" that people "get caught up in" and "commit their existences to". These persons may exist within a "modern" context, but it does not follow that their relationships can be wholly accounted for in terms of this modernity.

Favret-Saada (1989:54) claims that witchcraft is primarily a matter of relational closeness and proximity. Contrastingly, the approaches sketched above emphasise the distant nature and foreign origin of the events and processes that are said to occasion witchcraft. In order to deepen Favret-Saada's point, I will discuss the case above in light of Sally Falk Moore's work in another part of Kilimanjaro, and question the postulated relationship between witchcraft and modernity. I argue that witchcraft concerns relational fragility, rather than a narrative about, and a means for dealing with, social changes. Moreover, by means of historical evidence, I will demonstrate that the notions and practices involved in the case above have a longer history in

---

5. For accounts of "multiple" and "alternative modernities", see Moore (1996:587) and special issues of *Dædalus* (2000, vol. 129, no. 1) and *Public Culture* (1999, vol. 11, no. 1).

the area, which transcend relatively recent, externally imposed events and processes. Consideration of historical processes, and especially conceptual and practical continuities, can thus contribute to a new approach to these phenomena (Sanders 2008:109). In this manner, I will add my voice to the growing coterie of writers who question the close relationship between witchcraft and "modernity".[6]

Land and witchcraft in Kilimanjaro

The rural majority of the Chagga-speaking people of Kilimanjaro are settled in separate homesteads on the slopes of the mountain, where they chiefly cultivate bananas for consumption and coffee for cash. Most homesteads keep a few heads of stall-fed livestock, whose manure fertilises the banana garden. Every homestead also possesses a plot in the plains, where maize, beans, eleusine and sunflowers are planted on a seasonal basis. Land is inherited patrilineally, in a process where the first- and the last-born sons are privileged. Middle-born sons inherit less land than their brothers, and, in Rombo district at least, this land is usually located away from their natal homesteads.[7]

Land is presently a scarce resource, partly due to tremendous population growth and partly due to coffee cash-cropping. According to Sally Falk Moore (1986:110), this situation is largely due to certain social changes that can be traced back to colonial rule and the introduction of Christianity. Coffee farming was initially introduced by the Catholic Church to fund its mission activities, but was soon championed by the colonial authorities as a means of involving the people of Kilimanjaro in the cash economy. Cash-cropping increased the value of land, and changed people's attitude towards it. At the same time, Christian denigration of polygyny and local birth-spacing practices increased fertility, while missionary-provided medicine lowered infant mortality. Cumulatively, this resulted in enormous population growth, which made land a scarce resource. Due to the inheritance practice, the effects of this situation are unequally distributed; and, in turn, this unequal distribution is in Moore's view intimately related

6. See for instance Ellis (2002), Englund (2007), Favret-Saada ([1977] 1980; 1989; 1990), Green (1994; 1997), Kapferer (2002), and Sanders (2003; 2008).
7. Moore does not specify what the practice is in the areas where she did fieldwork. The concrete case she analyses appears to involve three brothers who remain each other's neighbours (Moore 1975:129ff), while she elsewhere refers to middle brothers being required to "cultivate bush" (Moore 1986:306).

to witchcraft accusations. To Moore, the social and demographic changes associated with colonialism occasioned specific changes in social relations that contributed to an increased frequency of witchcraft accusations and related practices.[8]

Moore (1986:306) argues that the scarcity of land, and the relative favouring in terms of inheritance, makes the middle-born sons and their wives vulnerable to witchcraft accusations from their elder and younger brothers. Middle sons are considered to be resentful of their lot in life, so when the favoured brothers are struck by illness, death and misfortune, the middle brothers or their wives are accused of harming them by means of witchcraft. In this process, which Moore (1975:136) elsewhere calls a "selection for failure", the middle sons are socially ostracised and sometimes even forced off their land. According to Moore's account, witchcraft is locally considered an illicit means by which the disadvantaged try to level the differences between agnates that largely result from recent social changes. In actual fact, however, the accusations serve to bolster the position of the privileged eldest and youngest brothers. The middle sons are thus structurally "selected for failure", and witchcraft accusations both express and entrench this fact. Collectively, Moore (1975; 1986) links witchcraft in Kilimanjaro with certain changes pertaining to colonialism, Christianity and cash-cropping, which the accusations represent and respond to in a teleological manner.

The fact that MaSway, in the case outlined above, pointed to Herman's brother's wife suggests that similar circumstances are at play in this case. However, Herman's situation does not fit the profile Moore suggests. First of all, Herman and his brother were their father's last- and first-born sons, respectively. They jointly inherited their natal homestead, and harboured no resentment towards each other because of land. Their two middle-born brothers, meanwhile, inherited land several kilometres away, from where they were considered to be too distant to bewitch Herman's daughter. Secondly, although the relationship between Herman and his eldest brother was at times strained, this was not because of a conflict over land, but due to Herman's brother's tendency to spend his days drinking the illicit brew *gongo* instead of working to provide for his family. Rather than his brother and his brother's wife being united in envy of Herman, it was Herman and his sister-in-law who resented their brother and husband, respectively, for

---

8. In my experience, there is a strong local conviction that witchcraft accusations and activities are on the increase. However, there is no evidence to corroborate such a claim.

his drunkenness. In other words, the requisite relationship of resentment does not intersect with the suspicion of bewitchment in the manner that Moore describes. Thirdly, Herman never suggested that it was his brother's wife who had bewitched his child; on the contrary, both Herman and his brother were convinced that the elderly wife of an unrelated neighbour was the perpetrator. Both of them claimed that she was widely considered to be a witch, and that she has bewitched children in the area for many years. In fact, they said that she bewitched their sister when they were children. Due to their fear of this woman, both Herman's and his brother's families restricted their interaction with this neighbour to an absolute minimum. Contrastingly, and in line with the mutual absence of suspicion, the relationships between the members of Herman's and his brother's homesteads were very close, and the two brothers, their wives and children spent hours together working and socialising every day.

Against this background, it is clear that the case of Herman's daughter deviates from the dynamics Moore describes. In my view, the reason for this is an over-emphasis on the determining nature of the relationships between the phenomena Moore sees as crucial. Historical evidence reveals that these interconnections are less strong than assumed.

Historical changes in Kilimanjaro

Historical sources suggest that the interrelationship between colonialism, coffee cash-cropping, population growth and land scarcity is less strong and more complex than Moore (1986) contends. This renders problematic a unilineal conception of the causation and purposefulness of Chagga witchcraft. Based on demographic research, Setel (1999:42ff.) argues that the population in Kilimanjaro was growing strongly in late pre-colonial times and that land was already then becoming scarce. Although these dynamics were exacerbated by colonial rule and the advent of Christianity, they cannot be attributed to them. The processes and relationships that Moore accords decisive weight seem not to coincide historically as she suggests.

A further factor, which neither Moore nor Setel sufficiently accounts for, is the fact that population density and land scarcity – whatever their causes – affected the different parts of the mountain unequally. Both Moore and Setel generally treat Kilimanjaro as a homogeneous area that was uniformly impacted by colonial rule, Christianity and cash-cropping. In 1943, however, the Commissioner for Moshi district reported on the relative population density in four areas of central Kilimanjaro, including most of the areas where Moore (1986:xiv) subsequently did fieldwork.[9] In Mamba, the density was 700 people per square mile, while neighbouring Mwika only held 300 people in the same area. For Kilema, the District Commissioner reported 400 people per square mile, while next to it Kirua Vunjo had only 250 people per square mile, and "...much land is still under bush for want of cultivation" (TNA 5/63/11).[10] No exact figure is provided for any part of Rombo, but the Commissioner's claim that Usseri in northern Rombo was the only place in Kilimanjaro where large numbers of cattle were grazed suggests that the population was even less dense here. Necessarily, population growth and cash-cropping had very different impacts on these areas. Consequently, they cannot be accorded the same dynamic around the mountain.

The picture is further complicated by the fact that the proliferation of coffee cultivation was not homogeneous within Kilimanjaro. Reports from the colonial Department of Agriculture reveal great disparities in the number of coffee trees between the different chiefdoms. Cultivation began in the early 1900s, but the number of trees dipped slightly between 1916 and 1922, due to a halt in planting and the neglect of trees during the First World War (TNA 5/AB427). In 1922, more than half of the 36,265 coffee-bearing trees were located in a single chiefdom, and nearly all of the trees were concentrated in four clustered chiefdoms. These included both of the chiefdoms that were described as densely and less densely populated by the District Commissioner, where coffee cash-cropping must have had different effects. At the same time, there were only 45 coffee-bearing trees in the whole of Rombo, which comprised several chiefdoms. Close to 90,000 trees were planted in 1922, but only 5,000 of these were in Rombo (TNA 5/AB425). There was a great push in coffee planting during the following years, but the colonial authorities' continued conviction that Rombo was too arid for the crop ensured that they were largely planted elsewhere.

The regional diversity within Kilimanjaro means that the advent of coffee cash-cropping cannot be described as a general event that affected the whole area in a uniform manner. When combined with the regional variation in population density, the upshot is that Moore's suggested confluence of colonialism, Christianity, cash-cropping, population growth and land scarcity cannot be generally maintained. If the relationships between these

---

9. Moore (1986:xiv) did fieldwork in the neighbouring areas Kilema, Marangu, Mamba and Mwika. She also visited primary courts in Moshi and in Keni-Mriti-Mengwe. The latter is located in Rombo district, not far from the site of my fieldwork.

10. TNA refers to Tanzania National Archives, followed by accession number.

phenomena are weakened, the account of the origin and teleology of Kilimanjaro witchcraft is undermined. The regional diversity allows for the possibility that the phenomena align in the way Moore suggests at specific sites around the mountain. However, historical evidence – including from areas where Moore did fieldwork – calls into question the uniformity of these occurrences, as well as the strong connections between them.

Historical continuities in Kilimanjaro

The idea that witchcraft is a consequence of, and reaction to, social changes is further unsettled by descriptions from the early 20th century that resemble the claims and activities contained in the case of Herman's daughter. In 1924, the colonial administrator Charles Dundas (1924:164) and the German missionary Bruno Gutmann (1924:46) published separate accounts of how a local healer, *mhanga*, smells out and removes objects that have been inserted into the victim's body by means of witchcraft, *wusari*.[11] These accounts concur closely with the activities of present-day Rombo healers. Unfortunately, neither Gutmann nor Dundas says anything about who the witches and their victims were. In other words, they give no indication of the relationships between the people who tend to suspect or accuse each other of witchcraft.

In 1911, Gutmann's slightly older colleague Johannes Raum published an article that largely consists of the translation of a manuscript compiled by a local man named Yohane Msando. Not much is known about Msando, but Raum (1911:160) says he was a Christian Chagga teacher, and it is likely that he was one of the first people baptised by the missionaries from the Leipzig Lutheran Mission Company.[12] Both Raum's (1911:202) remarks and Msando's main account contain descriptions of how a healer detects foreign objects that have been lodged in the victim's body. These objects are removed from the patient's body by making incisions and sucking them out, which remains the main activity of the majority of healers in Rombo.

---

11. The difference in terminology from the one used in the previous case reflects the variation of dialect between Old Moshi, where Dundas and Gutmann mainly worked, and Rombo. However, *mhanga* and *mwanga* are clearly cognates, as are *usawi* and *wusari*.

12. According to Winter (1979:45), the Leipzig missionaries celebrated their first baptisms in 1898. Raum's article was published in 1911, but the text was probably translated and annotated between 1908 and 1909, when Raum had home leave to Germany (Winter 1979:48).

Importantly, Msando (Raum 1911:211) informs us about the witch's motive:

> The main reason why people bewitch one another is resentment or envy. This you attract if you exceed others in beauty or in estimation by other people, if you possess more cattle than others, if you know better how to farm than others, if you have more children, and in many other ways. A woman who perceives that her husband loves the second wife more than herself becomes jealous. Or her resentment is called forth by the circumstance that her co-wife has children, while she has none.[13]

Judging by Msando's account, it is your successful engagement in productive and reproductive activities that makes people resent and become envious of you. Although he does not explicitly say so, Msando seems to imply that, by bewitching you, the envious person tries to dispossess you of your advantage. There is no mention of "development", coffee, and cash, but the basic themes are remarkably similar to the present-day discourse on witchcraft in Rombo.

These early accounts are refracted through the eyes and minds of some of the people who were involved in the introduction and expansion of colonial rule, Christianity and cash-cropping to Kilimanjaro. There were, moreover, multiple overlapping and mediating relationships between these people, which might have influenced their accounts. As already mentioned, Gutmann and Raum were colleagues in the same mission company. Both served in Kilimanjaro for a long time: Raum from 1897 until his death in 1936, and Gutmann between 1902 and 1938. There is no evidence that Dundas was personally acquainted with either of them, but he had at least knowledge of Gutmann's earlier publications. Dundas was District Commissioner in Moshi from 1919 until 1924, where he promoted coffee cash-cropping and probably oversaw the great expansion in the number of trees in 1922 mentioned above. Dundas's interpreter and main informant was Josefu Merinyo, a Christian convert and student of Gutmann's, who had worked as a servant for Dr. Emil Förster, a German settler who became Gutmann's father-in-law. Dundas also acknowledges a debt to Nathanael Mtui, another student of, and informant for, Gutmann. When the first local coffee co-operative was set up in 1925, Dundas's successor made Merinyo president

---

13. All translations from the German have been done by the author.

and Mtui vice-president.[14] Many of the actors in the accounts above were hence centrally located in the processes that Moore highlights with regards to Kilimanjaro witchcraft.

Despite their important and fascinating interrelations, as well as their intimate connections to Chagga "modernity", it must be emphasised that Dundas's, Gutmann's and Raum's accounts date from a time when colonial rule, Christianity and coffee farming were in their infancies. Msando's manuscript is particularly important, as it represents a vernacular voice from the early colonial period. As an adult convert, already educated as a teacher at the start of the 20th century, Msando probably represents a pre-colonial informant by Vansina's (1990:22) criteria. Msando's description of notions and practices pertaining to witchcraft – which strongly resemble the present-day discourse and activities – hence points to a remarkable historical continuity that Moore's conception is unable to account for. Even if we choose to disregard this continuity, the internal variations in population density and coffee cultivation mean that the concurrence between Msando's description from central Kilimanjaro and the present-day proceedings in Rombo cannot be reduced to a uniform trajectory. Historical complexity and temporal continuities thus subvert the determining interrelationship between social change and witchcraft.

The most likely conclusion must be that witchcraft in Kilimanjaro is not primarily about modernity, but about something else. In my view, Favret-Saada points to this when she describes witchcraft as a lived reality and emphasises its intimate connection to the social relationships people are entangled in. Witchcraft is primarily a matter regarding relational closeness and proximity, rather than global processes of historical change. This is of course not to argue that these phenomena represent a pristine pre-colonial reality, but to acknowledge that concepts and practices pertaining to witchcraft have a long history that cannot be explained in terms of societal "needs" that arise from social changes (Green 1994:43).

Conceiving of witchcraft as a matter of relational proximity, rather than the outcome of social change, enables me to take up a neglected strand of Evans-Pritchard's (1937) analysis. As Douglas (1970:xiv; 1980:25) points out, Evans-Pritchard's account is not primarily about social tension, but

---

14. For excellent accounts of the roles of, and relationships between, these people see Moore (1986:177ff.) and Winter (1979:53ff.). They differ somewhat in the importance they accord the different actors, with Moore emphasising the role of Dundas, and Winter emphasising the role of Förster.

concerns the social constitution of experience and knowledge.[15] In line with this, I will argue that the notions and practices of Rombo witchcraft concern local experiences of relational fragility. In my view, the vernacular discourse on witchcraft reveals the nature of social relationships, and the fact that these can always be disrupted by the people who partake in them. The discourse discloses how relational fragility occurs between people who are both socially and spatially close to each other – a fact that is also contained in Moore's account. Early ethnographic descriptions show that this predicament has a long history, which has become overlaid and made to articulate with more contemporary concerns. However, the abilities of such recent phenomena to interact with these concepts and practices are restricted, except to the extent that they play a role in the constitution of local social relationships. In order to demonstrate this, I shall consider another case of witchcraft and a further form of bewitchment, which overlaps with the kind described in the previous case.

Food stuck in the body

In addition to objects lodged in the body, Msando describes *kireyo*, bewitchment by means of food, which resembles one of the deepest concerns of the people in present-day Rombo. According to Msando, bewitchment by means of food are of two kinds. The first involves adding a substance to the food, which harms the victim once he or she eats it. Msando (Raum 1911:208) says:

> Someone is talked into eating and it (the food and the magic) sticks in the body, so that you either die straight away or after a few days. It also happens that one gets physically ill and carries the illness around for a whole year until it leads to death.

The second kind of food bewitchment does not involve substances, but works by means of a spell or a curse that operate on the food. Msando (Raum 1911:209) says:

> Secondly there is evil magic whereby a cursing formula is uttered either with the mouth or in the thoughts. If you are nearby food, a magician can, if he is close to you or you are inside the house together, look at you and bewitch you so that you die or become ill. If a woman is nursing her child, the magician can bewitch the child by means of the milk that it drinks.

---

15. Similarly, Englund (2007:298) argues for a conception of witchcraft as "an aspect of experiencing and imagining the world".

The notion that the people of Rombo talk about is an intermediary between these two kinds. It is not performed by means of a substance that is added to the food, nor by a spoken spell or a curse, but by someone gazing at the victim while he or she is eating. As in Msando's description, the food is made to stick in the stomach, causing illness, emaciation and eventual death. No one professes to know how this is done, only that it is performed intentionally, *makusudi*, by a witch, *musavi*, who possesses an ability to harm people by means of his or her eyes. In this respect, it resembles the form of witchcraft involved in the case of Herman's child, where the objects were said to have been inserted in her body by the witch gazing at her. Another case that took place during my fieldwork illustrates what is at stake in this kind of bewitchment, and in Rombo witchcraft more generally.

The case of William

Albert Moshi, a former lorry driver, is a son of the last "chief", *mangi*. During his days as a driver, Albert lived alone in Moshi and commuted to see his wife and children, who lived on the plot Albert received from his father in Rombo. When Albert retired and moved back to Rombo, most of his 12 children were grown up and married, and some of his sons had established their own homesteads on plots that Albert had sectioned off from his land. One afternoon, as we were walking to his favourite beer club, Albert told me that he was very concerned about William, an older classificatory brother whose homestead is close to Albert's. William had been ill for some time, with severe pain in his throat, and had great difficulties in eating and swallowing. William had just returned from Mount Meru Hospital in Arusha town, roughly 110 kilometres from Rombo. Due to the medication William had received, the doctor had instructed him not to drink alcohol for the next six months. Like Albert, William liked to spend his evenings in the beer clubs, but he was now just sitting at home, and Albert's worry was that William was growing increasingly resentful at the situation.

When we arrived at the beer club, two unrelated men who were younger than Albert were present. The two men asked Albert about William's condition, and they began to discuss his illness. Albert told us that before going to Mount Meru Hospital, William had visited a renowned healer called Richard in a neighbouring village. Richard diagnosed William and told him: "You have been bewitched by meat," *"walhuwa nyama"*. Richard gave William a local medicine to bring out the meat, and told him to come back a few days later. William took the medicine as instructed, but felt no improvement afterwards. Instead of going back, he therefore went to see Richard's younger brother Hippolyt, who also works as a healer in the same village. Like Richard, Hippolyt diagnosed William by placing a horn on his throat and chest, and smelling it repeatedly. Eventually he too concluded that William had meat stuck in his body. In response to this, the two men in the beer club said in unison: "Ah, it must have happened at the last *matanga* ceremony you had." Albert burst out laughing at this, and claimed that Richard and Hippolyt were just saying this in order to keep William coming back and giving them money. Instead of acting on Hippolyt's diagnosis, William travelled to Arusha, where he received the medicine he was now taking.

Food and relationality

Accounts like this were frequent during my fieldwork, mostly told by people who had been subject to this kind of bewitchment and subsequently cured by a healer. Meat is considered the most common form of "food that is made to stick in the stomach", *kelya kieyra ndeuni*, although banana beer and milk are also mentioned.

Like Msando's claim above, people in Rombo emphasise that the person who makes the food stick in the stomach must be physically close to the victim in order to do so. This is part of the reason why the two men in the beer club assumed that William was bewitched during a *matanga* ceremony. *Matanga* is the largest ceremony held on behalf of a deceased person, and can take place as many as 10 years after he or she has died. It is held at the dead person's homestead, to which the members of his or her agnatic descent group are required to contribute banana beer. The ceremony only concerns the deceased's descent group, but anyone can legitimately arrive and claim a share of the beer. In actual fact, the *matanga* ceremonies are the largest social occasions in Rombo, and none come bigger than those held by the members of Albert and William's descent group: their father *mangi* Tengia had 37 wives and 80 sons, meaning that Albert and William's agnatic descent group is the largest in the area. Consequently, they organise several carefully planned *matanga* ceremonies every year, which involve enormous amounts of banana beer and attract hundreds of people from several different villages, as well as family and friends who have migrated away and arrive from Tanzania's cities and towns.

During the *matanga* ceremony, the descent group slaughters one head of cattle and one goat. People with specific relationships to the deceased are entitled to particular sections of meat from the slaughtered animals. The meat is presented to them raw, and the recipients may bring the meat to their respective homesteads. However, dividing the meat between all those entitled to it is a cumbersome affair. The meat is therefore nearly always prepared at the homestead where the ceremony takes place. When the meat is cooked, the different sections of meat are placed on fresh banana leaves and presented again to their rightful recipients. Each group then finds a secluded place in the banana garden, where they can eat at a safe distance from the gaze of the people who have congregated at the homestead's courtyard. Nevertheless, each group comprises a large number of people, so someone usually urges those present not to exercise their witchcraft ability, euphemistically called "the bad thing", *kindo kiwiishwa*, if they possess it. Despite these precautions, some people hold their hands in front of their mouths to prevent the witch from looking at the food when they eat it. Others let the first piece of meat fall on the ground before they put it in their mouths, as this is considered to immunise it against bewitchment. Others, like my adoptive mother MaSway, simply refrain from participating in *matanga* ceremonies altogether, in order to remain on the safe side.

The members of each meat-sharing group have the same relationship to the deceased, and therefore address each other with reciprocal kinship terms. In the case of men, this entails that the group consists of either classificatory brothers or classificatory affines. In the case of women, the group is either made up of classificatory sisters or of *waeri*, classificatory co-wives, or women who have married classificatory brothers. For a *matanga* in Tengia's descent group, William and Albert share meat with their classificatory brothers – a group that in theory includes 80 people.[16] Many of them are not just brothers but also live in neighbouring homesteads, due to the inheritance practice. Not far away when they eat their meat is the group consisting of their wives, and somewhere in the banana garden is the group made up of their classificatory sons, who have received land from their fathers, married, and established their own homesteads. Affines who have married women from Tengia's descent group are also entitled to meat, along with affines from the descent groups that have provided Tengia's descendants with wives.

Thus, when William and Albert sit down to eat with their brothers, most of their neighbours are either members of the same group, or they are seated in other nearby groups scattered throughout the banana garden.

---

16. I say in theory, as obviously not all are still alive and many do not show up for these occasions.

These groups are partially hidden from each other, but it is always possible for someone to throw a glance over the shoulder and catch a glimpse of you when you eat. The possibility of someone gazing at you as you eat is always present. Furthermore, this gaze is most likely to come from someone who is close to you in both physical and relational terms. The threat of bewitchment is hence greatest from the people you are closest to, both spatially and socially.

Witchcraft and neighbourliness

In accordance with this, the people involved in the case of Herman's child suspected a neighbour of being the person who had harmed the child. MaSway suspected Herman's brother's wife, while Herman and his brother suspected the wife of an unrelated neighbour. Like Favret-Saada's (1990:54) informants, the people of Rombo emphasise that it is one of your neighbours who is most likely to bewitch you. Similarly, Moore's account also concerns witchcraft accusations between neighbouring brothers. Msando's claim above that bewitchment takes place between co-wives stems from a time when polygyny was the norm, and co-wives occupied neighbouring homesteads. Now, as then, neighbours are physically close and therefore able to bewitch you. Neighbours also have knowledge about you, your family and your homestead. Neighbours thus know about your "development" and are more likely than others to be envious of you; they therefore have a reason to bewitch you.

The Chagga term for "neighbour", *mamrasa*, is derived from the word for "boundary", *mrasa*, and literally means "person of the boundary". As a term of address, however, *mamrasa* is used for more people than those whose homestead borders yours. Connoting closeness and equality, the term is situationally used to address people over quite a large area. In fact, it is not uncommon for marriages to take place between the children of people who address each other as neighbours.

Combined with the pattern of inheritance, the geographical extension of the term "neighbour" entails that relations of neighbourliness overlap and intertwine with agnatic and affinal relationships. The concept *mamrasa* is therefore often co-extensive with the terms "father", "brother", "son", "sister", "brother-in-law", "sister-in-law", "mother's brother", "father's sister", and *watoi* – the term of address used between people whose children have married each other. The upshot of this situation is that physical and relational proximity articulate and interlock in everyday life. As in Favret-

Saada's (1990:54) case, Rombo neighbourliness is a "topo-social" phenomenon, which interrelates spatial, relational and affective proximity. Moore (1975:122) makes the same point when she outlines "[t]he community described here, the neighbourhood that joins kin and nonkin in permanent physical and social contiguity...". At the *matanga* ceremony, when the groups of people sit down to eat in the banana garden, this web of overlapping and interweaving relationality is reformed and compressed on an even smaller area, which heightens the everyday danger of being bewitched.

Witchcraft and relationality

The cases above thus demonstrate that witchcraft presupposes, and operates through, social relationality. However, it does not work through one specific kind of relationship, but can operate through any of the agnatic, affinal and neighbourly relationships that constitute the complex web of sociality that every person is implicated in. The threat of witchcraft is hence greatest from the people with whom your existence is most intimately bound up, but its scale and context are indeterminate (Englund 2007:306). Furthermore, in the case of food that is stuck in the victim's stomach, bewitchment works by means of the substances that are constitutive of this web of sociality. Meat, milk, and banana beer make up the better part of the bridewealth prestations, and are the substances that are offered to the ancestors (Myhre 2003). In both the bridewealth exchanges and the ancestral offerings, these substances are shared between, and consumed in the company of, the members of the agnatic descent group and their affines. It is precisely at such occasions of commensality that the risk of bewitchment is greatest. Witchcraft and sociality, therefore, are two sides of the same coin. Paraphrasing Geschiere (1997:11), we can say that witchcraft is the dark side of relationality. Witchcraft is not a distant phenomenon of foreign origin, but a social fact that lies at the heart of relationality itself. Social relations are fragile phenomena that can always be subverted and disrupted. Moreover, these disruptions are perpetrated from within, by the parties to the social relationships. Shadowing the network of social relations, there is a web of mutual suspicion, and each person is implicated in the latter by virtue of being entangled the former.

The web of mutual suspicion entails that social relationships are ambiguous and ambivalent to the people who partake in them. The ever-present threat of bewitchment means that people must be vigilant and circumspect in their dealings with each other. Moreover, incidents of illness and accounts of bewitchment prompt people to scrutinise and consider the relationships that surround the victim. In the case of William, the specific symptoms of his affliction, combined with the two healers' diagnoses, immediately suggested to the two men in the beer club that his problems were due to the public and communal consumption of meat at a recent *matanga* ceremony. If Albert had not dismissed their suggestion, the two men would have proceeded to speculate over possible perpetrators, and chances are they would have first scrutinised William's relationships with his neighbours. As both a neighbour and a classificatory brother, Albert himself could have been suspected.

As Favret-Saada (1990:45) shows, claims about bewitchment make people reconsider their lives and the social relationships they are entangled in. In this process, they bring hidden aspects out in the open and reveal what is normally concealed. These cases demonstrate that it is not just the victim who does this, but also the people surrounding him or her. The process of reconsideration is hence "infectious", and reverberates through the web of relationality that ties people together. The fact that bewitchment takes place by means of objects and practices that are normally constitutive of social relationality entails that the air of ambiguity and the processes of reconsideration are extended to these too. In this way, the mechanics of sociality that are normally taken for granted are temporarily disclosed to the participants. They are thus able to see the fragility of social relationality, and the uncertain character of an existence that is founded on such relationality. In this manner, witchcraft reveals the true nature of social relationality to the people who are entangled in it. Witchcraft makes evident that relationships can always be disrupted, that such disruptions are perpetrated by someone who is spatially and relationally close, and that relationships thus are fragile phenomena.

Repeated incidents of bewitchment make the victim and her family try to determine who the witch is and minimise their interaction with this person. Sustained suspicion that a particular person is harming you ultimately forces you to try to sever your relationship to the witch altogether. Msando (Raum 1911:210) describes the same phenomenon: "If you know that someone is a bad magician, you prevent this person from visiting you often. It is exactly when someone has made a friendship with the evil magician that he will bewitch that person". However, disrupting social relationships with people who are relationally and spatially close is not an easy task. Herman said that his family had tried to avoid engaging with their elderly female neighbour for as long as he could remember. Since she is an immediate neighbour, however, it is impossible to completely avoid her, which leaves open a continual possibility of bewitchment. People moreover take great care in not insulting or offending a suspected witch when they meet him or her. If the witch feels that the person is retracting, his or her resentment may increase, which adds to the risk of bewitchment. It is important to show circumspection, but the fact remains that you cannot completely avoid the witch. Disruption, illness and death are therefore ever-present possibilities in social encounters.

The case of William reconsidered

Keeping in mind that witchcraft relates human illness, misery and death to the disruption of social relationships, we can briefly consider why William suspected his problems to be due to bewitchment, and in need of attention from Richard, the healer in the neighbouring village.

Like the majority of the people in the area, William and his wife were Catholics, and had raised their children to be Catholics. Some time ago, however, William's eldest son joined the Seventh Day Adventists, one of several revivalist churches in the area. The eldest son's wife also joined the church, and eventually they converted his mother and all of his siblings. They all tried to convince William to join the church, but he steadfastly refused to give up Catholicism. Some claimed that in order to incense his family further he joined one of the saintly orders in the parish church in-stead. As born-again Christians, his wife and children were staunchly op-posed to drinking alcohol and to participation in ancestral offerings. They constantly tried to persuade William to give these things up, but he refused to do so. Eventually, the situation deteriorated to the extent that relations were terminated between William, his wife, and most of his children. The wife moved out of the marital homestead and into that of the eldest son, which was the closest neighbouring homestead. Three of their other sons had also received land, and after their marriages had set up their homesteads as William's neighbours. At the commencement of my fieldwork, William was therefore living alone, surrounded by his closest relatives with whom all relations had been cut off.

Two months before Albert told us that William had been to see the two healers in the neighbouring village, William called some senior members of his descent group for a meeting at his homestead, in order to discuss his inheritance. Due to the family situation, William did not want his youngest son to inherit his homestead as planned. The youngest son lived and worked in Moshi, but had allegedly not visited his father for the previous four years. Instead, William wanted to give his homestead to the teenage son of one his daughters, who lived and worked in Arusha. The daughter and her son were also born-again Christians, but they visited William regularly and brought him store-bought supplies, such as cooking oil, soap, sugar, salt and tea. It was rumoured that William's wife and sons immediately walked out of the meeting in protest at the fact that he had prepared banana beer. In any case, they did not receive William's decision well. In particular, William's eldest and youngest sons were strongly opposed to their sister's son inheriting the homestead that they considered the youngest son's rightful claim. William's wish only entrenched their disagreement and brought them further apart than ever before. William's sons lobbied the elders of the descent groups, but many of them sympathised with William and disliked his children for having turned their backs on their father. The elders' failure to decide whether William was allowed to leave his homestead to his daughter's son left the way open for William to do as he pleased. At the time of his death six months later, William's wife and children discovered that he had prepared a legally binding will, bestowing the homestead on his grandson.

Considering the situation William was in after this meeting, it is perhaps unsurprising that he immediately suspected his illness to be due to bewitchment. On an everyday basis, William lived surrounded by his closest relatives, but their relationships were cut off due to their mutual resentment. Broken relationships and feelings of resentment are not a novelty, and, as already mentioned, people try in such situations to minimise their interaction with each other. That also applied in this case, but the fact that they were immediate neighbours meant that William, his wife and their sons were bound to bump into each other as they went about their daily lives. Even if they did not speak to each other, they could always see each other as they were tending their banana gardens and feeding their livestock; and according to the local notions of witchcraft that is all it takes for someone to be able to harm you. Knowing that his closest neighbours and relatives resented him, and that they were constantly in a position to harm him, William could not rule out the possibility that his illness was due to their bewitchment. It was therefore worth his time and money to go to the healer in the neighbouring village and follow his prescriptions. It was only when the second healer diagnosed him with the kind of bewitchment that he had already taken medication for that William was convinced that his problems were not due to his neighbours, but rather must be attended to by means of hospital medicine.

Like all relationships, however, this also had another side to it. After his death, William's family told people about his repeated attempts at harming them by means of cursing. They undoubtedly had something to gain from portraying William in a bad light, but the majority of these stories actually came from William's grandson who inherited his homestead, and was now shunned by his maternal uncles. Members of William's descent group, who had no direct involvement in the case, moreover corroborated these accounts. William's grandson claimed to have found evidence of different kinds of cursing activities carried out at his grandfather's homestead, but the fact that William's relatives were "saved" meant that the curses had had no effect. If these curses were performed, they might have been attempts on William's part to control the situation he found himself in. However, the recounting of these stories after his death is also a testimony to the fear with which his wife and children had lived. The fear of living in the vicinity of someone you have broken off social relations with was not restricted to William, but also applied to his wife and sons. Just like William, they knew the dangers of disrupted relations and resentment, and that living in neighbouring homesteads meant that William was able to harm them at any time.

Conclusion

Neither of these cases fits Moore's (1975:112) account of witchcraft as a "selection for failure", where specific people are identified as bad characters in a process where "...the community must slough off some members in order to survive". Furthermore, historical source material from Kilimanjaro destabilises the interactions between the elements that are purported to give rise and purpose to the notions and practices pertaining to witchcraft. Rather, it demonstrates how these phenomena have a long-term continuity in the region. Colonial and postcolonial developments may have interacted with these ideas and activities, but only to the extent that these developments play a role in the constitution of local social relationships. This is not to deny the existence and importance of social change, nor that it impinges on social relations. Nevertheless, the combination of historical source material and contemporary field observations subverts the idea that witchcraft notions and practices have their origin in relatively recent social changes.

The cases illustrate how witchcraft relates illness, suffering and death to disrupted or undermined social relationships between people who are physically and socially close. A person's existence is intimately bound up with the overlapping network of agnatic, affinal and neighbourly relations, but these can for myriad reasons always be disrupted. The concept of witchcraft is not restricted to any specific relationship among these, nor does it occasion a collective response on the basis of a determinate relationship. However, the fact of relatedness remains at the core of the concept of witchcraft. As Englund (2007:306) points out, witchcraft does not exist outside of sociality, but serves to imagine the limits of social relationships on an indeterminate scale. Witchcraft thus reveals to the people involved the ambiguous and fragile nature of social relationships, and the vulnerability of the existence that is founded upon this human relationality. There is an element of uncertainty or indeterminacy at play in social life, which lies beyond the power of any individual. Surrounding the web of sociality, therefore, there is a web of mutual suspicion and constant consideration, which makes clear this vulnerability and uncertainty to the people entangled in them. In the words of Lienhardt (1951:316), we can say that "[w]itchcraft is a concept in the assessment of relations between two people". Or as Moore and Sanders (2001:20) say, it is "… a set of discourses on morality, sociality, and humanity: on human frailty". Even when these relationships are disrupted, the people involved in them remain in each other's vicinity, which heightens the possibility that they will harm each other by various means. Witchcraft, therefore, concerns the fragility and uncertainty of social relationships, in the sense that it is an ever-present possibility that they can be subverted from within.

Acknowledgements

I would like to thank the Institute of Social and Cultural Anthropology, Oxford University, the German Academic Exchange Service (DAAD), the Norwegian Research Council and St. Antony's College, Oxford, for funding different portions of my research. I am furthermore grateful to the Tanzanian Commission for Science and Technology (COSTECH) for granting research clearances. Earlier versions of this paper were presented at the Medical Anthropology Seminar, University College London; the Sir Edward Evan Evans-Pritchard Centenary Colloquium, Oxford University; the African Studies Seminar at St. Antony's College, Oxford; and the Nordic Africa Institute's conference "Uncertainty in Contemporary African Lives" in Arusha. I am grateful to the participants at these events for their incisive comments and thank Murray Last, William Beinart, Wendy James and Liv Haram for their invitations to these events. Last but not least, thanks are due to David Parkin, Nick Allen, Chris Wingfield and Kathleen M. Jennings for reading and commenting on earlier drafts, and to the publisher's anonymous reviewers.

References

Comaroff, John and Jean Comaroff, 1993, "Introduction", in John Comaroff and Jean Comaroff (eds), *Modernity and Its Malcontents*. Chicago: Chicago University Press.

Douglas, Mary, 1970, "Thirty Years after *Witchcraft, Oracles and Magic*", in Mary Douglas (ed.), *Witchcraft Confessions and Accusations*. London: Tavistock.

—, 1980, *Edward Evans-Pritchard*. New York: The Viking Press.

Dundas, Charles, 1924, *Kilimanjaro and Its People*. London: Witherby.

Ellis, Stephen, 2002, "Witch-Hunting in Central Madagascar 1828–1861", *Past and Present*, Vol. 175, No. 1, pp. 90–123.

Englund, Harri, 2007, "Witchcraft and the Limits of Mass Mediation in Malawi", *Journal of the Royal Anthropological Institute (N.S.)*, Vol. 13, No. 2, pp. 295–311.

Evans-Pritchard, Edward E., 1937, *Witchcraft, Oracles, and Magic among the Azande*. Oxford: Oxford University Press.

Favret-Saada, Jeanne, 1980, *Deadly Words: Witchcraft in the Bocage*. Translated from the French by Catherine Cullen. Cambridge: Cambridge University Press. Originally published as *Les Mots, La Mort, Les Sorts* 1977.

Favret-Saada, Jeanne, 1989, "Unbewitching as Therapy", *American Ethnologist,* Vol. 16, No. 1, pp. 40–56.

—, 1990, "About Participation", *Culture, Medicine and Psychiatry,* Vol. 14, pp. 191–199.

Geschiere, Peter, 1997, *The Modernity of Witchcraft: Politics and the Occult in Postcolonial Africa*. Charlottesville: University of Virginia Press.

Green, Maia, 1994, "Shaving Witchcraft in Ulanga: Kunyolewa and the Catholic Church", in Ray G. Abrahams (ed.), *Witchcraft in Contemporary Tanzania*. Cambridge: African Studies Centre.

—, 1997, "Witchcraft Suppression Practices and Movements: Public Politics and the Logic of Purification", *Comparative Study of Society and History,* Vol. 39, No. 2, pp. 319–345.

Gutmann, Bruno, 1924, "Der Beschwörer bei den Wadschagga", *Archiv für Anthropologie*, Vol. 20, pp. 46–57.

Kapferer, Bruce, 2002, "Introduction Outside All Reason: Magic, Sorcery and Epistemology in Anthropology", in Bruce Kapferer (ed.), *Beyond Rationalism: Rethinking Magic, Witchcraft, and Sorcery*. Oxford: Berghahn.

Lienhardt, Godfrey, 1951, "Some Notions of Witchcraft among the Dinka", *Africa*, Vol. 21, No. 4, pp. 303–318.

Marwick, Max G., 1950, "Another Modern Anti-Witchcraft Movement in East Central Africa", *Africa,* Vol. 20, No. 2, pp. 100–112.

—, 1952, "The Social Context of Cewa Witch Beliefs", *Africa,* Vol. 22, No. 2, pp. 120–135, No. 3, pp. 215-233.

—, 1965, *Sorcery in Its Social Setting: A Study of the Northern Rhodesian Cewa.* Manchester: Manchester University Press.

Moore, Henrietta L. and Todd Sanders, 2001, "Magical Interpretations and Material Realities: An Introduction", in Henrietta L. Moore and Todd Sanders (eds), *Magical Interpretations and Material Realities: Modernity, Witchcraft and the Occult in Postcolonial Africa.* London: Routledge.

Moore, Sally F, 1975, "Selection for Failure in a Small Social Field: Ritual Concord and Fraternal Strife among the Chagga, Kilimanjaro, 1968–1969", in Sally F. Moore and Barbara G. Myerhoff, (eds), *Symbol and Politics in Communal Ideology.* Ithaca: Cornell University Press.

—, 1986, *Social Facts and Fabrications. 'Customary' Law on Kilimanjaro, 1880–1980.* Cambridge: Cambridge University Press.

—, 1996, "Post-Socialist Micro-Politics: Kilimanjaro, 1993", *Africa,* Vol. 66, No. 4, pp. 587–605.

Myhre, Knut C., 2003, "The Grammar of Healing. A Study of Eclecticism and Historical Continuity among the Chagga of Rombo District, Kilimanjaro Region, Tanzania." Unpublished D.Phil. Thesis, Institute of Social & Cultural Anthropology, Oxford University.

Raum, Johannes, 1911, "Die Religion der Landschaft Moschi am Kilmandjaro. Originalaufzeichnungen von Eingeborenen", *Archiv für Religionswissenschaft,* Vol. 14, pp. 159–211.

Richards, Audrey I., 1935, "A Modern Movement of Witchfinders", *Africa,* Vol. 8, No. 4, pp. 448–461.

Sanders, Todd, 2003, "Reconsidering Witchcraft: Postcolonial Africa and Analytic (Un)Certainties", *American Anthropologist,* Vol. 105, No. 2, pp. 326–340.

—, 2008, "Buses in Bongoland: Seductive Analytics and the Occult", *Anthropological Theory,* Vol. 8, No. 2, pp. 107–132.

Setel, Philip, 1999, *A Plague of Paradoxes: AIDS, Culture, and Demography in Northern Tanzania.* Chicago: University of Chicago Press.

Vansina, Jan, 1990, *Paths in the Rainforest: Toward a History of Political Tradition in Equatorial Africa.* London: James Currey.

Willis, Roy G., 1968, "Kamchape: An Anti-Sorcery Movement in South-West Tanzania", *Africa,* Vol. 38, No. 1, pp. 1–15 .

Winter, J. Christoph, 1979, *Bruno Gutmann 1876–1966 – A German Approach to Social Anthropology.* Oxford: Oxford University Press.

Yamba, C. Bawa, 1997, "Cosmologies in Turmoil: Witchfinding and AIDS in Chiawa, Zambia", *Africa,* Vol. 67, No. 2, pp. 200–223.

– CHAPTER 6 –

Coping with Mental Distress in Contemporary Dar es Salaam

Mary Ann Mhina

Introduction

> [Mental health in Africa] is a really important subject and there are two basic institutions that come into play: the traditional African family structure and modern hospitals. However many countries are currently hurting due to years of misrule and corruption. The traditional family still stands but the modern hospital is barely staggering, if not on its knees. Caught in between – like so many other needy segments of society – are the mentally ill…. (Wilson Wanene)[1]

Working on mental illness in Tanzania was a challenge; a challenge that took me, time and time again, back to the debates at the heart of anthropology and of African studies. How can anthropology deal with mental illness? What of "traditional African family structure"? How about the "modern hospital" on its knees? How can my experience relate to these claims? What can I say about these issues? Moreover, to what extent is madness, and indeed sanity, a construct of a society, a culture, a time and a position? As Wanene suggests in the quotation above, our understanding of mental health cannot be detached from our understanding of families and of the health care system. By focusing on the lives of mentally ill people my research in Dar es Salaam has looked at a group of people for whom both of these institutions offer only temporary protection and relief. Here I seek to voice some of the uncertainty experienced by mentally ill people and their families whose suffering has largely been forgotten by all but a few psychiatric professionals operating with minimal resources and support. I identify that bio-medical intervention offers a level of hope and some control over the uncertainty mentally ill people experience, but also that it offers little response to social marginalisation and, in fact, to some extent, perpetuates it.

---

1. www.bbcnews.talkingpoint.debates.african, Tuesday, October 9, 2001.

Mental health in Tanzania

Tanzania was created in 1972 by the union of the newly independent Tanganyika and the islands of Zanzibar and Pemba. Tanzania has an estimated population of almost 36 million people, many of whom live in rural areas, although the populations of the country's urban centres – Dar es Salaam, Mwanza and Arusha – have grown in recent years (Central Census Office 2003). Tanzania has experienced an unrivalled peace for an African country since the 1970s, but the socialist politics, which produced this stability, and made some considerable advances in sectors such as education and health, also crippled economic development. Since economic liberalisation in the 1980s Tanzania has struggled to catch up economically with its neighbours and the reality is that life, for the majority of Tanzanians, remains very tough.

Post independence, Tanzania's policies centred on the provision of basic services for all citizens.[2] This has meant that since the 1970s the Tanzanian government has envisaged the provision of basic health care at village level as a guiding principle behind general health policy (Heggenhoughen 1984), and it remains a goal to provide basic mental health care at "grassroots" level (Ministry of Health 2002). Institutions like the national psychiatric hospital, Mirembe, and indeed the psychiatric department at Muhimbili, the country's national referral hospital in Dar es Salaam, exist as referral facilities for the most severe cases of mental illness. Meanwhile, Tanzania currently has about a dozen practising psychiatrists. There are also a number of trained psychiatric nurses, but in practical terms generalist primary health care workers are expected to provide basic mental health care at the village level.

In 1980 the National Mental Health Programme was established. This programme, funded by the World Health Organization, DANIDA (Danish Aid) and the Tanzanian government, was a three-year pilot project which began in Morogoro and Kilimanjaro regions. After the pilot was completed a review was undertaken and an appraisal report appeared in 1991 (Schulsinger and Jablensky 1991). The report explains that the pilot concentrated on the provision of services right down to dispensary level. It was anticipated that dispensary staff would, at minimum, be able to recognise five basic categories of mental health problems and offer appropriate referral or treatment. To this end the programme emphasised the training of general health workers. However, the external funding for the National Mental Health

2. These policies followed Nyerere's ideological bias towards the maintenance of communal Africanness – which he termed Ujamaa.

Programme was withdrawn after the pilot was complete. The Tanzanian government thereupon sought to extend it to ten regions but with limited success. During the 1990s the achievements of the programme were steadily reversed and very little was done in the field of mental health care.

In recent years the state's ability to finance the health care system has deteriorated (Illiffe 1998), and donors have become key financers of the health care system. The transference to neoliberal economics and a multi-party electoral system over the past 20 years has made patients increasingly pay for any health care they receive. Whilst some mentally ill people are still receiving free health care, the drugs which they need are often unavailable or in short supply.

Under subsequent government health sector reforms it is now up to each individual district to decide how to allocate funds for health care (Green 2002). This means that it is up to District Medical Officers to allocate sufficient funds for community mental health care. In practice, psychiatric services are, for the most part, only available at a regional level and the care which is being provided is limited to acute care facilities for the severely mentally ill. Maia Green (2002: 18) has made the observation that: "Decentralisation does not in fact give poorer districts more control. It merely increases their responsibility for provision while retaining overall dependence on central funding through a granting mechanism." The result is that the burden for the provision of health care services falls locally, but the macro decisions affect the district's ability to shoulder that burden. The kind of budgets available to district health care teams are currently insufficient to meet the burden of mental health care even if district officials have placed it as a priority. The real influence in terms of funding allocation remains with the state and, beyond it, with donor organisations contributing to government spending; those organisations which currently concentrate on acute illnesses, and HIV and AIDS, have yet to think seriously about mental health care (WHO 2001).

Mental health care in Dar es Salaam

The most recent census suggests that the population of Dar es Salaam is currently approaching 3 million.[3] The city is divided into three districts: Kinon-

3. In 2002, the total recorded population was 2,497,940 spread over the three districts of Dar es Salaam (Central Census Office 2003:3). However larger numbers were recorded in the smaller, more settled, more affluent area of the city, suggesting that perhaps the data underrecorded the actual population.

doni, Ilala and Temeke. Decentralisation has meant that health services are budgeted for and run by the three district administrations in the city and, therefore, mental health services in the city are provided by each district. Consequently, the level of service available varies from district to district. The Mental Health Unit at the central Ministry of Health also allocates a district mental health co-ordinator to each district in the country. This person is usually a psychiatric nurse who is also employed by the district in question to provide psychiatric services. In most cases they are provide these services singlehandedly. Central units like the Mental Health Unit take a supervisory and advisory role, providing resources, training and advice.

Community mental health services began in Dar es Salaam in 1984 (Barantanda et al. 2000). Existing psychiatric nurses were trained to take mental health care skills out of Muhimbili down to district level facilities and below. This programme was developed during the course of the National Mental Health Programme of the 1980s.

As a research associate I was based at the Department of Psychiatry, Muhimbili Hospital in Dar es Salaam between 2002 and 2004. My research work of talking with patients in Dar es Salaam was mostly carried out in Kinondoni district. There were five functioning clinics in Kinondoni district.[4] In 2002 those clinics served 5,194 psychiatric patients.[5] The clinics are staffed by psychiatric nurses who, where possible, manage patients without referral to Muhimbili. Other districts of Dar es Salaam are less well served. Temeke currently has only one functioning mental health clinic, usually staffed by one psychiatric nurse who last year saw a total of 491 patients. Psychiatric care in Ilala is provided by two psychiatric nurses based at the district hospital, Amana. They occasionally make visits to other health facilities in the district. Their data suggests that between them they have been treating a few thousand patients every year.

I interviewed patients in Swahili, which is the national language of Tanzania and a language in which all my informants were fluent.[6] I asked patients using facilities in Kinondoni about their illness and how it began. I asked them about the treatment they were receiving and about other therapies they might have used. I also asked questions about other aspects of their lives: their families, their income and social life. Often, I also talked to patients' families and carers; sometimes I spoke only to a family member

4. Mwananyamala, Magomeni, Lugalo, Oyster Bay and Tandale.
5. Data collected by collating records kept by psychiatric nurses in clinic facilities.
6. The majority of people in Tanzania have a good command of Swahili even if the language is not their mother tongue.

when patients themselves were unable to communicate with me. I talked to a total of 50 patients and in more than 35 of those cases a relative was involved in the conversation. I was constantly aware of ethical questions raised by my research project. I am uneasy about telling the stories of people who almost unanimously did not wish to be identifiable. I have, therefore, taken great care to conceal identities in the excerpts I reproduce here and all names are pseudonyms.

I also spoke with psychiatric nurses in all the districts of the city about their work and the problems they faced. Without exception they talked of resource constraints, of the heavy case load, and of the stigmatisation of themselves as psychiatric specialists amongst their fellow health care workers in the facilities where they work. Without exception the physical space allocated to mental health care is the smallest, and the resources allocated are the most minimal. Psychiatric nurses are also expected to bear the additional burden of providing treatment to the growing number of drug users in the city (Gilbert 2002).

Stories

In my research work I set out to collect narratives of people suffering from mental illness in Dar es Salaam. The material I have collected is neither strictly narratives of illness, nor constitutes comprehensive life stories of patients. In reality, my material hovers somewhere in between. The narratives talk about "traditional families" and "modern hospitals" and a wealth of things besides. People's stories are not only confined to their experience of being mentally ill; "being mentally ill" can be both an identity and a non-identity. Categories shift and boundaries blur. "Being mentally ill" also relates to both a space and a time in which you are categorised as such by yourself and/or by others. The stories I have collected provide some insight into the reality of the mental health care provided by the "modern hospitals" and the continued existence of "traditional families", which escape easy description. They also tell a story about what being mentally ill means for your relationship not only with your family and health care systems but also with the rest of the world around you.

Of illness narratives

Narratives, or the things people chose to tell me, are conditioned by multiple factors. The location in which they are taken, the individuals' own position vis-à-vis those to whom they are telling a story, the way the story is elicited, and much more besides (Bury 2001). Bio-medicine has what Hyden has called an "ambiguous" approach to the stories of patients (1997), preferring to base its diagnosis on biological science rather than the somewhat less definable symptoms found in patients' narratives. In the field of psychiatry, however, things become a little less clear. While a number of mental illnesses have specific biological indications, some patients may have no obvious biological symptoms at all. The problems inherent in diagnosis are, perhaps, best illustrated by the frequency of multiple diagnoses found in many of the patients' files that I consulted during the course of my research. Illness which is classified as "mental", and therefore a sickness of the mind, brings with it an inherent problem for bio-medical science.

For a psychiatric diagnosis the story must have increased importance, since it is often only through the stories of the patient and/or their family and friends that the symptoms can be explained and a diagnosis sought. It is, perhaps, in psychiatry that the limitations of a strictly bio-medical approach to the treatment of illness are most keenly felt, and where questions of wellness and illness come most under scrutiny and answers are less easily found (Precin 2002). Take the following case, for instance:

> My name is Stephen and I am 43 years old. Now I live in Tandale, I moved there last year from Temeke. My problem is that I have fits and I make a lot of noise. If I use the medicine then I don't have fits any more. Here, the clinic was the first big hospital which I came to and I haven't visited traditional healers.[7] I only started getting these fits in the year 2000 and my relations were very surprised and couldn't understand why I was getting them. At the time I was working as a builder – the people I was working for saw my problem and I lost my job just like that. Now I am looked after by my relatives and I do small jobs if there are any around but I am no longer employed. I encounter lots of problems – this thing has "reversed my development" [*Imenirudishia nyuma kimaendeleo*]. I am engaged to a woman who is living in the village, but she is suffering there from small illnesses. I

7. What are termed "traditional healers" (*waganga wa asili*) in this chapter are not a homogenous group. Their means of treatment range from the simple use of herbal remedies known for their medicinal properties to those whose treatment is based on their perceived possession of spiritual power to ascertain the cause of suffering and to carry out remedial rituals. The latter are also often referred to as *waganga wa kinyeji* (best translated as "local healers"). This chapter does not question the distinction between different means of healing. Rather, it juxtaposes "traditional healing" (encompassing a number of healing methods) with a bio-medical, state-funded approach to dealing with mental illness.

had the plan to marry her but I have not done so yet. Now I have medicine and I want to work but the illness prevents me. I would really like to work. Before this happened I was living with my fiancée – it was the illness that made me go back home to my family by force (his family came to collect him). They have told me but I can't remember how it all happened, though now I have medicine I am there freely and there is no problem.

Mental illness changes people's lives. It makes those lives that little bit harder. It makes coping even more difficult than it already was. In a case like that of Stephen it makes the planned processes of life uncertain, and the things he had once depended upon appear to have collapsed. Mental illness makes an individual less acceptable as a marriage partner or as an employee. In Steven's case it makes life difficult even though he is among those fortunate enough to be receiving treatment. Though he has medicine, he is still unable to work, not only because of some serious side effects but also because of a pervading belief on the part of those around him that he is incapable of work; indeed, it seems he is also thought incapable of maintaining a relationship.

> My name is Salma. I am 26 years old and I live in Sinza. I have a mental illness; I feel dizzy and my senses leave me. It all started in 1993. I lived in a village in Morogoro region and I didn't have any treatment. I went to "local doctors" (*waganga wa kiwnyeji*) and used their plant medicines but they didn't help me at all. I didn't know at all about hospital treatment. People in the village didn't know what to do – they couldn't do anything. I went to visit so many different healers – at least 15 of them. I came to Dar es Salaam with my brother but now I live by myself. I depend upon myself and he is on his own. Here in Dar es Salaam I went to about three healers but they didn't really seem able to help me. Then in 2002 I was given the idea by people around me to come to the hospital. I came to the clinic at Mwanyamala because I was told that they would help me here and it is true the treatment I have received here has helped me. Sometimes I feel that the darkness is coming into me and that there are insects crawling inside my head. I live alone with my partner, I do business here in the city and I depend upon myself but I do get drugs. My heart beats very quickly and I get some worries – it just happens like that and I don't know the cause.

Salma talks about a life in the village where she was unable to access treatment for her illness. She talks about visiting a variety of practitioners in town and about accessing bio-medical services at one of the city's clinics. Because my research has been carried out alongside psychiatric facilities, all

147

of the people I interviewed had accessed those services. The reality is that the majority of mentally ill people in Tanzania probably never access bio-medical facilities. A story like Salma's suggests that the so-called "traditional family" and indeed the "traditional healing system" to which it looks for healing does not always find satisfactory ways to cope with mental illness. It also suggests that people do not always have a coherent understanding of, or explanation for, the mental health problems they face.[8] Another problem is the ambiguous and indeterminate accounts of the symptoms that people with mental illness provide. Phrases such as "insects crawling in my head" belong to a realm of discourse in which traditional healers might seem more comfortable than bio-medical practitioners.

The pluralistic nature of the healing strategies employed by the mentally ill people I spoke to is emphasised by Osman's story. Osman came to the clinic at the hospital to collect his medicines. He told me that he had been suffering from fits since he was very small. He explained to me that people, including his parents, believed that a curse of some kind had been placed upon him. In order to try and remove the curse, Osman was taken to a "local healer" (*mganga wa kyenyeji*). The healer gave him some medicines derived from plants to use. For six months Osman felt much better but after that he began to have fits again. Four years ago, when Osman was 13 years of age, his parents brought him to the hospital. There the psychiatric nurses diagnosed Osman with epilepsy and now he is being effectively treated with medicines provided by the hospital. Osman told me that he knows that his illness was initially caused by some kind of curse but that the medicines he gets from the hospital help to keep that curse under control.

The causes of illness and healing are explained by different people in different ways. The same person, like Osman, can believe both in a curse and the bio-medical drugs that appear to be curing it. Medical anthropology uses the concept of medical pluralism to describe people's tendency to look for treatment, and indeed causality, in more than one place (Feierman and Janzen 1992).

Osman has been taking drugs prescribed for a condition called epilep-

---

8. Additional research which I carried out, talking with mentally ill people in Mt-wara region in southern Tanzania, where bio-medical mental health care is minimal, showed that the vast majority of mentally ill people living in rural areas are unaware that bio-medical therapies exist for their problems. A small acute ward at the regional hospital in Mtwara town and a small hut in Masasi are the only structural facilities. A handful of psychiatric nurses provide limited hospital-based care.

sy.[9] In all three East African countries I visited, [10] epilepsy is allocated to the government official responsible for mental health. But as Patel (2003: 70) writes: "Epilepsy is not a mental illness." The causes of epilepsy are neurological and therefore medicine considers it not to be a mental illness. Scientific categorisation relates us back to biological function. The reality in the "modern hospitals" of Eastern Africa is that patients think epilepsy is a mental health problem and psychiatric specialists treat epileptic patients. The World Health Organization also considers the burden placed on communities by epilepsy as contributing to that placed on them by mental illness in general (WHO 2001:34). So, whilst medicine as a discipline categorises epilepsy as a physical rather than a mental illness, the WHO places it in the category of mental health, because of similarities in terms of symptoms and treatment in many parts of the world. Osman, moreover, has another understanding about the problems he has faced. Rather than relating them to electrical charges in the brain (WHO 2001), he relates them to a curse placed upon him as a child.

Osman did not in fact discount the explanation, offered by Patel, that epilepsy is caused by electrical charges in the brain. He simply told me that it was a curse that initially triggered his problems. We might infer that he believes that a curse caused the charges in his brain (rather than that he rejects the biological explanation of what has happened to him). Whenever I visit a psychiatric clinic in Tanzania a large proportion of patients are recorded to be suffering from epilepsy. The psychiatric nurses in Masasi in southern Tanzania have conducted their own studies in which they suggest that untreated malaria in children might be an important factor in the significant number of epileptics who seem to be seeking their help.[11] But the bio-medical data is sill incomplete. We may know that epilepsy means electrical charges in the brain, but complete knowledge, particularly about prevalence in specific areas, seems to have escaped us (Mugarura 2000).

> My name is Julius and I am 54-four. I am mentally ill and I have been coming to this clinic for quite a while. I live on the other side of town with my

---

9. Epilepsy, unlike other mental illnesses has a name in Swahili which is well known and is not a modern translation from English, which is why patients and their relatives use the term. The term is *kifafa*, which I translate as epilepsy. However, as often the case with indigenous terms, *kifafa* might often denote other conditions that are not always diagnosed as epilepsy.
10. Tanzania, Kenya and Uganda.
11. Discussion with informants, 2003.

mother and my children, and my wife who I married is there. I come here every month, just to get the drugs. My problem started not very long ago, and it was simply that I just couldn't sleep and if I don't get drugs then yes, I can't sleep. The problem was malaria, it went to the head but now it doesn't go up. I was a machine operator. But when I take drugs, I sleep, so I can't work. I look after my own children. A long time ago I was at Muhimbili [hospital]. When I was in Rufiji area (in the south of Tanzania), I went to see a "local healer" and he gave me some plant medicines. A long, long time ago I was admitted for only a week. This is just malaria. I have six children, they are two boys and four girls. They are studying but one has finished. The treatment I get here is all right and they seem to have enough drugs, but life is a struggle.

Julius tries to explain his problems in different ways; lack of sleep, severe malaria and so on. He also has tried to solve his problems in what we might call a "medically pluralistic" way (Feierman and Janzen 1992). Macarthur's ethnographic work with healers in Dar es Salaam led him to suggest that a characteristic of traditional healers[12] might be their own ability to adapt their forms of therapy (Macarthur 1999). So, perhaps, it is not only patients but even healers themselves who are sometimes medically pluralistic, borrowing from different therapeutic traditions and rationalities in their treatment of their patients (Macarthur 1999).

Caring for mentally ill relatives

To care for the mentally ill is, as the following narrative illustrates, a heavy bunden for the closest family – often with dire cosequences.

My eldest daughter Amina was born in 1960 and she was fine and smart as a child. She schooled up to form six (final year in secondary school). After her father died, I married again and my new husband and other children lived well together. But towards the end of her schooling, Amina started having these problems. She would make a lot of noise and say things that made no sense to me. In the end, she stopped going to school and never got her leaving certificate. Her mental state deteriorated and eventually one of my brothers suggested I should take her to see a doctor. We went to the doctors at Muhimbili one day when she was really bad and she stayed in that place for nearly a month. They gave her their medicines and she came home for a

12. Macarthur does not question the concept of "traditional healer" and simply translates it into Swahili as *mganga*, which can refer to a practitioner of any kind including a bio-medical doctor.

while. Then she was better, to some extent. She used to go to Muhimbili and collect her medicines. But then the problems got worse again. I sent Amina to stay at my brother's place in Tabora, because I could no longer manage with small children at home in those days. In that place Amina could no longer get medicine, they would take her to those "traditional healers", but her disturbance got worse. When I visited Amina, I found her tied up behind the house, thin and uncared for.

When people are mentally ill they often disturb their families and cause economic strain. Of course that strain is felt most keenly by families who are already struggling to get by. In many cases, I have found that families respond by seeking the best way in which they can get by. Sometimes this means restraining the mentally ill person to minimise the damage they may cause. In other cases, as in the case of Mwadime, the simplest answers may be to do very little.

A long time ago Mwadime used to go to the hospital and get those medicines. In the beginning they were free. Later he could only get them if we paid for them. When he takes the medicines he talks a lot, he might seem more normal but he is still hard to handle. And those medicines cost a lot of money these days. I don't want to take him back to the hospital because I am afraid when he goes there they might make him stay and that place is not nice any more. The place is horrible and I don't want a child of mine staying there. So when he is violent or angry I prefer to lock Mwadime in his room until he stops. Sometimes he doesn't talk for days, other times he is so noisy, but I prefer we deal with it ourselves these days.

Severely mentally ill people place an unimaginable strain on their families and carers. In a tough economic climate where health care is not always certain, getting by sometimes means limiting the possible negative consequences as best you can.

My name is Juma and I have come here with brother Abdallah. We are from Songea in the south of Tanzania. Abdallah began to suffer from this epilepsy when he was only just born, before he reached his 40th day. Over the years Abdallah visited so many of these local healers who were local to Songea and was given different kinds of plants as medicine. I moved here to Dar es Salaam about five years ago, looking to make a better life for myself. I went home and brought Abdallah here to the city seven months ago. He can't communicate and he doesn't work or do anything for himself. His mind is not well. He used to have fits about three times a month before I brought him but since he has started using medicine he doesn't have fits anymore. We always thought that someone had done something bad to us or that it was God's will. But here in Dar one of my neighbours had an epileptic in his family and that person was getting treatment. He told me that the hospital has treatment for that kind of thing and we came straight here to the clinic at Magomeni. He just stays at home and sits there – everything is done for him as we are always afraid that he might have fits again.

The stories of mentally ill people in Dar es Salaam do not offer us an easy definition of mental illness, rather they offer us some insight into the daily experiences of one of the most marginalised groups in Dar es Salaam and their strategies for dealing with the unavoidable uncertainty of being mentally ill.

As Wanene says in quotation at the beginning of this chapter; "The traditional family still stands", but do the stories that I was told really bare witness to this? Is it really the "barely staggering…modern hospital", as he suggests, that lets them down? If the traditional family believed mental illness to be a curse, many of the narratives bear testament to the persistence of a curse as a casual factor in the onset of mental illness, but they also suggest that families often offer the mentally ill person a coping strategy. Stephen is looked after by his family after he is forced to leave his fiancé; Juma is kept at home by a protective family; Julius says he is still able to care for his children; Salma goes on living with a partner but not with her own family; while in the case of Amina and Mwadime, the "protection" offered by the family seems to stifle life. To some extent it feels as though the coping mechanisms offered by the "traditional family structure" are partially in place, but that they work against the narrative of healing offered by bio-medicine. They appear rather to assist in the maintenance of a view in which a mentally ill person needs protection and, when necessary, physical restraint.

The storytellers have all benefited from bio-medical intervention, which has offered them, at least for a period of time, an element of control over their illness. But do the healing systems on offer give mentally ill people a chance of long-term healing or social acceptance? Hearing these stories gave me an overwhelming, sometimes unbearable sense of mentally ill people as marginalised and socially unacceptable. The intervention of bio-medicine seemed to have offered only control but not social healing. Socially, they remained incapacitated, unable to work or marry, struggling to convince others of their capabilities.

The stories present a reasonably positive vision of bio-medical services provided by the "modern hospital". All of the narrators have used the services and many have found some relief and been able to take some control of their lives as a result. The modern hospital would therefore seem not to be on its knees. Instead, it seems able to offer some relief to mentally ill patients. However, the marginalisation not only of mentally ill people, but also of the professionals who specialise in psychiatric treatment, suggests a deep social marginalisation, which the modern hospital has failed to overcome.

Mental health and traditional medicine

A history of mental health care in Tanzania would show that there has been a medically plural approach to the treatment of mentally ill people. As in many other countries that were at one time colonial states, Tanzania has a psychiatric institution dating from colonial times. It also has psychiatric professionals who have been trained in a bio-medical approach to mental health care. On the other hand, there are also a number of other beliefs and ideas about mental health and illness which co-exist with those of the psychiatric establishment. Traditional healing (*uganga wa asili*) is another complex story. It cannot be seen as a coherent body of practitioners, though associations of healers do exist. Healers offer patients multiple explanations and treatments, but for some patients their assistance is clearly not sufficient.

Talking with mentally ill people in Tanzania has illustrated that parallel healing systems exist co-evally and that most patients themselves have a medically plural approach to seeking care. No one person or institution can present a composite picture of mental health in Tanzania. Nor can any intervention, whoever it is designed by, or for, present an all-encompassing answer to the problems mental health care faces. Whilst the stories which I heard from mentally ill people were undoubtedly constructed by them and presented the view of their circumstances and of their illness which they wanted me to hear there was an overwhelming sense of resignation in many of the voices that I heard. In addition, I spoke at length with families, practitioners and policy makers.

Although all the narratives I heard were constructed by their narrators I cannot get away from an overwhelming sense of negativity, an overwhelming sense that a very large group of people (most of whom have never accessed bio-medical services) live, because of their experiences of mental illness and because of the effect of their illness on their relationships with the world around them, in a protected, marginalised world from which healing systems do not seem to offer much offer of hope or release. Without doubt many of the mentally ill people I spoke with have already been let down by multiple narratives: by narratives of healing and family, which we might call local; and by narratives of health care provided by a supposedly developing state, because despite the promise of healing offered by bio-medical institutions social marginalisation is not addressed – rather it is perpetuated within the health system itself by the marginalisation of the staff providing psychiatric treatment.

There are many examples in my interviews of different kinds of "rationality" and their mutual existence in one space and time and indeed in one person's mind. Many people are less confident about the all-solving properties of medical science, preferring to see it as a means to solve some biological problems but not an all-solving medicine for all (Good 1994). We might note that bio-medical science has produced pharmaceutical cures for mental illnesses but even Western science recognises the role of other forms of therapy as being crucial to the treatment of the mentally ill. Almost all the psychiatric patients I interviewed had consulted "traditional healers" (*uganga wa asili*) of different kinds. Most of these explain their patients' ailments as originating in a curse or disagreement of some kind. Some of the patients had experienced forms of treatment which involved spiritual possession of some kind. Others had been given medicine derived from plants. Many traditional healers run a kind of inpatients' unit where severely mentally ill people are kept for some time, and usually this treatment involves physical restraint of some kind. The majority of my informants told me that their treatment by traditional healers had had limited, or no positive effect. However, it must be considered that I was interviewing patients who were, for the most part, using hospital services and initially viewed me, to some extent or other, as a part of them. When I visited traditional healers in the countryside in southern Tanzania, I also encountered a number of patients who had used hospital services, been dissatisfied with them, and returned to seek the help of traditional practitioners.

James Ferguson (1999) has set the narrative of modernity surrounding the Zambian copper belt in the 1970s against the experiences of the men he found there. He looks at the way the narrative of modernisation has worked to encourage what he calls "dis-connection" amongst workers who struggled for an idealised modernity, which has continued to exclude them. A number of patients told me about a home place in the countryside and a recent emigration to town. As such, mentally ill people, like many other urban dwellers in Dar es Salaam, are new immigrants to the city, accessing a new kind of life, and for many patients I spoke to it was the move to the city that facilitated the access to bio-medical services. They experienced frustration as well as hope.

Mentally ill people are let down by the promises of both bio-medicine and traditional healing systems which, though they may offer some temporary relief, seldom offer the chance of social acceptance or indeed a feeling of having really "got better. The people whose stories I have re-told here seemed forever consigned to the periphery of life – cared for by relatives, relieved by drugs or ceremonies, but not able to fully participate in the world around them.

Cultural psychiatry has sought to contest the Eurocentric nature of psychiatric discourse (Littlewood and Lipsedge 1997). Predominantly concerned with the treatment of "aliens" in the United Kingdom, Littlewood and Lipsedge contested the British medical profession's tendency to conclude that people from certain societies have a tendency towards experiencing psychological problems. They, like Fanon before them (Fanon 1967), suggest that psychiatry is a Eurocentric project, and that, as such, it therefore conforms to a particular society's understanding of what is normal. Littlewood has continued to investigate these ideas and has subsequently published *Colonialism and Psychiatry* (Littlewood and Bhugra 2001), which investigates the links between colonialism and psychiatric understanding of people's state, showing the extent to which psychiatry assisted in the colonial project of inferiorising the "native". Littlewood and Bhugra argue that we should give "local understandings of self and illness" as much credibility as "psychiatric theories" (Littlewood and Bhugra 2001:2).

In the context of this chapter the traditional family structure is alive but faces serious challenges from mental illness and a globalised world. The modern hospital has in Africa largely failed its users. In general, it continues to provide sub-standard health care to the minority. In particular, it tends to fail those with mental illnesses, for whom appropriate treatment is seldom available. Traditional healers are perceived often as being more effective in treating mental illness but do not always bring long-term relief. Five mentally ill men tied up outside the home of a traditional healer was one of the most challenging things I encountered during my research. Physical shackles provided relief for families, who slept by their side and prepared food to sustain their existence. When those same families told me that they had visited the local hospital but had not been able to access effective treatment, and that they had therefore returned to a local healer who could provide a means of therapy which made their lives easier, the challenges of this situation hit me in the face.

Conclusion

Healing systems are not on an evolutionary continuum, rather they exist
co-evally in the same space and time. Many patients use bio-medicine and
"traditional healing" interchangeably in an attempt to find a way to manage
the constant uncertainty with which they live and to mitigate against it. The
protection which is sometimes offered by the traditional family structure, as
well as by traditional methods of healing, play an important part in both the
management of illness and the protection of the individual from harming
themselves or others. The bio-medical relief offered by modern hospitals offers some temporary relief and brief periods of a "normal life". Yet, without
exception, the mentally ill people I spoke to described themselves as marginalised, and their social marginalisation seemed to be reinforced by the
special marginalisation of the psychiatric services in the "modem hospitals"
of Dar es Salaam. Psychiatry, therefore, offers some means to cope with
uncertainty: an extra strategy, perhaps, unavailable to those in rural areas,
far from the concentration of bio-medical services that one finds in the
city. However, the coping mechanism is not an answer to all the challenges
mentally ill people face. The social marginalisation, which often translates
into extreme protection at the hands of their families desperate for a means
to cope, makes life uncertain and confused for mentally ill people as they
struggle to find a place in a society that finds them difficult to comprehend
or accept.

Mentally ill people everywhere suffer from misunderstanding and marginalisation. Nowhere is this felt more acutely than in countries like Tanzania where resources are scarce and rights elusive. For families living with a
severely mentally ill person life is always uncertain and the burden is often
great. My research evidences the capacity for coping with uncertainty that
characterises contemporary life in Tanzanian, but it challenges any tendency
to characterise a specific approach to mental illness in Tanzania or indeed
in Africa. When we think about mental illness in contemporary Tanzania
we must consider that resources at every level, from the family unit to the
national government, are stretched beyond belief. We need to understand
that in such an environment mental illness presents an inordinate challenge
to families and communities and that any "traditional approach" to contemporary problems is being challenged locally by those concerned. The
increasing urbanisation of contemporary Africa and the boom in television
and mobile communication is irrevocably changing Tanzania and in prob-
ability most of Africa. But the lessons which Ferguson has drawn from the

Zambian copper belt remain pertinent. Will these changes mean anything to those whose lives are forgotten and marginalised by mental illness? How much will increased globalisation affect the weakest in society whose lives are in a state of constant uncertainty?

References

Barantanda, E., S. Kaaya, et al., 2000, "Community mental health services in the context of health sector reforms in Kinondoni district, Dar es Salaam". 18th Tanzanian Public Health Association Annual Scientific Conference, Dar es Salaam.

Bury, M., 2001, "Illness narratives: fact or fiction?", *Sociology of Health and Illness*, 23(3):263–285.

Central Census Office, 2003, *2002 Population and Housing Census General Report*. Dar es Salaam, National Bureau of Statistics, President's Office, The United Republic of Tanzania.

Fanon, F., 1967, *Black Skin, White Masks*. New York: Grove Press.

Feierman, S. and J. Janzen, 1992, *The Social Basis of Health and Healing in Africa*. Berkeley: University of California Press.

Ferguson, J., 1999, *Expectation of Modernity–Myths and Meanings of Urban Life on the Zambian Copperbelt*. Los Angeles and London: University of California Press.

Gilbert, S., 2002, *Drug Prevention Campaign*. (Unpublished document.) Save the Children.

Good, B., 1994, *Medicine, Rationality and Experience: An Anthropological Perspective*. Cambridge: Cambridge University Press.

Green, M., 2002, *Social Obligations and Health Services: The Imagination of Health and Development in Tanzania*. London: School of Oriental and African Studies 19.

Heggenhoughen, H.K., 1984, "Will Primary Health Care Efforts be Allowed to Succeed?", *Social Science and Medicine*, 19(3):217–224.

Hyden, L., 1997, "'Illness and Narrative'", *Sociology of Health and Illness*, 19(1):49–69.

Illiffe, J., 1998, *East African Doctors–A History of the Modern Profession*. Cambridge: Cambridge University Press.

Littlewood, R. and D. Bhugra (eds), 2001, Colonialism and Psychiatry. Oxford: Oxford University Press.

Littlewood, R. and M. Lipsedge, 1997, *Aliens and Alienists*. London: Unwin.

Macarthur, G., 1999, *Traditional Healers in a Changing State*. Department of Anthropology. Maynooth, National University of Ireland 112.

Ministry of Health, 2002, *Medium Term Expenditure Framework 2002/2003–2004/2005–Policy Statements and Performance Review*. Dar es Salaam, The United Republic of Tanzania.

Mugarura, A., 2000, *A Socio-Economic Perspective of Epilepsy among rural people: A Case Study of Rubindi Sub-County, Mbarara District*. Development Studies. Uganda, Mbarara University of Science and Technology 63.

Patel, V., 2003, *Where There is No Psychiatrist*. London: Gaskell.

Precin, P., 2002, *Client-Centered Reasoning*. Boston: Butterworth Heinemann.

Schulsinger, F. and A. Jablensky, 1991, *The national mental health programme in the United Republic of Tanzania*. Copenhagen: Munksgaard.

World Health Report 2001–Mental Health: New Understanding, New Hope. World Health Organization 178.

– CHAPTER 7 –

Female Suicides in Dar es Salaam: The Ultimate Uncertainty and Despair

Noah K. Ndosi

Introduction

One of the most drastic consequences of uncertainty, the feeling of utter in-ability to cope with one's life, is that of giving up altogether, of being driven to terminate one's life as the final solution. Suicide is a truly philosophical problem, as Albert Camus once observed (Camus 1975:51). The ontology of life and living, our physically being in the world, manifests and affirms the specificity of (our) life. Therefore choosing to terminate that life not only contradicts the essence of being, but raises larger issues, one of which is whether we have the right to end our own life in the first place. Or, whether being here in the world also entails a responsibility for perpetuating life and trying to deal with any difficulties that we encounter on the journey of life, quite simply, by just living on. It is partly for such a reason that most religions proscribe suicide, making it both a moral and an ethical issue. The uncertainty and distress that the phenomenon of suicide causes in the lives of those left behind is also partly what makes it such a difficult and profound problem.

In this chapter, I am concerned with neither the existential nor the philo-sophical implications of suicide, but approach it from the perspective of a medical doctor and a neuro-psychiatrist – one of a score of mental health specialists in present-day Tanzania. My concern, apart from portraying the determinants involved in suicide, is that of showing how some unfortunate women, in present-day Tanzania, perceived no worthwhile possibilities or scope in their life, so that taking their own life was for them the only option.

My study is limited to the individual characteristics of women who fa-tally poisoned themselves as a result of despair. In doing so I hope to ex-plore and discuss the various factors that contributed to the self-poisoning of these particular women. The established determinants of suicide and the types of poisons employed to carry out the suicide are considered in the light of other studies in order to increase understanding of this tragic loss of human lives. Ways of preventing or limiting suicide are urgently needed.

Suicide as a reason for death is unique to humankind A suicidal action may be impulsive or may have been contemplated over a long time. Usually it is a result of low self-esteem, a history of losses, a depressed mood and troubled relationships between individuals. Self-annihilation is among the top 10 causes of death in most countries that report suicide rates (Desjarlais et al. 1995:68). Among people aged between 15 and 25, suicide is the third leading cause of death worldwide. Rates of suicides have been said to be low in Africa due to a paucity of depressive conditions and increased frequency of communal clashes that divert the aggression in the direction of others (Nwosu and Odesamni 2001:259). This view is no longer tenable because depression in Africans is not readily recognised as it presents with a cluster of physical complaints, bodily expressions, rather than feelings of guilt and self-reproach, which is the common mode of presentation among depressed patients in Western cultures (Reza et al. 2001:104; Morgan 1979). Acts of suicide carry serious implications for victims, their families and other dependants. A shortened life causes both immediate and long-term distress, including economic disadvantages.

There is an acknowledged scarcity of analytic studies on suicide which focus on males and/or females separately (Desjarlais et al. 1995:85). Reports on suicide in Tanzania are not only patchy but also erratic. Studies that investigate various factors associated with suicide in Tanzania are lacking. However, Tanzanians have recently been alarmed by an increase in acts of suicide, particularly within communities of the commercial city of Dar es Salaam. An editorial in one of the newspapers in Tanzania, *The Guardian*, reported as follows:

> Suicide cases in Tanzania seem to be increasing at an alarming rate. This disturbing trend calls for urgent attention. Our experts need to find out the major cause behind it so that counselling can be done (April 3, 2001, p. 6).

Escalating suicides have sparked debates as to why people decide to kill themselves. Remedial measures need to be effected to contain this tragic loss of human life.

Fatal self-poisoning by women is immersed in worrisome and painful suffering, which often results from extreme tensions that have built up within interpersonal relationships or families. Although data on this subject is lacking, hospital-based observations indicate that, currently, suicide constitutes a major public health concern. However, information on suicides has to be interpreted cautiously because it is from selected samples that more in-depth information can be obtained than from country statistics. Required capacities to intervene and prevent suicidal acts should be fostered through a better understanding of the various factors involved in precipitating them. A high annual population growth of 2.8% aggravates poor housing, malnutrition, infectious diseases, accidents and psychological stress. A profile of 100 suicides in Dar es Salaam was recently studied (Ndosi et al. 2004).

In the following sections I will first account for the methodological procedures employed in this study and the obtained results. The causes of suicides are then investigated and the findings are compared and discussed in the light of other studies.

Setting and methodology

Tanzania is among the poorest countries in the world. According to World Bank development indicators in 2006, the annual per capita income in Tanzania is estimated to be US$ 340 (World Bank 2006 (http://www.worldbank.org/data). The financial resources available for amenities of life are severely limited and nearly half of the Tanzanian population live below the poverty line of US$ 0.65 a day. A quarter of an estimated 36 million Tanzanians live on less than US$ 0.5 a day. A high annual population growth of 2.8% aggravates poor housing, malnutrition, infectious diseases, accidents, and psychological stress. Urban hard-core poverty which affects young women more severely accounts for 10% of the total poverty affecting the Tanzanian population (World Bank 2006 (http://www.worldbank.org/data).

In the last four decades, the urban population in Tanzania has increased from 7% to over 30% of the total current population. Over half of the increase in this population has occurred in the city of Dar es Salaam (Ndosi 2005:196–208). Here, unemployment amongst men during 2004–5 was 24.3% but amongst women it was double (National Bureau of Statistics 2005:37–39). Underemployment is also higher among women than men, and much of the work available to women is poorly paid and labour-intensive. Many women engage in informal sector activities of petty trading and subsistence farming. Low-income women among urban slum dwellers in Dar es Salaam live under stress at home when the social support of their spouses is lacking. They suffer from deprivations aggravated by unemployment in addition to frequent attacks of malaria and high rates of HIV infection. These disadvantaged living conditions cumulatively arouse feelings of powerlessness and hopelessness.

This study was carried out at Muhimbili National Hospital in Dar es

Salaam, the largest referral centre in Tanzania, which is also a university teaching institution with an admission capacity of 1,500 beds. The Department of Morbid Anatomy and Pathology is one of 18 departments under the Faculty of Medicine and has seven pathologists. Currently, Dar es Salaam region has a population of 2.5 million people (http://www.tanzania. go.tz/census/dsm.htm). All medico-legal post-mortems from Dar es Salaam region are conducted here. The Muhimbili mortuary is designed to accommodate 25 bodies at a time but it is often overloaded with up to 60 bodies piled up in a single cold room. About 1,000 post-mortems are conducted here annually. Usually, any person suspected to have committed suicide is reported to the nearest police station without delay by relatives or responsible ten-cell leaders.[1] The District Criminal Investigation Officer sends investigating officers to the site of the suicidal act. They in turn look for the people who best knew the deceased, mainly close family or neighbours to identify the deceased reliably. The investigators note the position and general state of the dead body. They then describe the environmental surroundings, record any obvious means employed to commit suicide and any other relevant observations before taking the body with an official medico-legal post-mortem form to the Muhimbili mortuary.

From September 1, 2000, to October 31, 2001, all suspected suicides from the three districts of Ilala, Kinondoni and Temeke (which constitute Dar es Salaam region) were duly identified by the police and relatives or persons who knew the circumstances leading to death of the deceased well. Successful suicide attempts reported by Muhimbili Hospital, district and private hospitals and health centres within the region were also included. A total of 111 suicides were reliably identified but in four instances, grieving relatives refused to volunteer information pertaining to the deceased on the grounds that they were not in a position to disclose private family problems. Some Tanzanians do not volunteer such information because suicide is legally prohibited. They fear to implicate their families in breaking the law.

In the case of seven other suicides, information regarding individual characteristics, reasons for suicide and circumstances surrounding their deaths was inadequate, and they were thus not included in the study. Additionally, any available information as to details pertaining to circumstances and motives surrounding the completed suicide acts was sought from the

---

1. A ten-cell leader is a political spokesman entrusted with the responsibility of overseeing 10 households in a small community as part of a village or an urban street.

police and courts of law. To protect confidentiality, the courts of law normally provide only limited information that leads to the verdict of suicide or not suicide.

After individual circumstances surrounding the self-annihilation had been carefully established, medico-legal autopsies were conducted at the hospital mortuary by the pathologists on call to establish the causes of death. Means employed to complete suicidal acts including any other significant but relevant findings were recorded. In each case, samples of blood, urine, stomach contents, liver and kidney tissues were taken to the Government Chemist to determine the types and blood concentration levels of poisons ingested to cause death.[2] Since people infected with the human immuno-deficiency virus have been reported to attempt or commit suicide secretly, a sample of blood was also taken in each case to test for HIV infection (Gielen et al. 1997; Van der Straten et al. 1998).

The key informants were adult family members, spouses and workmates, close friends of the deceased and/or any other persons who had reliable information on the deceased after they had willingly given informed consent. Prior to the interviews, I assured the key informants that the suicides would only be recorded as numbers to prevent any leakages of information about individual suicides to unauthorised persons during the research period. Equally, I would be responsible for ensuring that all information from the interviews was kept strictly confidential. To ensure privacy, I conducted the interviews – each of which lasted between 30 and 60 minutes – in a quiet room in the Department of Psychiatry. However, when the information acquired was inadequate, other family members or friends of the deceased were interviewed on subsequent days to validate the reasons for committing suicide.

Ethical considerations

Permission to carry out the study was sought from the Criminal Investigation Department and the medico-legal authorities in Dar es Salaam after we had explained the aims of the study to them. The autopsies were conducted after official authorisation from the Criminal Investigation Department had been procured.

Furthermore, the main objectives of the undertaking were explained clearly to each key informant, and informed consent was obtained, prior

---

2. The Government Chemist in Tanzania is officially responsible for all national medico-legal laboratory analyses.

to the investigation each subject of the study cohort. The findings were not communicated to other persons.

Results

Out of 100 reliably identified suicides, 46 women committed suicide by poisoning. The 46 female suicides were aged between 15 and 39 years. Thirty-one women (66.7%) were aged below 25; 14 women (30.4%) were between the ages of 25 and 30 and only one was above 30 years. Forty-one subjects (89.1%) had received primary education and five (10.9%) had received secondary education. Thirty-one females (66.7%) were unmarried, 11 (23.9%) were legally married, three (6.5%) divorced and one separated. Twenty-eight women (60%) were unemployed while seven were housemaids, six worked in the informal economic sector as petty traders, and one was a teacher. Employment status could not be established in four subjects.

Reasons for fatal self-poisoning were established in 32 women (70%). These included disappointments in love relationships, grave conflicts emanating from infidelity among cohabiting partners, perturbing family and marital conflicts. According to key informants the interpersonal conflicts between partners frequently consisted of observed acts of physical, psychological and sexual violence. Dislocation of joints, bruises, bone fractures and mouth bleeding were some of the reported injuries that some of the women were seen to have suffered from. Their male partners often heaped insults on female counterparts, such as, "prostitutes", "dogs"[3], "mules" and "thugs".

In two instances, women who feared that their partners could have contracted HIV were repeatedly forced into sexual intercourse. Five women suffered from severe physical illnesses (pulmonary tuberculosis, AIDS, severe skin infections) and three had been afflicted by recurrent major mental afflictions, namely: schizophrenia, psychotic depression and severe disturbance of elevated mood. Nine women (20%) were reported to have drunk alcohol regularly while four (9%) were known to be alcohol-dependent. The alcohol-dependent women were observed to have been unusually loud, emotionally explosive, and they were frequently embroiled in quarrels after prolonged drinking of alcohol. One woman had been observed to be

---

3. A dog is a derogatory term meaning sexually loose or a greedy person who readily accepts offers. A woman who accepts many lovers easily is sometimes referred to as a dog or a bitch. A mule refers to a dull-witted person who is also stubborn. Women who refuse to obey their husbands are sometimes abusively called mules.

heavily inebriated 12 hours prior to committing suicide. Pregnancy and dramatic loss of money through theft were separate single causes of death. Only one woman out of the total of 46 had previously attempted suicide. Ten women (22%), with an average age of 27.6 years, were found to be HIV sera-positive.

Although fatal poisoning was reliably reported and observed in all 46 women, it was chemically proven in only 14 suicides (30%). Failure to detect toxic substances from submitted samples of blood, urine, vomited material and body tissue samples in 32 women (70%) was largely due to lack of machines for chemical analysis and the needed chemical reagents. Moreover, some samples decayed in store during the wait for new consignments of chemical reagents after the available stock had been exhausted. Chloroquine poisoning was reported in 17 subjects (37%) but chemically proven in ten (22%). Pesticides (organophosphates) were reported in four instances (9%) but only confirmed in two instances (4%). Two women were reported to have poisoned themselves with quinine but chemical analysis confirmed only one. Ampicillin and aspirin were reportedly ingested singly; however, only ampicillin toxicity could be confirmed. To carry out their fatal self-destruction, the majority of women committed suicide in their bedrooms and ingested the poisons when no other people were expected to be around.

From post-mortem findings, only three women (7%) revealed typical poisoning findings as normally expected by pathologists, such as frothing at the mouth, aspirated vomited material in gullets, airways and congested lungs. Of the five severely emaciated women (11%) who had suffered from AIDS, three (6.6%) had pulmonary tuberculosis accompanied by pleural effusion, including signs of gross anaemia and oral thrush. Five young women (10.9%) were found to be between five and six months pregnant. However, it was in a single instance that unwanted pregnancy was established as the reason for fatal self-poisoning.

Until the end of the last century, chloroquine was the first drug of choice in treating malaria throughout Tanzania. In recent years, malaria parasites have been noted to be increasingly resistant to chloroquine. This drug has now been substituted with fansidar (sulphadoxine/pyrimethamine). In a previous study conducted at Muhimbili Hospital (Ndosi and Waziri 1997:55), female suicide-attempters were reported to have swallowed an average dose of 1.5 gm of chloroquine. In this study, chloroquine was the main drug of choice employed in overdoses to complete the suicidal self-destruction. Although its use was reported in 17 suicides (37%), and chemically confirmed in only 10 (21.7%) of the subjects, more women could have ingested chloroquine with other drugs without proven fatal chloroquine toxicity. When given in doses of over 3.5 mg/kg body weight, chloroquine causes heart problems, dilatation of blood vessels and low blood pressure, and even death (Cook 1996:1129). The analysed serum concentration from the suicides was as high as 34.4 mg/kg body weight on average while that of stomach content was 58.0 mg/kg body weight. Quinine was reportedly used in two (4.3%) cases of poisoning. In overdoses of 0.6 gm per day, quinine stimulates the higher centres of the brain, depresses and paralyses some brain centres, which results in death (Goodman and Gillman 1996:972). Clinical experience has shown organophosphates to be one of the most commonly used pesticides in the country to commit suicide. When taken in overdoses, they cause twitching of muscles, body weakness, high pulse rate, and loss of reflexes. Overdoses of organophosphates can cause confusion, fits, coma, respiratory depression and death (Lister and Wilson 1990:807). Female teenagers and young women in Zimbabwe have been reported to use organophosphates more frequently than other poisons as a means of committing suicide (Dong and Simon 2001:333). Moreover, during 1995–2000 in Zimbabwe, organophosphate poisoning was noted to have increased by 320% and the resulting deaths were found to constitute 8.3% of total mortalities in that country. In this study, aspirin and ampicillin were differently detected in two female suicides but these drugs had been taken in combination with chloroquine to complete suicide.

Agents employed for self-poisoning

The prevailing health policy in Tanzania controls preferences for methods of suicide because patterns of prescribing medicines influences trends in substances used in overdose (Hawton et al. 2001:1203–1207). Under the Tanzania Pharmaceutical and Poison Act of 1978, prescription of drugs was authorised to registered medical practitioners, dental practitioners and veterinary surgeons. Even though these professionals are the only persons legally responsible for prescribing medicinal drugs, misuse of the Pharmaceutical and Poison Act is rampant because of inadequate supervision of the dispensing of treatment drugs. In their quest for profits, the mushrooming pharmaceutical stores in Dar es Salaam dispense drugs without valid prescriptions or medical surveillance (Mbatiya 1997). Thus, people who decide to poison themselves can easily procure enough doses to kill themselves. Many of the drug shops are not duly qualified to dispense the drugs used to commit suicide and some of them operate far from prescribing health centres (United Republic of Tanzania 2003). In an attempt to curb the wor-risome uncontrolled dispensation of drugs in the country, the government passed the Tanzania Food, Drugs and Cosmetics Act of 2003 to replace the 1978 act (Nsimba et al. 1999:12). The pharmaceutical council of the new act plans to operate more effectively. A study on usage of medicinal drugs at household level during 1994 in Dar es Salaam observed that 83.3% of 400 households in Kinondoni district practised self-medication, which con-sisted of inappropriate self-medication and indiscriminate use of antibiotics and injections (Mlavwasi 1994). It is therefore not surprising that rates of deliberate self-poisoning in recent years appear to be increasing, particularly due to over-the-counter easy availability of therapeutic drugs. Usually, in-dividuals intending to kill themselves by poisons tend to choose chemical substances known to them to have the desired fatal effect (Morgan 1979). During 2002, a third of outpatients in Tanzania were treated for malaria for which chloroquine was the drug of first choice (Ministry of Health, Tan-zania, 2002:1). Chloroquine is one of the most commonly used drugs for suicide attempts in malaria-prone regions (Van Rooyen et al. 2002:652).

I interviewed the key informants focusing on individual demographic attributes (both of the informants themselves and those of the deceased). These included information on age, residence, religion, educational level, marital status and occupation, as well as the length of relationship with the deceased, date and place of suicide, substances ingested, reasons for self-poisoning, important health problems of the deceased including hospital admissions and the kind of medication which had been taken by each wom-an.[4]

Emphasis was also laid on whether the deceased had suffered from a pre-vious mental illness which could have manifested with behavioural abnor-malities like social withdrawal, over-talkativeness, talking nonsense, mood swings and inappropriate tearfulness, apparent self-neglect, inappropriate laughter, previous attempted suicide or any other significant observed in-congruence of behaviour. Habitual alcohol intake, in particular the types of beverages, the frequency of drinking and the amounts consumed by the deceased, were enquired about. Drugs of abuse, like heroin, or of poten-tial abuse, like painkillers or sleeping pills, were also enquired about. Key

---

4. Some individuals give relevant hints when they are about to attempt or com-mit suicide. To keep watch over them and to keep away dangerous objects like knives, belts and drugs can, in some instances, contribute to averting suicide. Knowing the likely places of committing suicide can in future contribute to valuable preventive measures.

informants were also asked whether the woman concerned had in recent weeks experienced any noteworthy social conflicts or had come into conflict with the law. Hospital clinical notes from previous admissions were sought so as to establish the medical diagnoses and treatments given and thus any diseases or drug overdoses that could have contributed to suicide. Messages left by the deceased and any other relevant information related to the self-poisoning were also studied in the attempt to understand the motives behind the suicidal intent and the means of suicide employed.5

Discussion

Suicide is a complex phenomenon associated with psychological, biological and disabling social factors. Physiologically, it follows severe exhaustion under a continuing assault of stressors when the suicidal individual is no longer able to cope with life. Desjarlais et al. (1995:68) underscore Durkheim's views concerning variation of suicide rates according to the extent of individual ties with domestic, occupational and religious groups. Although these views are quite old, they are still valuable (Desjarlais 1995:76). The prevailing impact from the processes of globalisation, together with economic pressure on indigenous cultures, has contributed to a weakening of the extended family in Tanzania. Rapidly expanding populations in urban areas have become particularly vulnerable to social isolation and loneliness (Ndosi 2005:196–208). Individuals lack people to confide in when they encounter emotional crisis. Overwhelming emotional problems drive them towards self-destruction. A century ago, suicides were rare in African culture (Thwala 2005:18). Many traditional African societies fear suicide and it is one of the strongest prohibitive taboos (Sorri et al. 1996:3). In East Africa, in particular, suicide is a terrible event not only for the involved person, but also for the family and close friends (Swift 1977:118). In this study, 27 (58.7%) of the women were Christians. A Christian suicide is commonly excommunicated and the priest does not attend the burial ceremony. Accordingly, the suicide's destined life after death is considered to be uncertain and he or she is buried silently in his or her own compound. Suicidal behaviour is morally condemned by church authority. Consequently, suicidal

---

5. After the above investigations had been completed in each case, I rechecked the data for any omissions or errors for corrections. I then entered the data in the computer using data sheets of Microsoft Excel to calculate the frequencies of the items on the questionnaire, the average age and amounts of toxic poisons ingested.

cases could be underreported due to the fact that the family of the deceased might wish to avert some of the negative social consequences. Under Islam, too, committing suicide is prohibited. To commit suicide is perceived as interfering with God's plan for that individual's life. However, unlike with Christians, the burial and the mourning ceremonies of suicides proceed formally, as after the deaths of other Muslims. Muslims leave suicide in the hands of God.

Relationship between socio-demographic attributes and suicide

In this study, female suicides peaked at adolescence and early adulthood. This finding is consistent with recent World Health Organization data on suicides for those aged between 15 and 25 years (Sayil and Devrimci-Ozguyen 2002:11; Chishti et al. 2003:108). In a study of parasuicides in Dar es Salaam, Ndosi and Waziri (1997) also found a correspondingly young age spectrum. Thirty suicides (66.7%) in this study were unmarried and nearly 90% of the women had only seven years of formal education. The literacy rate among these women was higher than the national literacy rate of 56.8% for females in 1995. Rural literacy rates in Tanzania are comparatively lower than urban rates not only because there are fewer schools in rural areas but also because in towns, women are more likely to struggle to reach a higher educational level so as to enable them to meet rising demands of adaptation and survival. Nevertheless, the relatively low educational level in the study cohort could have deprived the women of opportunities to qualify for careers that could have enhanced their individual economic independence.

According to the World Health Organization's 1995 data bank (WHO 1995), 51% of Tanzanians lived below the poverty line in 1993. Unemployment is currently an acknowledged and escalating socio-economic problem faced by many young female urban dwellers, not only in industrialised countries, but also in developing countries like Tanzania (Curle 1996:14). In 1995, nearly a third of the youths and young adults in Dar es Salaam were reported as unemployed or underemployed (Tungaraza and Ndosi 1995). Women aged 15 and above in Dar es Salaam constitute a quarter of the estimated 2.5 million inhabitants of the city and the majority of these women live below the poverty line, in congested shelters and slums with unhealthy sanitation (Ndosi 2005:196–208).

In sub-Saharan Africa, many anguished women with limited help carry the heavy burdens of providing financially for their families as well as their extended families (Nwosu and Odesamni 2001:259). In particular, women residing in poor urban settings are more openly exposed to stressors, and they are also more vulnerable to stress than their male counterparts (Conger et al. 1999:54). Whereas 28 (60%) of the women in this study were reported to be unemployed, the rest were petty traders, housemaids or peasants who negotiated for a difficult existence in the city. It is known that economic pressure increases the risk of emotional distress that can generate suicidal ideation (Hardiman 1982). The remaining three were divorced and one was separated. These findings may suggest that adolescents and young single females in Dar es Salaam live in circumstances that expose them to vulnerable impulses of deliberate self-destruction.[6]

Social reasons for self-poisoning
According to the World Bank (1993), a third of Tanzania's population lives in urban areas and about half of the urban population lives in the expanding commercial city of Dar es Salaam. Rapid urbanisation in Dar es Salaam city during the last three decades has witnessed increasing social stresses that have enhanced maladaptive patterns of living, particularly among the unemployed and poor females (Ndosi 2005:196–208). The identity of Tanzanian women, like that in many sub-Saharan countries, is deeply embedded in a cultural context that is characterised by male dominance. Many women are pushed into silent defeat and helplessness, which makes them vulnerable to unbearable suffering. Such women remain in abusive relationships for years due to fear of losing economic support, fear of losing face in the community, and emotional ties to the abuser (Mujinja 1997). Culturally, women's behaviour tends to be strictly controlled. Whereas there is a general attitude of permissiveness towards men having multiple sexual partners, such behaviour in women is disapproved of morally, or even condemned. Thus women conduct their lives in relative powerlessness. There is significant evidence that some women, can resort to suicide as a means to communicate despair (Kabeer 1994:3). Social triggers for self-poisoning in this study were established in 22 suicides (47.8%). Infidelity among cohabiting partners was reported in about half of these 22 cases. Infidelity, the betrayal of companionate love, can arouse intense anger and loneliness in the aggrieved partner as in the following example.

A 23-year-old female teacher from Kinondoni district lived in an inti-

6. Despite cultural differences, similar findings have recently been reported in North European studies, which also found a higher prevalence of suicidal expressions among young women, especially those living alone in urban areas (Wanderlich et al. 2001:332; Renberg 2001:429).

mate relationship with her boyfriend of a similar age. When the man developed a relationship with another female lover, the woman became emotionally so intensely pained and upset that she decided to end her life by swallowing poison. She left a piece of paper behind with the following brief message: "Darling dear, I am sorry for what I have done but it is too much to bear! Only God and me alone know what was in my heart for you. I have dearly trusted you all that long. Since I came to know you, I never had any other man. Today, you came up with all that you told me. I loved you and still love you so much. You will never come across a lady who will love you as I did".

Infidelity and betrayals in relationships often leave women feeling abandonned, intensely jealous and unhappy, as well as anxious about sexually transmitted infections – including HIV (Fagan and Browne 1994). Gender-based violence is a widespread phenomenon, and in some instances associated with suicide (Institute of Medicine 1996:178). A recent study on HIV and partner violence in Dar es Salaam found that a lifetime history of violence was common among women attending the Muhimbili Health Information Centre (Maman et al. 2001). These women were physically and/or sexually abused. The distressed women in this study suffered not only from loss of personal esteem but developed enmity towards their partners and female sexual rivals. Observations from some key informants, about the women who had poisoned themselves, revealed frequent domestic quarrels that led to acute emotional crises and even physical violence. Whereas some women sustained bruises, sprains and fractures of limbs, others were frequently insulted and repeatedly forced into sexual intercourse, although their partners had multiple sexual partners concurrently. Consequently, anger, shame and despair and suicidal impulses attained such high levels that the women opted to poison themselves as an expression of their intolerable distress.

According to a study by Conner et al. (2001) African women are socialised to tolerate a high level of conflict in marital and family life as well as tolerance of male authority. A woman's refusal to accept her subordinate position in relation to her husband is likely to cause disputes and even violence. Suicide may be seen by a powerless person as a means of avenging herself and punishing her tormentor. Of the five women found to be in their second trimester of pregnancy, only in one instance was unwanted pregnancy a reported cause of fatal self-poisoning. The girl committed suicide after her boyfriend suddenly and unexpectedly terminated their relationship and abandoned her while pregnant. These findings suggest that female suicide due to unexpected or unwanted pregnancies without social support could be hidden in silence; further studies are needed, therefore, to investigate the seriousness and extent of the problem.

Some medical and socio-economic factors associated with suicide

The risk of suicide is greater among patients with physical illness than among the general population and a terminal illness can sometimes lead to suicide without conspicuous psychopathology (Desjarlais et al. 1995:74; Kishi et al. 2001:382). Ten suicides (21.7%), with an average age of 28 years, were HIV-positive but only a half of these were suffering from persistent illnesses of pulmonary tuberculosis and advanced AIDS. The chronic physical illnesses were the reported determinants of suicide in these women. The rate of HIV infection in this study cohort is about twice that of the current national rate of 10–15% amongst the sexually active population in Dar es Salaam (http://www.tanzania.go.tz/hiv aids.html). Studies conducted in four African cities have shown an increased rate of suicidal ideation, suicidal attempts and completed suicide in individuals with HIV and AIDS (Buve et al. 2001:117). Furthermore, a fifth of people living in sub-Saharan Africa have been reported as living below the poverty line. Women constitute a disproportionate 70% of this poor population sub-group. Sub-Saharan women aged between 15 and 24 suffer from HIV infection rates that are at least three times as high as in their male counterparts. The prognosis of AIDS among urban dislocated and unemployed women in urban African areas is often poor as the women lack nourishing diets and they cannot afford the needed medicines to treat associated infections (Rajs and Fugelstad 1992:234; Meel 2003:1). It is therefore not surprising that in a situation of socio-economic helplessness, some of the women in this study opted for suicide to end their prolonged physical and psychological suffering. Medical triggers among 300 attempted suicides in Dar es Salaam were recently established in 28 (9.3%) of attempters, of which physical illness accounted for 13 (4.3%) of the triggers (Ndosi and Waziri 1997:55). Recently, a young woman suffering from AIDS, as well as multiple sores following an operation in Muhimbili Hospital, committed suicide by jumping from a third-floor window in the hospital (Ndosi and Mtawalli 2002:41).

Although alcohol dependency and harmful use of alcohol has predominantly been observed to involve males, nine (19.6%) subjects under discussion were reported to be regular users of alcohol and four of them (8.7%) were alcohol-dependent. Their individual histories revealed multiple instances in which acute intoxication from alcohol in both conflicting partners was observed to have augmented the levels of aggressive exchanges and violence. Two other studies in different cultures have reported that a husband's alcohol use is frequently related to marital violence (Rodriguez et al. 2001:317; Quigley and Leonard 2000:1003).

Prospective studies show that close to 90% of suicides have diagnosable psychiatric disorders (Maltsberger et al. 2003:111). In this study, conspicuous mental problems (psychoses) were the associated causes of fatal self-destruction in three women with established reasons for successful suicide. Below is an example extracted from one of the key informants:

> A 39-year-old married woman with three living children from Kinondoni district in Dar es Salaam city developed a mental illness a year prior to committing suicide. Since 1981, her marriage was observed to be stable and they had four children. Two years prior to committing suicide, her daughter completed suicide by ingesting overdoses of chloroquine. Thereafter, a cousin hanged himself for reasons that were not clearly established. A year prior to killing herself, she had been admitted to the psychiatric unit at Muhimbili National Hospital because of a major mental illness (paranoid psychosis). The frequent drug treatments of her mental illness caused distressful side effects, which included loss of strength, involuntary muscle twitches, restlessness and stiffness of joints, which reduced her ability to walk properly. Although her family had been supportive during the times of illness, frequent recurrent mental symptoms due to poor drug compliance, the intolerable side effects of the medicaments and the demeaning gossip from the neighbourhood that she suffered from "insanity" (*kichaa*, in Swahili), pinned a burdensome stigma on her. She was heard to complain bitterly three days prior to the suicidal act. Driven to profound despair and uncertainty, she bought 30 tablets of anti-malarial chloroquine from a nearby shop without a prescription receipt. After locking herself in her bedroom, she swallowed all the tablets and died shortly thereafter.

Reasons for self-poisoning could not be established in 14 women (30.4%). It is possible that some of these women could have suffered from depression, one of the strongest triggers for suicide (Elliot 2001:163). This mental disorder is often not diagnosed readily in developing countries, due to the cultural tendency to somatise[7] psychological distress. More suicides could have suffered from depression without its detection prior to the suicidal act. Monetary loss as a determinant of self-destruction was observed in a poor

---

7. Somatised depression is a form of emotional disorder in which a lowered mood is expressed in a cluster of bodily complaints. These complaints are culturally more readily accepted than expressions of emotional complaints, which are often heavily stigmatised.

desperate woman who lost her money through theft. Poverty and economic pressure do increase the risk of emotional distress that can enhance ideation about deliberate self-destruction (Jin et al. 1995:529; Krysinska 2003:34).

Conclusion

Rapid population growth increases competition for education and employment and places a strain on society; the breakdown of stable society places particular pressure on urban dwellers (Desjarlais et al. 1995:22–23; Ndosi 2005:196–208). Marital and family problems have increasingly become individualised. Family elders are now able to exercise limited influence and women find themselves increasingly in weaker positions. Factors leading to fatal self-poisoning, as observed in this study, are considerably embedded in the female gender role. Predominantly young single females of low educational level who were unemployed or underemployed became vulnerable to severe stresses. The reasons for deliberate self-poisoning were associated with intense psychosocial distress, often triggered by problems within love-partner relationships, or marital or family conflicts. Physical and mental illnesses were the medical determinants of self-poisoning. The lives of these women were plagued by psychological stresses, which created deep uncertainties in their lives and culminated in self-immolation. These influencing factors have to be considered against a background of high HIV-infection rates, as well as frequent and excessive use of alcohol among the suicides.

Efforts to reduce mortality in this vulnerable population need strengthening. One way of addressing these fatal self-poisonings might be to look into precipitant conflicts with appropriate socio-cultural awareness. It is also quite important to assess the dispensing behaviours of drug-sellers and the prescribing practices of health-care providers, particularly those in private facilities. Further studies are thus urgently required to augment the understanding of this neglected, but important health hazard. Since a high rate of prescribing anti-malarial drugs without proven diagnosis exists, there is a burning need, for educational programmes to target persons empowered to prescribe treatment drugs.

Acknowledgements

I am grateful to the relatives and friends of the deceased who willingly volunteered information on the individual suicides. I am also thankful for a grant of TZS 900,000/- (the equivalent of USD 890) by Sida/SAREC's programme on Research Capacity Strengthening, at the Muhimbili University College of Health Sciences (MUCHS), which enabled me to meet part of the costs of this research undertaking.

References

Blakely, J.A., S.C.D. Collings and J. Atkinsons, 2003, "Unemployment and Suicide. Evidence of Causal Association", *Epidemiology and Community Health,* 57:594–600.

Buve, A., E. Lagarde, M. Carael, N. Rutenberg, B. Ferry, J.R. Glynn, M. Laourou, E. Akam, J. Chege and T. Sukwa, 2001, "Study Group on Heterogeneity of HIV Epidemics in African Cities. Interpreting Sexual Behaviour Data: Validity Issues in the Multi-centre Study on Factors Determining the Differential Spread of HIV in Four African Cities", *AIDS l15 Supplement,* 4:117–26.

Camus, Albert, 1975, *The Myth of Sisyphus.* Harmondsworth: Penguin, p. 51.

Chishti, P., D.H. Stone, P. Corcoran, E. Williamson and E. Petridou, 2003, "Suicide mortality", *Canadian Journal of Psychiatry,* 48:2.

Conger, R.D., M.A. Rueter and G.H. Elder Jr., 1999, "Couple Resilience to Economic Pressure", *Journal of Personality and Social Psychology,* 76(1)54–71.

Conner, K.R., P.R. Ruberstein, Y. Conwell, L. Seidlitz and E.D. Caine, 2001, "Psychological Vulnerability to Completed Suicide: a Review of Empirical Studies.", *Suicide Life Threat Behaviour,* 31(4):367–85.

Cook, Gordon, 20th ed., 1996, *Manson's Tropical Diseases.* ELBS with W.B. Saunders, p. 1129.

Curle, A., 1996, "Violence and Alienation: an Issue of Public Mental Health Medicine", *Conflict and Survival,* 12(1):14–22.

da Veiga, F.A and C.B. Saraiva, 2003, "Age Patterns of Suicide, Identification and Characterization of European Clusters and Trends", *Crisis,* 24(2):56–67.

Desjarlais, Robert, Leon Eisenberg, Byron Good and Arthur Kleinman, 1995, *World Mental Health: Problems and Priorities in Low-Income Countries.* New York and Oxford: University Press, pp. 68–86.

Dong, X. and M.A. Simon, 2001, "The epidemiology of organophosphate poisoning in urban Zimbabwe from 1995–2000", *International Journal of Occupational Environmental Health,* 7(4):333–8.

Elliott, M., 2001, "Gender Differences in Causes of Depression", *Women Health,* 33(3–4):163–77.

Fagan, J. and A. Browne, 1994, "Violence Between Spouses and Intimates: Physical Aggression Between Women and Men in Intimate Relationships", in A.J. Reiss Jr. and J.A. Roth (eds,), *Understanding and Preventing Violence,* Vol. 3. Washington DC: National Academy Press 27.

Gielen, A.C,, P. O'Campo, R. Faden and A. Eke, 1997, "Women's Disclosure of HIV Status: Experiences of Mistreatments and Violence in Urban Setting", *Women Health,* 25(3):19–25.

Goodman, Louis and Alfred Gilman, 1996, *The Pharmacological Basis of Therapeutics.* New York: The McGraw-Hill Companies, pp. 972–81.

The Guardian Tanzania, 2001, "Suicides: Urgent Need for Counselling Services", Editorial April 3, p. 6.

Hardiman Margaret and James Midgley, 1982, *The Social Dimensions of Development: Social Policy and Planning in the Third World.* Chi Chester, New York, Brisbane, Toronto and Singapore: John Wiley & Sons Limited.

Hawton, K., E. Towsend, J. Deeks, L. Appleby, D. Gunnel, O. Bennewith and J. Cooper, 2001, "Effects of paracetamol and salicylate legislation in The United Kingdom: opportunistic before and after study of suicide, liver from transplant, and self-poisoning and its consequences", *British Medical Journal,* 322:1203–1207.

I–TECH in Tanzania, 2005, http://www.tanzania.go.tz/hiv aids.html (accessed December 2006)

Institute of Medicine, 1996, *In Her Lifetime. Female Morbidity and Mortality in Sub-Saharan Africa.* Washington DC: National Academy Press, p. 178.

Jin, R.L., C.P Shah and T.J. Svoboda, 1995, "The Impact of Unemployment on Health: a Review of the Evidence", *Canadian Medical Association Journal,* 153(5):529–40.

Kabeer, N., 1994, *Reversed Realities: Gender Hierarchies in Development Thought.* London: Verso.

Kishi, Y., R.G. Robinson and J.T. Kosier, 2001, "Suicide Ideation Among Patients With Acute Life-threatening Physical Illness: Patients with Stroke, Traumatic Brain-injury, Myocardial Infarction, and Spinal Cord Injury", *Psychosomatic,* 42:95:382–90.

Krysinska, K.E., 2003, "Loss by Suicide. A Risk Factor for Suicidal Behaviour", *Journal of Psychosocial Nursing and Mental Health Services,* 41(7):34–41.

Lister, D. and C. Wilson, 1990, "Teenage Suicide in Zimbabwe", *Adolescence,* 25(100):807–9.

Maltsberger, J.T., H. Hendin, A.P. Haas and A. Lipschitz, 2003, "A Determination of Precipitatory Events in the Suicide of Psychiatric patients", *Suicide Life Threat Behaviour,* 33(2):111–9.

Maman, S., J. Mbwambo, N.M. Hogan, G.P. Kilonzo, M. Sweat and E. Weiss, 2001, *HIV and Partner Violence: Implications for Voluntary Counselling and Testing Programs in Dar es Salaam, Tanzania.* Washington DC: Population Council 2001 Research Report.

Mbatiya, Z.A., 1997, "The Availability and Use of Anti-malarial Drugs in Households in Kibaha District, Tanzania, 1996." Dissertation in Partial Fulfilment of the Requirements for the Degree of Master of Science in Tropical Diseases Control in the University of Dar es Salaam.

Meel, B.L., 2003, "Suicide and HIV/AIDS in Transkei, South Africa", *Anil Aggrawal's International Journal of Forensic Medicine and Toxicology,* Vol. 4., p. 1.

Ministry of Health, Tanzania 2002, *National Malaria Medium term Strategies Plan 2002–07,* pp.1–2.

Mlavwasi, Y.G.W., 1994, "Availability and Usage of Medicinal Drugs at Household Levels in Kinondoni District, Dar es Salaam, Tanzania". Dissertation of Master of Pharmacy, University of Dar es Salaam.

Morgan, H.G., 1979, *Death wishes? The understanding and management of deliberate self-harm.* Chi Chester: John Wiley & Sons Limited.

Mujinja, Phares, 1997, "Poverty and Health; Socio-economic and Political Determinants of Health". Scientific Paper Presented at Tanzania Public Health Association annual conference, November 1997.

National Bureau of Statistics, 2005, *Tanzania Demographic and Health Survey 2004–2005.* Dar es Salaam: National Bureau of Statistics, pp. 37–39.

Ndosi, Noah, 2005, "The Challenges of Psychiatry Amidst Economic Deprivations and Social Change in Dar es Salaam Tanzania", in Joe Lugalla and Kris Heggenhougen (eds), *Social Change and Health in East Africa.* Dar es Salaam: University Press Ltd., pp. 196–208.

—, M. Mbonde and E. Lyamuya, 2004, "Profile of Suicide in Dar es Salaam", *East African Medical Journal,* (81):207–211.

—, and M.L. Mtawali, 2002, "The Nature of Puerperal Psychosis at Muhimbili National Hospital: Its Physical Co-morbidity, Associated Main Obstetric and Social Factors", *African Journal of Reproductive Health,* 6(1):41–49

—, and M. Waziri, 1997, "The Nature of Attempted Suicide in Dar es Salaam", *Social Science & Medicine,* 44:55–61.

Nsimba, S.E., A. Maselle, M.Y. Warsanme and G. Tomson, 1999, "Prescribing Patterns of Anti-malarial Drugs in Urban Health Facilities in Dar es Salaam, Tanzania", *East and Central African Journal of Pharmaceutical Science,* 12–15.

Nwosu, S.O., W.O. Odesamni, 2001, "Patterns of Suicides in Ile-Ife Nigeria", *West African Journal of Medicine,* 20(3):259–62.

Quigley, B.M. and K.E. Leonard, 2000, "Alcohol and the Continuation of Early Marital Aggression Clinical and Experimental", *Research,* 24(7):1003–10.

Rajs, J. and A. Fugelstad, 1992, "Suicide Related to Human Immunodeficiency Virus Infection in Stockholm", *Acta Psychiatrica Scandinavica,* 85:234–7.

Renberg, F.S., 2001, "Self-reported Life-worries, Death Wishes, Suicidal Ideation, Suicidal Plans and Suicidal Attempts in General Population Surveys in North Sweden", *Journal of Social Psychiatry and Psychiatric Epidemiology,* 36(9):429–36.

Reza, A., J.A. Mercy and E. Krug, 2001, "Epidemiology of Violent Deaths in the World", *Injury Preview,* 7(2):104–11.

Rodriguez, E., F. Lasch, P. Chandra and J. Le, 2001, "The Relation of Family Vi-
olence Employment Status, Welfare Benefits and Alcohol Drinking in the
United States", *Western Journal of Medicine,* 174(5):317–23.
Sayil, J. and H. Devrimci-Ozguven, 2002, "Suicide and Suicidal Attempts in An-
kara in 1998; Results of the WHO/EURO Multi-centre Study of Suicidal
Behaviour", *Crisis,* 23(1):11–6.
Sorri, H., M. Henriksson and J. Lönnquist, 1996, "Religiosity and Suicide", *Crisis,*
17:123–127.
Swift, Charles, 1977, *Mental Health Rural Health Series 6:* African Medical and
Research Foundation, p. 118.
Tanzania National Website, 2003, *2002 Population and housing census,* http://www.
tanzania.go.tz/census/dsm.htm (accessed December 2006)
Thwala, W., 2005, "Suicide up in Southern Africa", *Africa, News,* 10:18.
Towsend, E., K. Hawton, L. Harris, E. Bale. and A. Bond, 2001, "Substances Used
in Deliberate Self-poisoning 1985–1997: Trends and Associations With Age,
Gender, Repetition and Suicide", *International Social Psychiatry and Psychiat-
ric Epidemiology,* 36:(5)228–34.
Tungaraza, Felicius and Noah Ndosi, 1995, "Unemployment Crisis Among the
Youth in Tanzania". Paper presented at SOSMED Workshop for Youth and
Related problems, The Kilimanjaro Hotel, Dar es Salaam, Tanzania.
United Republic of Tanzania, 2003, *The Tanzania Food, Drugs and Cosmetics Act
No 1.*
Van der Straten, A., R. King, O. Grinstead, E. Vittinghoff, A. Serufilira and S. Al-
len, 1998, "Sexual Coercion, Physical Violence and HIV Infection Among
Women in Steady Relationships in Kigali, Rwanda", *AIDS and Behaviour,*
2(1):61–73.
Van Rooyen, M., T. Kirsch, K. Clem and J. Holliman, 2002, *Emergent Field Medi-
cine.* New York: McGraw-Hill Medical Publishing Division, pp. 652–63.
Wanderlich, U., T. Bronisch, H.U. Wittchen and R. Carter, 2001, "Gender Differ-
ences in Adolescent and Young Adults With Suicidal Behaviour in Munich
Germany", *Acta Psychiatrica Scandinavica,* 104(5):332–9.
Watt, J.R., 1996, "The Family, Love, and Suicide in Early Modern Geneva", *Journal
of Family History,* 21(1):63–86.
WHO (World Health Organization) 1995.
World Bank, 1993, *World Bank Report 1993 Tanzania: a Poverty Profile.* Dar es
Salaam: World Bank.
—, 2006, *World Bank Development Indicators 2006* http://www.worldbank.org/data
(accessed December 2006).

– CHAPTER 8 –

Surviving AIDS?
The Uncertainty of Antiretroviral Treatment

Hanne O. Mogensen

Introduction

Patent, profit and poverty have been key words in the debate about accessibility of anti-retroviral treatment (ART) for people in Africa and elsewhere in the world. Questions of cost-effectiveness and sustainability, as opposed to global responsibility and equity, have framed the debate. International and national activists, driven by the ideal of human rights and global equity have been challenging the market ideology governing access to drugs and the notions of cost-effectiveness governing health care delivery. As a result of this prices went down immensely, shortly after the turn of the century. As a result, in many African countries, including Uganda, which is the focus of this article, treatment with antiretrovirals (ARVs) could no longer be dismissed as totally unrealistic. But, for may people, costs are still too high and access so difficult that the drugs were causing disruptions of everyday life. Drugs were available, but largely inaccessible, and in the space between availability and inaccessibility there is room for uncertainties that cause, not only economic, but also social disruption.

These new uncertainties, I will argue, have been ignored in the debate about whether and how to make ARVs available to poor people. For two decades HIV and AIDS have caused immense uncertainty in African lives. Ironically, the solution to the problem, the treatment that can reduce the viral load and, therefore, reduce infection and contagion and potentially keep people alive for an extensive period, are likely to cause not only hope and better health for some, but also further disruption, suffering and uncertainty for others. In the following I will use this situation to explore more general questions about uncertainty and potentiality, and how social relations are reconstituted as a result of ARVs.

AIDS is by now a well-known global health problem that respects no borders but is unequally distributed across these borders. But it is also a health problem that is at present undergoing many changes. It is, as social scientists have extensively discussed for over two decades, transmitted through various kinds of connections in a global network of human interaction – through international movements of labour, goods and services. It is shaped not only by the virus but also by global forces of international political and economic relations (Farmer 1992, 2001; Packard and Epstein 2001; Schoepf 1991, 1995). It is the result of poverty, social disruption and, in the case of Uganda, also shaped by war and civil strife (Bond and Vincent 1991). And now, we have to add, it is furthermore shaped by the increasing availability of a treatment for the disease. ART has entered the scene, as a solution to the problem, but also, I will argue, as a new force, the influence of which is embedded in international political and economic relations, and beyond the control of people with the disease.

Some tenacious assumptions in the international discourse are, on the one hand, that lowering the prices of the drugs and thereby giving people the choice to buy them is the "human-rights-thing-to-do", as long as we cannot make them freely available to everybody. On the other hand others argue that these drugs are not cost-effective, and that cost-effectiveness of the health care system is what in the long run will create prosperity and equity and thus in the end possibly enable people to get access to the drugs. Both of these assumptions, I suggest, ignore the complex social reality of people who face the dilemmas of life and death flourishing in the space between availability and inaccessibility. There is a need to look at AIDS not only as a global problem, but also at the ways in which the changes in the epidemic manifest themselves in local social worlds. We have to confront the dilemmas of AIDS and of ART by dealing with the nexus of family, social support, cost and complex issues of adherence to medicine in general. We have to understand how people navigate in a sea of uncertainties and potentialities, and of social relations and power relations, none of which are transparent, and become even less so when life and death are at stake and people are struggling to find ways of getting access to life-saving medicine.

The aim of this chapter is thus to raise questions concerning the social consequences of ARVs and point to dilemmas, which we need to be aware of, as ARVs become increasingly available in the years to come. For this purpose, I will turn to the life of social actors in Uganda among whom I have carried out fieldwork on health-related issues for a number of years, and whom I have seen become increasingly caught in the grid of AIDS and ART.

Boundaries and responsibilities

Alongside other research in Uganda I have become increasingly involved in the life of the members of one extended family, some of whom live in the rural areas of eastern Uganda, others in the capital, Kampala, while some move back and forth between relatives in various parts of the country. I lived with the family while carrying out 12 months' fieldwork in eastern Uganda in 1995–1996 and I have been visiting them regularly since then, both returning to the original field site and staying with family members in other parts of the country, mainly Kampala. In 2001 I spent a month collecting personal narratives from three women in the family (a mother and two adult daughters). During this stay, Kate, one of the daughters, asked me to help her get an HIV test done, which turned out to be positive. The previous year her older sister had died, presumably of AIDS, and all of the women were still struggling to come to terms with her death and with the presence of AIDS in their lives. In the following I will take as my starting point these women's and other family members' increasing awareness of the approaching death of the second daughter, Kate, and use it to reflect on social consequences of the AIDS epidemic as it enters its third decade, shaped by new possibilities for treatment and new uncertainties.

Uganda is well known for having been in the forefront with respect to recognition of, intervention against, and openness about AIDS. It is a country often hailed for its efforts to fight AIDS through preventive measures, and it was one of the first places where infection rates started declining. The response to AIDS has in Uganda been characterised by openness and political support from all levels of government, and internationally recognised Ugandan NGOs have been key players in promoting the discourse of openness and in helping people to "live positively with AIDS". TASO (The AIDS Support Organisation), founded in 1987, is one of the best known of these (see for example Kaleeba et al. 1997). Being able to join TASO has until recently been the most commonly mentioned reason for getting an HIV test done. In TASO there is, potentially, medicine – even if just aspirin and chloroquine; counselling – even if your counsellor may not always be available for you; and sometimes even food or other kinds of assistance.

The government health care system, however, has not had much to offer in terms of treatment for AIDS patients. The government per capita expenditure for health care was about US$ 4 in Uganda in 1999 and has long been strained by the presence of the many AIDS patients. That ART is not cost-effective in the present setting is evident. Already, health services are highly dependent on donor support, as would be any attempt to introduce ART. Yet the Ugandan government has, like all other African governments, been drawn into the discussion of global equity as opposed to cost-effectiveness and has been seeking ways to make the drugs available in Uganda. In

2003 (the time of the writing of this chapter) ARVs were not yet found in government health facilities, but the situation is changing rapidly and every month new funding and new channels of access appear.

The global era, states Paul Farmer (2001:xix, 4), has made it increasingly difficult to live in ignorance of the suffering of others. This, however, he adds, has not led to a more just distribution of the fruits of science and technology. It has not avoided inequalities in the spread and outcome of infectious diseases either. AIDS like other epidemics may well be a global phenomenon respecting no borders, but attempts are anyway made to set up borders when it comes to dealing with it. One way of doing this is through policies of decentralisation and notions of cost-effectiveness and sustainability. Inherent to the idea of sustainability is an idea of the local, and a notion that borders can be set up which cut off global forces and global connections. If a treatment is not affordable and cost-effective within one locality it will not be available there. Farmer (1999:2001) advocates an image of the world in which no such borders exist and where money and medicine can flow to areas in need of them. He tries to infuse new life into the health-care-for-all movement that ran out of steam as the millennium approached and it became clear that it had not achieved its goal of health for all by the year 2000. We cannot, he says, meet the highest standards of health care in every situation but "it is an excellent idea to try to do so" (Farmer 1999:1492). When he and his colleagues channelled significant resources to patients with TB and AIDS in Haiti, Boston and elsewhere, "we didn't argue that it was cost-effective nor did we promise that such efforts would be replicable. We argued that it was the right thing to do. It was the 'human-rights-thing-to-do'" (1999:1493). The wealth of the world has not dried up; it has simply become increasingly unavailable to those who need it most (Farmer 2001:xii). As this debate shows, the dilemma of global equity and local cost-effectiveness comes down to a question of where to set borders between local and global, or in other words how to set limits to responsibility.

Farmer, an outspoken member of the academic community, is not the only one imagining a global community and a sense of responsibility extending beyond national borders. So do many activists and African politicians. Initiatives have been taken around the world to increase access to ART for the poor. One of these initiatives, launched in May 2000, is the "Accelerating Access Initiative" within UNAIDS, which has assisted a number of countries, including Uganda, in negotiating with the pharmaceutical industry to make drugs more affordable in developing countries. The prices of a number of important drugs have decreased dramatically in recent years. In January 2002 *The New Vision* (Ugandan national newspaper) announced that the price of the cheapest possible ARVs had been reduced from US$ 1000 per person per month in 1998 to US$ 40 in 2002. In March 2003 it was down to US$ 28 and there is reason to think that prices will continue to drop. In 2003 treatment, however, was still only available in Uganda in a few NGO facilities and as part of clinical trials, and for most people it is impenetrable how one becomes one of the lucky few who get access to it. The drugs are still largely inaccessible. In addition, US$ 28 per month for the actual treatment plus all the other costs coming along are a far cry from the US$ 4 per capita per year that the government spends on health. And it is a far cry for Kate who does not even have an income high enough to pay the US$ 5–10 per month that it costs to rent a one-room house in town somewhere near facilities where she could get access to the treatment. The struggle over limits to responsibility does not only take place on international levels and within nation states. It is manifested in the uncertainties of everyday life of those who have the disease, and they are the ones I now wish to turn to in an attempt to explore the dilemmas and challenges of this struggle.

The uncertainty and potentiality of ART

Kate's parents divorced when she was only a few years old. She spent her early childhood with her father, her sisters and the father's new wife, but as a result of the political instability and turmoil of the 1970s and early 1980s her father had to escape from his home village in the eastern part of the country, was imprisoned, and ended up settling in Buganda in the central part of Uganda. Kate spent the rest of her childhood and youth moving back and forth between primarily matrilateral relatives, and occasionally also staying with her own mother. She has two sons, but she never married the fathers of her children and she receives no support from either of them. Thus, neither Kate nor her sons have any significant contact with or support from their patrilineal clans. Kate and her sons have spent most of their lives staying with various relatives of Kate's mother, sometimes together, sometimes the sons separately from their mother. Occasionally, Kate has supported herself with the income from a job or a small business that has usually not lasted for long. She is in many ways living on the margins, not just of the world economy, but also of the local social support system. From another perspective, however, she is at the centre of the extended family network. Marginalised, unsettled relatives moving around like her can be seen as nodal points around which connections and a shared sense of responsibility among relatives are maintained.

Kate had been seriously sick and ailing for some time when in 2001 she asked me to accompany her to have the HIV test done. While the answer, of course, was a shock to her, she was not completely taken by surprise. She had suspected she was positive, but as she said to me the day after the test: "I used to think that even if I got sick one day, they would have already found the medicine by then. But now I am sick and still there is no medicine. So maybe AIDS is the end of the world." To this thought of hers I had to answer: "Kate, they actually did find some medicine that can make people stay alive longer. But it is still very expensive and difficult to get here in Uganda." Kate, however, seemed not to hear what I had said and continued: "I think it is the end of the world. Here in Uganda people say like that. OK, I know that God is not bad, but I don't know why he cannot help people and teach them how to find a cure so that we can all get medicine. So that is why I think that maybe it is the end of the world." I did not pursue the topic, knowing already that I would not be able to provide the medicine for her. In August 2001, it seemed likely that her AIDS diagnosis probably was going to be the end of her world. She did not know the term "antiretroviral" yet. She did not know what I was talking about when I said that medicine actually had been found. She sometimes read newspapers if she found somebody to borrow one from, and she sometimes listened to the "teaching about AIDS" on her neighbour's radio. But all she knew when, at her request, we went to the "AIDS Information Centre" to have her tested for HIV, was that were she to be HIV- positive it would be a death sentence, as it had been for everybody else she had seen with this disease.

Still, Kate had been determined to know her HIV status. She wanted the paralysing uncertainty with which she had lived for long to be replaced by certainty – certainty about the direction in which she was going. Yet, this certainty was accompanied by a whole range of new uncertainties: questions about how to be able to move on, now that she knew which way she was going, and how to prepare for her children's life after her death. Based on Hanna Arendt's ideas about human beings as never merely "doers" but always at the same time "sufferers" (Arendt in Mattingly 1994:819), Mattingly discusses life in time as a place of possibility, but also of uncertainty. Doing and suffering are opposite sides of the same coin – and so are potentiality and uncertainty. When we act upon the potential of a moment we also act upon its uncertainty, and the question is how ambiguity, doubt and uncertainty are engaged by people; how a person enters a story in which she will not suffer passively, but can work towards desirable endings and search for possibilities that lead in hopeful directions (Mattingly 1998:813, 819).

With her discussion of narratives as being lived before they are told, Mattingly carries narratives and emplotment into the arena of social action (1998:813). Not only when we tell stories, bu also when we act, we emplot – that is, we act on the basis of an interpretation of the past and with an eye to the future. We act to get something done, and we do so with an awareness that in order to get somewhere we need to negotiate with other social agents so that we can move towards desirable goals cooperatively. We have to get others to agree to our plots, and even though our actions are taken up, reworked and redirected by the responses of other social agents we have some success some of the time in getting other people to work with us towards endings that we care about. As Mattingly says, we live in the midst of unfolding stories over which we have only partial control (1994:813).

In the midst of the uncertainties created by Kate's fear for her health and later by the HIV test itself, she started telling me the story of her life and her suffering. Telling and acting became two sides of the same coin. Telling the story created a sense of agency for her, a sense of being a subject defining her own life rather than an object being acted upon by others (cf. Ricoeur 1991; Jackson 1998). But she also told me her story in exchange for my involvement in her life and her suffering; an involvement which did indeed have practical implications for her life. My interest in her gave her a particular position in the family that was not always to her advantage since it also created jealousy and tension. My involvement also resulted in material benefits for her, and it was what had given her the courage to have the HIV test done. It also made her ask me to reveal the result of the test to some of the influential members of the family – something she would not have had the courage to do herself. Kate's experience with all of this, as well as her experience with her childhood, her lovers and their abandonment of her and her children, her parents' divorce, her mother's mental confusion, her sister's prostitution, her grandparent's cursing, her innumerable jobs and attempts at petty trade, and much more, is what she talks about on the many tapes we recorded together right after the test and over the years that followed. It was a storytelling, and it was an attempt to act and make life move towards desirable endings (cf. Mattingly 1994). It was a part of her struggle to turn uncertainties into potentialities.

The process of getting Kate to tell the story of her life became for me an entry point for participating in the negotiations over her life and death and helped me catch sight, not only of her attempts to turn uncertainties into potentialities, but also how in the course of this she became entangled in new uncertainties. I was part of the dilemmas and questions of responsibility that developed while I held the tape recorder and I thereby gained insight into the ways in which boundaries and questions of responsibilities created uncertainties and possibilities in the everyday life of people with HIV. I spent the first month after Kate's HIV test with her and I have been in regular contact with her ever since. Her life had not yet come to an end, but her life as she used to know it had. She asked me, not only to help her get the HIV test, but also to get a padlock for the suitcase in which she keeps most of her belongings, so that she could lock up any papers with the words HIV orAIDS on them. She initiated an intense struggle not to let anyone but a couple of strategically selected people know. But alongside this Kate's sisters showed an intense interest in discussing Kate's health with me and in trying to make me reveal what they thought I knew, which they could not ask Kate about directly. I, however, had to go along with this game of mutual deception. As mentioned, Kate asked me to inform some of her more prosperous family members that she was HIV-positive, hoping for various kinds of assistance from them. After I had told one of them, he stared at the floor with empty eyes for a long time. "Do you know what an awfully difficult situation you have put us in?" he said. "Of course we all suspected that she was sick. But now she has the proof, and she knows that we know. Soon she will also know about antiretroviral drugs[…] They are there. They talk about them on the radio, in the newspapers. She will understand and she will know that we understand. But will she understand if we decide we cannot help her get them? And what if somebody else in the family decides to get tested also?"

His family had until then provided for her and her sisters, on and off, for years. They were the daughters of a divorced sister. They had all failed to finish school and to marry. They had had a number of children anyway and were roaming around restlessly, moving from one job to another, and from one relative to another, occasionally turning up at one of these uncles' places for assistance of various kinds, including a place to live. While all this was taking place Kate and one of her sisters had stayed for some months at one of the uncles' homes. A few weeks later they no longer did. Clearly her test had added to the complexity and tensions that had long been involved in her search for food and shelter. Not because of her relatives' fear of AIDS, contagion or death, but because of the fear of what they could not do for her. They knew about ART. They knew how to get it, and they knew what kind of sacrifices they and other family members would have to make if

Kate was to receive the medicine. But they also knew that saying no would be a way of making her forthcoming death explicit – a death they all knew about and had managed to live with as long as it was implicit. The involvement with the anthropologist, the test, and the presence of ART in Uganda had made her death explicit.

What will happen as these drugs increasingly become available is difficult to say. Or rather, many different things are likely to happen. Families will react in different ways. The need to know one's HIV status will differ from situation to situation and at different stages in the process. There is no simple relationship between these drugs and the desire to know or the solution to the problem. But the point arising from this discussion is that death and social responsibility can be made part of life in implicit ways that are broken down when they become explicit. ART makes them explicit.

Surviving AIDS is not only a matter of curing the disease, but also of surviving as a social person. As Kate had previously said to me when discussing her sister's death: "She died like a poor person who does not even have relatives. Not even a bed sheet. Only an old blanket. Not that everyone should die like a rich person, but at least that you have people who take care of you. OK, being poor is not only that you don't have money, or you don't have any relative who is rich. Being poor is also about how your relatives look after you". Relatives are wealth in Uganda in more than one way. Sometimes they actually have some wealth to distribute. But even if they do not, then maybe, even more importantly, you are not poor if they are there for you when you are dying. For some people with AIDS, they are not. Their disease, others' fear of the costs associated with it, and the aggravation of this caused by ART, have the potential of making people with AIDS poor indeed. But ART also has the potential to do the opposite.

It was not the existence of ART as such that caused the withdrawal of Kate's relatives. It was the fact that ART made the strains and tensions in their social relations as well as her forthcoming death explicit. The idea that everybody is part of the same family and has rights and access to help from the others could no longer be maintained. The Ugandan kinship system is based on an ideal of what Sahlins (1972) would refer to as generalised reciprocity – that is, the idea that transactions are unselfish and made between those who have more and those who have less, a kind of redistribution of wealth within the kin group. This does not mean that reciprocity is absent, but expectations to the counter-gift are diffuse, returns can be made with long delays or never take place, without necessarily having the consequence that the relationship dissolves.

One of the "counter-gifts" expected in the Ugandan kinship systems is "respect" towards the ones who give, and the uncles of Kate and her sisters often criticised them for having disregarded this through their behaviour, for example their inability to complete school and enter into proper marriages, rather than extramarital relations, which had also resulted in pregnancies and HIV infection. The generalised reciprocity in the Ugandan kinship system is far from unproblematic. There are ongoing considerations about how, how much and to whom one should give food, pay for health care, school fees, and so on. There are many uncertainties, conflicts, disappointments and negotiations of social relationships and trust going on in these acts of giving, receiving and if possible returning some kind of counter-gift or the other. Assistance is never equally distributed among the members of the kin group, but the idea is that we share what we have, can be kept alive and thereby contribute to keeping connections between people alive, as long as certain things are implicit. Kate received some kind of help here and there, on and off, as long as her marginal position and the tensions surrounding her situation were kept implicit. But ART made them explicit. In other situations, for other people, ART may make explicit the extent to which a person occupies a more respected and central position in the family network than Kate did and how sacrifices are therefore made to help this person gain access to the medicine. These drugs are going to become increasingly available in the years to come – though most likely they will not be universally and freely available. The story of Kate and her family is but one example of what may happen. Other families may respond in very different ways, and this family may respond differently later, in another situation concerning another person. But that is exactly why Kate's story about of reminds us about the urgent need to explore the new uncertainties and dilemmas that these people are faced with. The availability of ART, whether accessible or not, changes people's lives for better and for worse, sometimes in unpredictable ways.

Crossing boundaries – making connections and
discovering potentialities

In December 2002 I received the following letter from Kate:

> Please do not be very surprised that I ask you this, but I think it would be good for me to have a cell phone. I know the many expenses you have already had on my health. But I think it can help me in very many ways. I

will handle it with much care and economise very much, but it will make it possible for me to get in contact with many people. Also it can help me in asking questions on the radio every Tuesday where they have the programme "Capital Doctor". You can ask them things about your disease and they sometimes talk about the tablets that can make you live for a long time, but which are very expensive and that you have to take for the rest of your life. If you stop it will be your end, so I think it is only good for someone to take it who can afford it. And please do not be surprised that I have a radio. Don't think I am wasting my money. I have just bought the radio to listen to only health programmes, because now it is the only important thing in my life. And it is a very good radio programme. Whenever I listen to it, it encourages me not to get worried and to be strong. Only that I never get a chance to talk to those people on the radio, because I do not have a phone.

Kate's uncles were right. She did find out about ART. In this letter, she illustrates that more than information and technology have crossed boundaries and reached her. She also shows that she and her perception of the problem is changing. She is turning the coin and looking at the side of potentialities rather than uncertainties. She is realising she can make connections that can help her cross that which she may previously have perceived of as boundaries – connections with the radio, and with me. Her uncles "did not want to know", maybe precisely because they did care but could not afford to act. But in the process of realising this, Kate has discovered that there are alternatives to the connections on which she used to rely. I interfered in her uncles' project of the uncles "not knowing", and I interfered in Kate's view of her options and the connections that it is possible for her to make. The point is not that her relatives' sense of responsibility is limited and that my involvement makes this a unique situation. Rather, it is that we all constantly respond to other people and each other's projects, to that which we learn and experience, and to the new information and technology entering our lives. Communities and social relationships are the outcome of action and are recreated every day (Barth 1992). It is in these daily encounters and recreations of social relations that we understand the consequences of the flow of information and technology like, for example, ART. And it is only through participation in these encounters that we understand their dynamics. It is through my interaction with Kate and with other people in her social surroundings that I understand the dynamics between her and them. And it is because their interaction goes through me and I become part of the struggle to find out how to interfere or not to interfere that I learn about the doubts, uncertainties and possibilities of living with AIDS and with the availability of ART.

The kind of knowledge we as researchers get from involving ourselves in the doubts, dangers and uncertainties that shape people's lives is different from the knowledge Farmer gets from his experience of intervening as an expert with medical as well as anthropological expertise and vast financial resources. He succeeds in illustrating that which he sets out to illustrate: that it is practically possible to provide treatment for poor people. He describes the situation from the perspective of having something with which to help people. I have tried to describe Kate's situation from the perspective of walking along with her, without having much to offer her at all. There are things we do not hear and do not see unless we take this walk along with people and notice the dangers they are heading towards or managing to avoid, and see the alternative roads and other directions in which they can also choose to walk – that is, the altrnative connections they make.

Social relations are emergent and often unpredictable. So are the consequences of a new technology like ART. All we know is that its availability, whether accessible or not, has changed the lives of Kate and her relatives, for better and for worse. It has given her hope, and it has contributed to tensions within her family. ART has many other consequences in addition to that of keeping alive those who take the drugs. And only by entering people's lives, and stumbling over the dilemmas they are faced with, can we understand these consequences. There is nothing new in this. It is but another way to say that participant observation is important. It is, however, a point I feel like making yet again in the light of the remarkable lack of attention being given to it in relation to the way ART is changing the AIDS epidemic right now.

Conclusion

In 1997 Bond and Vincent identified three paradigms of AIDS research in the first decade of the epidemic. During the "bio-medical paradigm" target populations were identified, sought out and blamed for the behaviour leading to their infection. This was followed by a "community paradigm" where the anthropologist turned into a social worker and started focusing on *caring* rather than *curing*, on orphans, widows and widowers, households, and so on. Rather than seeking out and blaming the victim, this phase tended to focus on the social dislocation caused by the sickness and death of the victim (Bond and Vincent 1997:91). In the early 1990s a third paradigm appeared, as both medical and social scientists adopted a more critical tone and started exploring the epidemic of economic, social and political responses to AIDS and restoring the historical and social context shaping the spread of the disease (Bond and Vincent: 93).

Since then, ARVs have entered the stage and are integral to any discussion about AIDS. This, I would argue, has brought new life to the bio-medical paradigm and hence to the need to challenge it. The development in ARVs has brought a long-awaited optimism that science is about to gain the upper hand against HIV. But alongside this optimism there is a renewed tendency to blame the victims – those who are sick as well as those who care for them – for being incompliant, uneducated and poor, and hence not qualifying for treatment. We need to move on to consider not only the *cure*, but also the *care*. We must not forget to care for those who can do nothing but imagine the treatment – or who suffer from other people's wishes that they could do more. We must not reduce the discussion to either one or the other. Implicit in the debate about cost-effectiveness and human rights is also an assumption that prevention and treatment are independent of each other and that investing in one will reduce the amount of resources available for the other. However, we do not as yet know anything about how the two influence each other. The case presented in this chapter is an example of how the availability of ARVs brought about increased uncertainty. It is, however, important to note that it took place back in 2001–2002, that prices continue to fall, new channels of access continue to appear and many questions have yet to be answered. How are treatment and prevention mutually interlinked? What will happen to stigma, secrecy and disclosure when AIDS is no longer necessarily a death sentence? How will this influence people's perceptions of the uncertainties and possibilities in their lives?

The story of Kate calls for a new critical paradigm that does not cover up human suffering in a discourse of cost-effectiveness and sustainability. Such a paradigm should also not be one that uncritically accepts ART because it is the "human-rights-thing-to-do", without paying attention to the new uncertainties and social situations that arise from this "human-rights intervention". While it is an excellent idea to work towards a realisation of equal access to health, as Farmer says, it is not a bad idea to pause and look at the social conhe story of Kate calls for a new critical paradigm that does not cover up human suffering in a discourse of cost-effectiveness and sustainability. Such a paradigm should also not be one that uncritically accepts ART because it is the "human-rights-thing-to-do", without paying attention to the new uncersequences of this approach, by walking along the paths taken by people with AIDS, whose lives, even under the threat of imminent death, are still full of life.

Post scriptum

The chapter is based on a paper prepared for the conference "Uncertainty in Contemporary African Lives, convened by the Nordic Africa Institute in 2003. Since then the situation of antiretroviral treatment in Uganda has changed dramatically. In 2005 antiretroviral drugs started becoming widely and freely available in Uganda, largely due to funds from President Bush's AIDS plan, PEPFAR (The President's Emergency plan for AIDS Relief) and the Global Fund. The space between availability and inaccessibility of antiretroviral treatment (ART) described above has therefore been considerably altered. For an update on the situation in Uganda see Mogensen (forthcoming). Nonetheless, the availability of ART has not increased to the same extent all over Africa, and the dilemmas of uncertainty explored in this chapter are also still of importance to other aspects of Ugandan lives and health care.

Acknowledgements

Kate, whose full name is Catherine Abbo, wishes that her own name be used when I write about her. I am immensely grateful to her for all that she has taught me about life and about struggles for survival. I am equally grateful to the rest of her family for having assisted me in all possible ways since I first arrived in Uganda in 1995. I would also like to express my appreciation of my colleagues at the Child Health and Development Centre, Makerere University, with whom the Institute of Anthropology at the University of Copenhagen has carried out collaborative research since the early 1990s, and in particular Susan and Michael Whyte who are a never-ending source of inspiration for my work. Finally, I wish to thank the Danish Development Agency (Danida) and the Danish Fulbright Commission for supporting various stages of the research process.

References

Barth, Fredrik, 1992, "Towards greater naturalism in conceptualizing societies", in Adam Kuper, *Conceptualizing society*. Routledge: London and New York, p.17–33.

Bond, George C. and Joan Vincent, 1991, "Living on the edge: changing social structures in the context of AIDS", in Holger B. Hansen and Michael Twaddle, *Changing Uganda*. London: Fountain Press, p. 113–129.

Bond, George C. and Joan Vincent, 1997, "AIDS in Uganda: The first Decade", in Bond, G.C. et al. (eds), *Aids in Africa and the Caribbean*. Colorado and Oxford: Westview Press, p. 85–97.

Farmer, Paul, 1992, *AIDS and Accusation. Haiti and the Geography of Blame*. Berkeley: University of California Press.

—, 1999, "Pathologies of Power. Rethinking Health and Human Rights", *American Journal of Public Health*, 89(10):1486–1496.

—, 2001, *Infections and Inequalities. The Modern Plagues*. Berkeley: University of California Press.

Jackson, M., 1998, *Minima Etnographica. Intersubjectivity and the Anthropological Project*. Chicago: University of Chicago Press.

Kaleeba, N., S. Kaleeba, M. Kaseje et. al. (1997) Participatory evaluation of counselling, medical and social services of The AIDS Support Organization (TASO) in Uganda. *AIDS Care*, 9 (1): 13–26.

Mattingly, C., 1994, "The concept of therapeutic 'emplotment'", *Social Science & Medicine*, 38(6):811–822.

Mogensen, Hanne O., 2009 (Forthcoming), "New Hopes and New Dilemmas: Disclosure and Recognition in the Time of Antiretroviral Treatment", in H. Dilger and U. Luig (eds), *Anthropologies of AIDS. The Morality of Illness, Treatment and Death in Africa*. Oxford/New York: Berghahn Books.

Ricoeur, P., 1991, "Life in Quest of Narrative", in D. Wood (ed.), *On Paul Ricoeur. Narrative and Interpretation*. London: Routeledge.

Packard, R.M. and R. Epstein, 1991, "Epidemiologists, Social Scientists, and the Structure of Medical Research on AIDS in Africa", *Social Science & Medicine*, 33(7):771–794.

Sahlins, M., 1972, *Stone Age Economics*. London: Tavistock Publications.

Schoepf, B.G., 1991, "Ethical, Methodological and Political Issues of AIDS Research in Central Africa", *Social Science & Medicine*, 33(7):749–763.

—, 1995, "Culture, Sex Research and AIDS Prevention in Africa", in H. ten Brummelhuis and G. Herdt (eds), *Culture and Sexual Risk. Anthropological Perspectives on AIDS*. Amsterdam: Gordon and Breach Publishers, p. 29–51.

CHAPTER 9

Uncertain Livelihood: Women Challenging the Hegemonies of Male Sexual Dominance

Liv Haram

Introduction

Soon a decade into the 21st century, the HIV/AIDS epidemic is continuing to spread, causing much illness and suffering. Although the prevalence in certain areas of Africa has dropped considerably during the last few years, the particular gendering of the epidemic is still a severe issue (WHO/UN-AIDS 2003, 2008). The blaming of women for the cause and spread of sexually transmitted infections (STIs), including HIV, is a global phenomenon (Bujra 2000; Middelthon 1992; Schoepf 2001; Walker and Gilbert 2001). By drawing on longitudinal anthropological research which I have conducted intermittently in Arumeru district and Arusha town, in northern Tanzania since 1989, this chapter illustrates how such processes of blaming are played out in everyday life and seeks to explore their social and cultural logic. It argues that HIV/AIDS has become a spatial disease identified with women who cross borders spatially, physically and morally. As I hope to illustrate, social space is constituted through practices and power relations. The spatial dimension is not an empty and passive "container" for human behaviour but is embedded in power relations and, in this particular case, in hegemonies of male sexual dominance, which is being challenged by women at the (spatial) borders.

I begin this chapter with the story of Mary and her married lovers. The story, I believe, shows how AIDS is conceptualised locally and how the "*virusi*" (HIV) targets the victim's body as well as her family and friends.

When I first met Mary in 1991, she was 30 years of age and worked in one of the many tourist hotels in Arusha town, roughly 15 km from her natal home on the slopes of Mount Meru, as the manager's personal secretary. She was a very attractive woman, always neatly and fashionably dressed, with her hair styled accordingly.

After primary education, Mary left her natal home, went to town, and was employed as a bar woman. She soon became the bar owner's "town-wife". The bar owner was wealthy and the owner of several bars in Arusha. His first and legal wife worked as a farmer on their land in Kilimanjaro (roughly 90 km from Arusha town) and reared their children. Mary and the bar owner lived together for several years and had a son. During these years, Mary was trained as a secretary and upon improving her skills she also got better job opportunities.

After co-habiting with the bar owner for nine years, Mary had by common consent finally "skinned" him and "eaten all his money" – local metaphors for having ruined him economically – and left him. The previously wealthy bar owner returned to his wife and farm in Kilimanjaro an impoverished man. Mary, however, subsequently got involved with another young and wealthy man, Paul. When they first met, Paul was legally married and lived with his wife and their three children in Arusha town. Although Paul and Mary tried to conceal their love affair, Paul's wife soon discovered what was going on. When Paul increasingly neglected his wife and their common children economically, she informed her Meru in-laws about the matter. Over a long period of time Paul's extended family made several unsuccessful attempts to reconcile the spouses. First, Paul's eldest sister and later his mother tried to reconcile them but even though Paul promised to behave, he soon returned to Mary. The clan elders then called Paul home to discuss the issue with his family and even though he once again made promises, he didn't end his love affair with Mary.

After several years with Mary as his mistress, he ultimately left his wife and children and moved in with Mary. Paul sporadically visited his wife and children, but he ceased to support them economically. Before Paul met Mary he was a reliable man with a good reputation. By living with Mary, and particularly in neglecting his family, he marginalised himself socially. His family therefore became suspicious of Mary's character. When Paul himself argues, "If I do not see her, my feelings towards her will grow like an abscess (*yuure*) in my heart. I just can't live without her!", the family suspects Mary of being a witch. For them, Paul's strong love for Mary is seen as unnatural and they believe that such feelings must be caused by his lover's witchcraft. Obviously, she is capturing his mind, causing Paul to lose control of his own will. According to Meru traditions, witchcraft "goes in the family", and because Mary's sister is also said to practise witchcraft and, moreover, lives with a married man as his (informal) second wife, their suspicion is further confirmed. Paul is, of course, scolded by his family and clan for his misconduct, but at the same time he is held innocent because his family strongly believes that he is "trapped" and victimised by his "outside

wife" (*nkaaoora*). Their rather stereotypical view of Mary is, moreover, confirmed, because ever since Paul met Mary, Paul's life has become "disrupted"
(*amevurugiwa maisha yake*). Recently he lost his previous job as a manager
and the many fringe benefits that went with it. One of the reasons, they
argued, was Paul's misuse of the company car to serve Mary's many needs.
Paul's family therefore held Mary responsible for "draining his wealth" and,
by capturing his mind, making him lose control of his will and senses, leading to the disruption of his life. Paul, once a wealthy and reliable person, has
become poor both in terms of money and respect. Mary has taken control
and they argue she "drives him like a car". Accordingly, Paul is the loser. A
man of his age and position should have built a house long ago at home for
his retirement. Mary, on her part, does not equally reciprocate Paul's strong
love for her and, more recently, she has asked Paul to return to his wife. People now say: Paul has become a poor man. Mary has skinned (*chinja*) him
and is now looking for another wealthy lover. [1]

With this introductory story in mind, I shall explore why AIDS and its
progression is seen as analogous to a female who, after exploiting a wealthy
and healthy (male) body of his vitality, then moves on to another, as with
Mary's conduct with Paul. The chapter argues that in order to understand
forms of blame there is a need to analyse why men and women perceive
sexually active women as both dangerous and threatening to men's health
as well as to their and their families' prosperity and wellbeing. In sexual life,
people explain, women are hunters, they ambush and lure men and they
milk them". Thus, according to the hegemonies of the masculine sexual and
moral order, AIDS is perceived as a woman who, after draining the wealthy
and healthy man of his life force, then moves on to another. Both the AIDS
virus and women might be perceived as in transit, targeting the healthy individuals of a population and draining them of their life force.

In order to better understand what follows, I will first situate Paul and
Mary within the socio-economic setting, with a focus on the local AIDS
discourse.

Situating the Meru and the AIDS discourse

When in 1989 I began conducting research among the agricultural Meru,
who live on the southern and eastern slopes of Mount Meru immediately

---

1. The word chinja has multiple meaning, such as "to slaughter" or "to kill", but in
   this particular context it means "to skin" a man by getting access to and stripping
   him of his material resources.

east of Arusha town, very few knew about the HIV/AIDS epidemic. Some referred to it as a disease of "the other" and of the "outside" – that is, outside the Meru home area. By this stage, HIV prevalence rate was roughly 7% in Arusha town, 3% in the semi-urban areas, and 1.5% in the rural areas (Mnyika et al. 1994). However, the situation changed quickly. Soon an increasing number of people came to learn about AIDS through infected relatives who had been living "outside" but now came home to be cared for by their family and kin before they died. The typical AIDS sufferer was a young or middle-aged man or woman who had lived outside Meru or had been commuting on a daily or weekly basis, was usually educated, and had often been involved in business. These lay observations were very much in accordance with early epidemiological findings from the area. Soon, however, AIDS became a disease in their midst, or as one male informant told me in mid-1995:, "Currently, we learn that even those of us who have not been outside get ill and die of AIDS." This observation increasingly became a fact over the coming years. According to the epidemiological factsheets of 2003, the prevalence rate in Tanzania had reached 20%, but in more recent years it has been dropping and is now roughly 8–10% (WHO/UNAIDS 2008). The epidemic, however, still shows a wide variation geographically, between the sexes, as well as between age-groups.[2] It should also be noted that the epidemic clearly shows a gendered bias – leaving the youngest women at highest risk of becoming infected with HIV.

In 2005, I looked systematically into the relationship between the frequency of death in the community and how people organised the many funerals (Haram forthcoming, 2009). Most of those I spoke with, in a survey where interviewees were selected randomly, were very concerned – especially about the young generation and their uncertain future. Dejected and weary, people explained, while pointing in different directions: "Yesterday we buried someone over there, today we are burying someone here, and tomorrow we will be burying yet another person over there. At times we have to break the mourning (*ikwiimbo rembo*) too early. We have to leave a funeral only to rush to attend to another funeral! The young generation will die!"

In Tanzania, antiretroviral therapy (ART) became available in the government health facilities in 2004. In spite of increased political will and

---

2. The World Bank estimates that because of the AIDS epidemic, life expectancy in Tanzania by 2010, will revert to 47 years instead of the projected 56 years in the absence of AIDS. The crude death rate in 1995 was 19.5, and in 2010 it is estimated to be 25.2 per 1,000 persons (UNAIDS/WHO 2002: 14; see also Foster, 2003).

commitment to financing HIV/AIDS diagnosis and ART in recent years, for most people access to such treatment is still very limited, particularly in rural areas. In 2006, less than a quarter of HIV-infected Africans received treatment. In Tanzania, an estimated 1.4 million people were infected with HIV in 2006, but only 77,066 patients –that is, 5.5% – received the life-prolonging medication (PlusNews 2007). In 2007 I conducted a study among co-infected TB and HIV/AIDS patients in Temeke district, in Dar es Salaam, and found that many – especially women – did not take antiret-rovirals (ARVs) in spite of being offered free treatment. One main reason, they argued, was due to the fact that they could not afford to eat sufficiently and thus their body was too weak to tolerate the heavy dose of the antiret-roviral drugs (Haram 2008).

Like most people in East Africa, the Meru associate the spread of HIV/AIDS with rapid social change and a weakening of the social fabric of a traditional way of life in general and more particularly with their notion of "modern life" and "development" – commonly referred to by the Swahili term *maendeleo* (meaning "progress" and "development"). But the increase in AIDS-associated death is, above all, held to be due to moral disorder; in particular, they believe it is uncontrolled sexuality that ultimately causes HIV and AIDS or "the disease of these days" (*ugonjwa wa kisasa*), as it is commonly referred to. Young and old are concerned about the lack of re-spectability and generally refer to the demise of the age-grade system which should guide the younger generation about how, when, and with whom to mix socially and sexually – dictated by the notions of "respect" (*wiindi*) and "shame" (*usutu*). Thus, this cultural logic links AIDS to a product of modern life. The older generations in Meru criticise the young men of mar-riage age for being guided by love and facial beauty in their choice a wife, and not by traditional principles such as a family's wealth and respectability, and lack of disease and witchcraft. Similar explanations are observed, for in-stance, among the neighbouring Chagga (Setel 1999) and among the rural Luo (Dilger 2003). According to my findings (Haram 1999; Haram 2005), however, there is also a particular gendering of modern life which I will briefly explore in the next paragraph.

While men have been involved in migration for decades, women, how-ever, have traditionally been socially and culturally held back from partici-pating in activities that takes them outside their homes on the mountain and into Arusha town. This is particularly the case among the young and as yet unmarried or the newly married women of reproductive age. More recently, however, women have gradually come to participate in different economic activities that take them outside their homes on the mountain and into town. This gender difference is partly a result of socio-economic changes, such as transformation of the agricultural sector, and overpopulation, with a resulting land shortage. These processes have been further escalated by the neoliberal policy pursued by the government. The gender difference is also closely associated with the moral principles inscribed in the local conception of space which tends to curb women's spatial mobility compared to men. Although Arusha town is close to the homesteads on the mountain and many travel to and from on a daily basis, the perceived gulf separating the socio-cultural construction of the two areas is considerable: the simple and morally esteemed life of the rural Meru versus the immoral and corrupting life of townspeople and townswomen in particular. For women, to move out of their homes on the mountain also means to move beyond male authority and the many restrictions/restraints that follow the male-dominant ideology and particularly the hegemonies of the masculine sexual order. However, in moving away from the "cosy" atmosphere of their mountain homes, to use Douglas's term, women such as Mary also lose "old protection" and, in turn, become vulnerable and exposed to HIV infection (Douglas 1994 :15).

Blaming the deviant women

Blaming women for the cause and spread of HIV and AIDS is not unique to the Meru: it has been extensively reported from other parts of Africa (cf., for example, Schoepf 2001 and Weiss 1993 for studies from Zaire and Tanzania, respectively).

One case which typifies some of the Meru's concerns, since AIDS has become a major problem, is that of Rose. A single mother with two children by different fathers, Rose died of AIDS in late 1992 at the age of 35. Like many other orphaned children, Rose's children were left in the care of their maternal grandmother. Roughly six months prior to her death, Rose left her job in town and returned to her natal home for care and treatment. During the funeral, at which her closest family, neighbours, friends and colleagues were mourning her and comforting each other, people also gossiped. Everyone knew that Rose had died of AIDS, and they all expressed concern for the youth of the community, so vulnerable to the new and deadly disease. People also talked about Rose's job and her many scholarships and other fringe benefits, including the many trips she had taken within Tanzania and to Europe, obtained through her relationship with her boss.

Whether or not the mourners' gossip gave a true picture of Rose, there is a general awareness about the vulnerable situation of young women and of single mothers like Rose in particular. Many in the community, and particularly older women, who increasingly have become the main caretakers of their grandchildren, as in Rose's case, sigh: "AIDS is going to kill the young generation." As indicated in the case of Rose, those women who remain unmarried or become single mothers, are frequently harassed or gossiped about in the community. An unmarried woman or single mother is frequently described as a "*malaya*", a loose or promiscuous woman. Some women who are rumoured to have multiple lovers are raped, even sometimes gang-raped.

Take the case of Felisto, for example. She became a victim because the wife of one of her lovers hired several men to attack her in a most loathsome way. She was not only raped by one man, but by a gang.

Felisto died of AIDS at the age of 25 (cf. Figure 1). She was a single mother with one child. In addition to her more steady relationship with her partner, Felisto had additional lovers of a more short-term nature. Most people considered Felisto therefore to be "promiscuous". According to rumours, the wife of one of Felisto's lovers knew about her husband's love affair with Felisto and she hired a group of young men to rape her. These men first befriended Felisto in a bar and after spending time drinking together they accompanied Felisto to her home. There they stripped her naked and raped her. Some neighbours got suspicious but when they arrived at Felisto's place, the men had left as their task was accomplished. The men had completed their job on Felisto by forcing a soda-bottle into her vagina which caused tears and heavy bleeding. Her neighbours brought her to the hospital where she was stitched.

Rape and even gang rape are reported from several parts of Tanzania and are not uncommon (see for instance, Green 1999).[3] It was also noted that blame is often put on the raped woman. Rape and gang rape are an invasion of the female body and a woman's most intimate area. Such acts both express the subordinate state of women and can be seen, in a sense, as strengthening solidarity between men. In Felisto's case, by inserting a bottle in her vagina, which caused severe tearing, the men both insulted her and did physical damage to her fertile body.

---

3. The troubled matter of gender violence, sexual harassment and rape is a major global issue. In Africa, as in the rest of the world, acts of violence against women often go unnoticed and thus convey the message that they are justified or will go unpunished (cf. Green 1999).

Notions of risky and safe partners

Blaming women is also expressed in people's perception of risk. When men are asked about their notions of risk, or rather how they differentiate between a dangerous or "dirty" (*kasha*) sexual partner and a non-dangerous, safe and "clean" (*utore*) one, many give responses similar to the following, from a young businessman:

> First, the dangerous woman is a very popular woman and her beauty strongly contributes to her popularity. Second, she is loose; she is always travelling here and there. Third, she purposely dresses fashionably, wearing expensive dresses to attract men and to drain their money. A clean woman, on the other hand, is confined at home and always busy working. Moreover, she does not care about fashions or a luxurious life (*starehe*), but dresses modestly and keeps her body clean. Therefore you can easily know in which category a woman fits by carefully studying her *mikaae* (behaviour, nature, character).

Although not all men express such a clear-cut perception of the "dirty" and risky versus the "clean" and non-risky women, this young man's attitude is more or less echoed by most men. Thus, the "clean" and non-risky woman who is confined at home and hardworking, is set in opposition to the "loose" and "dirty" woman who travels around and dresses up to attract men. Some men may even be cynical when choosing their lovers. Aware of the high infection rate among the young, they therefore choose their lovers among "older women" – that is, women who have given birth and therefore are held to be less risky because they have a "wider and looser vagina" than the very young women's more "narrow and dry vagina".

Nevertheless, many men find the young women irresistible. A commonly heard Swahili saying about AIDS is: *Acha Iniue, Dogo-dogo Sintaacha* ("Let it kill me but I will not leave the young girls").[4] Although this statement is sometimes heard from bragging men, it is not merely men's talk or a wishful expression of their maleness, but it also expresses a social reality in male-female sexual relations: in the literature such men of means are commonly referred to as "sugar daddies". Locally, such elderly and generous men are called, for instance, *mfadhili* (donor), *mbuzi*, which literally means billy goat, or *mwingi*, literally meaning "a man of many" (that is, many lovers). Such men are often favoured sexual partners both for *dogo-dogo* – young

---

4. The *dogo-dogo*, literally "small-small", are girls who are not merely young also sexually inexperienced and thus sexually "clean". It should be noted that this lay or popular abbreviation for AIDS at times has a slightly different meaning: "OK. Let [AIDS] kill me, slowly. But I will not cease [having sexual affairs]."

and as yet unmarried women – as well as for single mothers, like Rose and Felisto. For men, having multiple young lovers is a sign of their wealth and their virile bodies.

In addition to these more individualised strategies, there are some more community-based strategies which I will turn to now.

Manning the gates by "reading" sexual networks

A main thesis in Mary Douglas's *Purity and Danger* (1980) is that the human body is used as a social and religious symbol and that people's ideas about the human body correspond closely to their ideas about society. In *Risk and Blame* (1994) she further elaborates her theory on the body as a theory of risk. She asserts that risk in the social environment is likely to be projected onto a concern with the body, arguing that when a society is threatened by a common danger, its members turn to blameworthiness. This vignette is a near-quotation from Douglas (1994:19), where she further suggests that a society mans the gates by arming the guard in a communal strategy to defend itself, by manning the gates. She explains:

> The best immune system is the community; the body has not enough re-
> sources on its own. But the outside skin, the community, must be kept
> whole. It can be destroyed by wrong behaviour. Most of the efforts at preven-
> tion have to be focused on protecting this last protective layer. (1994:111)

In Meru society such communal efforts in guarding the whole and healthy body against evil penetration from outside is clearly at play with the dangerous spread of HIV and AIDS. A commonly used method of preventing the contamination of the community is to single out a (potentially) risky sexual partner or an AIDS victim in the community and to map or to "draw a sketch" of the person's sexual history and his or her sexual networks. But as I will illustrate, the communal effort of prevention does not target just any body, but the female and sexually active body. Or put differently, it is not the biological body *per se* but the feminine and sexually active body that is targeted.

By focusing on how people map sexual networks, I found that, most people perceive that all sexual networks begin with, or rather, can be traced back to, a woman who, in turn, is seen as the ultimate cause and transmitter of HIV/AIDS. In fact, the sexual networks are called by women's names, like, for instance, "Felisto's lovers" or "Salome's electric net" (cf. figures 1 and 2). "Electricity" or "lightning" (*umeme* in Swahili) is a commonly used metaphor for AIDS and underscores the unpredictable and random nature

Figure 1. "Felisto's lovers"   Figure 2. "Salome's electric net"

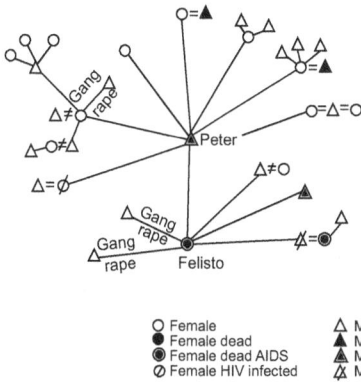

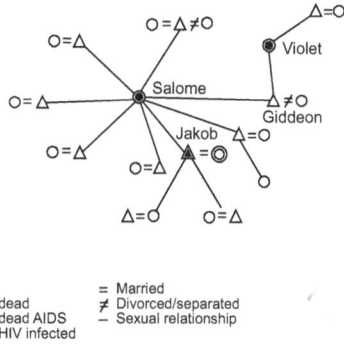

O Female	△ Male	= Married
● Female dead	▲ Male dead	≠ Divorced/separated
◉ Female dead AIDS	▲ Male dead AIDS	– Sexual relationship
⊘ Female HIV infected	⚡ Male HIV infected	

of HIV.[5] In this context electricity refers to the electric coupled circuits, and the similarity with a sexual network indicates the comprehensive and rapid spread of HIV. The way people observe and interpret such sexual networks, I believe, also expresses how the Meru defend themselves against the spread of AIDS because such knowledge informs people how to act and guides them in choosing the safe rather than the risky sexual partner. Although both sexes accept more or less tacitly that men "naturally" must have multiple partners because of their strong sexual urge, to have too many, however, may endanger their reputation and even their respectability. In spite of the fact that men have more lovers than women, the ultimate source in the spread of AIDS is held to be a woman. And since a man contracts the disease from a woman, he is conceived of as the victim while the woman is blamed as the cause.

But why do they blame women and why, in particular, do they place the ultimate blame on the single woman? First, it is linked to the Meru's notion of contagion. The outsider and the "dangerous other" are seen as "dirty" and dangerous to mix with socially and, above all, sexually. Thus, they are held to be sexually polluting, to be responsible for social and moral contagion. Second, blaming women is linked to the notion that female sexuality is ambiguous. I shall return to this point soon, but suffice it here to say that female sexuality is held to be both dangerous and life-bringing.

5. Another HIV/AIDS metaphor expressing the arbitrary and forceful nature that sweeps across the landscape is that of the heavy El Niño rainstorms that caused considerable damage in the area in 1997/98.

The close link between female sexuality and the (Meru) notion of contagion is clearly expressed by the first women who, on their own initiative, left their kin and home area and mixed socially and sexually with other ethnic groups. Or, as explained by one of the elders, an explanation which most people adhere to: "We call such women *makasha* (dirty women) because they brought sexually transmitted diseases, which previously had been unknown to us, from the outside."[6] Later I learned that Nkyeku, the grandmother in our homestead, was one of the women this man was referring to. While Nkyeku was still a young woman she refused to marry the man chosen for her by her father, and managed to escape to her older sister who previously had run off to Arusha town. Here Nkyeku, according to her own account, forged a livelihood by brewing and selling beer. She also involved herself in successive "marriages", as she referred to the informal conjugal relationships she got involved in, before returning home as a "separated" and middle-aged woman. Nkyeku never returned to her natal family, but remained a poor housekeeper in her extended family until she died in late 1993. Whenever she recalled her rather turbulent life history, she grieved: "Now I am an old and worn-out woman. If I had married a Meru, I would at least have had my own house and children to look after me in my old days."

The story of Nkyeku illustrates some different, but closely related themes. First, it informs us that the Meru consider "new", and as yet unknown, diseases to be ailments coming from the "outside" or from the "unknown world" of strangers and "dangerous others". A parallel with Sontag: "[T] here is a link between imagining disease and imagining foreignness. It lies perhaps in the very concept of wrong, which is archaically identical with the non-us, the alien" (Sontag 1989 [1988]:48).[7] Second, once people move around and cross physical borders they also cross moral borders and thereby become potentially dangerous to their social environment and the moral order. Hence, "dirt", or *kasha*, for the Meru is only potentially dangerous and becomes dirty once moral borders are crossed. In such a context, contagion is linked to social behaviour and the breaking of moral rules, in which contagion can be voided, through correct social behaviour.

Third, contagion is closely linked to their perceived and lived landscapes,

---

6. He is referring to syphilis and gonorrhea which are both referred to as *usetai* (cf. also Harjula 1976).

7. Sontag gives an illuminating case of the syphilis epidemic that swept across Europe in the last decade of the 15th century. She writes: "It was the 'French pox' to the English, *morbus Germanicus* to the Parisians, the Naples sickness to the Florentines, the Chinese disease to the Japanese" (1989:48).

which is also embedded within a gendered ideology and a male hegemonic sexual order. It both deals with the social role of women as well as their particular sexuality and their role as child-bearers. This is further underscored by the fact that many men went outside the Meru homeland on labour migration or for education a long time before women did so, but still women such as Nkyeku are held responsible for "bringing/giving" (*yombutia*) STIs to the Meru. As noted, women are also blamed because their sexuality is ambiguous and at times dangerous. In what follows, I will expound on this particular issue.

The lure of female sexuality and men who lose their mind

It is well documented that sexuality, in particular female sexuality, outside socially accepted unions is seen as the cause of pollution and even death (Bloch and Parry 1987; Ngubane 1977; Whyte 1990). Drawing upon her observations in Marachi, Western Kenya, Whyte argues, "Although a man's sexual behaviour could theoretically bring *ishira* (the state of danger which may follow immodesty between generations) upon his family, it was women's sexual affairs that were most often seen to cause trouble" (Whyte 1990: 105). As is common with many people, the Meru held that the female, and particularly the fertile and menstruating woman, is dirtier and potentially more responsible for contagion than the male. Women are even held to be "naturally" dirty because of their monthly menstruation. The particular danger of females transmitting STIs, including HIV, is also explained by the particularity of women's physical bodies. Both sexes argue that it is well-known that women tolerate or "hide" diseases (STIs) longer than men and explain that that is why women are referred to as "dirty" (*kasha*). The potential pollution and ambiguous nature of the menstruating and thus still fertile female body is also repeatedly commented on in the AIDS literature throughout the world (Ingstad 1990; Middelthon 1992; Obbo 1995). In a study among the patrilineal Giriama of Kenya, Udvardy (1995) found that women's bodies are conceptualised as "suitcases" for male blood. "Suitcases are special kinds of containers: they are vehicles in which goods are transported" (1995:326). In an analysis of the HIV epidemic in Norway, Middelthon (1992) very illuminatingly illustrates how women become both dangerous and polluting since they are perceived as the "containers" of HIV as well as the distributors of infection.

With the Meru, women like Nkyeku, who left their homes and marriage for Arusha town in search of an alternative livelihood, crossed not only physical borders but also moral borders. Thus, the Meru's theory of conta-gion is conceived in moral terms: people, particularly women, whose behav-iour transgresses the acceptable social order must be punished to maintain social order. In keeping with Douglas's (1980) theory of the relationship between the individual body and the social body, ideas concerning pollution and contagion, both physical and moral, are drawn upon to regulate social relations and thus reveal the underlying tension in a society, and in the case of the Meru, that between female sexuality and male hegemonic control.

Once women leave Meruland and are therefore "out of sight", as it is generally put, they move beyond male authority and control; it is thus as-sumed, correctly or not, according to the male dominant discourse, that they do not only trade their wares but are apt to trade their bodies. In short, such women refuse to accept the "conditions" (*masharti*) set by males and are thus perceived as uncontrollable. They are also perceived as "greedy" and "selfish" (*nnyuuku*). This way of reasoning is partly linked to the gendered ideology and embedded in a male dominant sexual order, as mentioned, and more specifically with men's perception of the particularity of women and their sexual and reproductive bodies. A "proper" and respectable woman should control her sexual lust, dress modestly and, above all, should not ap-proach men sexually. Thus, generally, men consider a sexually active woman to be potentially threatening to their health and wellbeing, or as they gener-ally put it, "she may capture their mind without their awareness". Women, men believe, employ certain techniques, primarily their sexuality, to attract a man's mind. Accordingly, men argue, "in sexual life women are hunters; women create a certain smell when they are hunting for lovers", a smell which men cannot resist. The logic goes that a woman's sweetness easily "traps" men because it is to sweet that it is irresistible to men's sexual lust.

Much ethnography from Africa shows that it is common to use meta-phors of food and eating to express sexual intercourse and sexual lust (cf., for instance, Emanatian 1996; Weiss 1996). Thus, expressions such as "he is eating at that place", refers to the man's lover and signifies the sexual relationship involved. It is, however, men that should consume and eat the sweet meat of women and not vice versa. Men gathered in a bar, for in-stance, may warn each other when they are attracted by a woman at the neighbouring table: "Watch out, if you are not careful, she will swallow you!" Female sexuality may be harmful to men not only because immoral women may intentionally employ sexual techniques as a means to control and dominate them, but also, and perhaps more importantly, because fe-male sexuality, regardless of a woman's intentions, is intrinsically dangerous for men unless they show some caution. Both men and women comment, "A man who 'eats' a beautiful woman (for her sexual sweetness), is likely to forget his other duties and may ultimately die" (*Ikoloviru latoongwa ni nse wa ikundu ikandefiiyao*). A commonly used metaphor among both sexes for the woman's sexual "juice" is *nse*, which is the sweet juice from ripe bananas. The logic goes that a woman's sweetness easily "traps" men because it is so sweet that it is irresistible to men's sexual lust. Men get "stuck". Thus, female sexuality is not only a threat to male virility and potency: simply, excessive copulation drains men's physical strength and wellbeing. The loss of semen is, of course, non-productive sex. Thus, a woman exploits men for no purpose. In other words, the (unmarried) woman who merely engages in sex for the purpose of money and not to bear children encourages men to engage in "useless" copulation. By engaging in unregulated sexuality, a woman not only sates her sexuality in a selfish and demanding manner, but through sexual intercourse she has the capacity to drain the life-force of a man. Unless men are vigilant and therefore in control of such women, they are not only "stuck", but are also sapped of their semen and, ultimately, they perish. Or, as it is expressed, "a woman ambushes and lures men and she milks men's money". To milk men's money is another way of expressing the milking of men's semen. In both cases, the man is drained of his physical strength and wellbeing. He is "skinned".

It is commonly held by both sexes that men have many sexual partners because of their great sexual desire. Is their male "nature" (*mikaae*), so to speak, and their sexual desire is thus naturally uncontrollable. According to the male-dominant sexual order, men are actually entitled to have multiple lovers as long as they do not boast about such affairs openly but exercise discretion (see Haram 2005b). Many of the younger and newly married women I have become acquainted with expressed some jealousy towards their "unfaithful" husbands. However, whenever they expressed such feelings, they were quickly corrected by older and more experienced women, that trying to control their husbands' extra-marital love affairs was, as they commonly said, a waste of their time and money: "You will simply get tired for nothing!"

Women, on the other hand, are commonly said to have multiple lovers not because they cannot control their sexual desires, but because they cannot control their "desire for money" (*tamaa ya pesa*) and luxurious commodities (*starehe*). Such a woman has become greedy and "eats" more than what rightfully and morally belongs to her. To consume more that her lot by taking from others is a type of behaviour that is strongly associated with witchcraft.

To satisfy the "greedy" needs of their lovers, many men do not provide for their families. Hence, unmarried women and single mothers as, for instance, Mary, Rose, Felisto and Nkyeku, who are likely to get attached to married men, threaten and even disrupt the family order and domestic life. Some men may even sell their most valuable resources, such as land and cattle to "keep women" and to meet their consuming desires. In turn, their wives and families suffer. Thus the single women also threaten and strike at the very structure of sound kinship and ultimately at the very reproduction of Meru society.

Married women, like men, draw upon the common manner of blaming when they feel that their own and their children's economic wellbeing and lives are threatened by "greedy" women. It is not difficult to understand why wives also blame the unmarried or single woman since she is likely to be their husband's short- or long-term lover and, therefore, may tempt him to spend his money on her and their common children. Frida, for instance, a 36-year-old woman whose husband is working in the southern part of Tanzania while she cultivates their Meru farm voices a common concern among married women: "Townswomen hijack our husbands, causing disharmony in marital life. A man may spend all his money on such women, and may even forget his economic responsibility towards his wife and family in the village." Such mistresses cause family hardship and may at times even cause separation. Consequently, they threaten the social and economic well-being. Simply, there are those who become greedy and thus make "too much" (*ovyoo-ovyoo*)" of it. *Ovyoo* means recklessly, at random, and saying "ovyoo-ovyoo" underscores the meaning. Such people are to be blamed.

The riddle of life and death:
Challenging the hegemonies of male sexual dominance

AIDS is not simply any disease. It is a death-bringing disease. The fact that AIDS threatens local populations precisely in the realms of sexuality and procreation makes it a big issue. The roles of sexuality, reproduction and gender relations are clearly at stake. The following quotation taken from Sally Falk Moore's study among the neighbouring Chagga of Kilimanjaro is also valid for the Meru:

> The riddle of life and death was joined with the puzzle of sexuality . . . The proper combination of male and female in marriage was in keeping with social order and produced healthy new life. *The wrong combination, out of*

wedlock, incestuous or anomalous in some other way, made disorder, sickness, and death. One of the practical and philosophical problems was to keep separated that which should not be in contact, and to combine that which could be connected, each at the right time and in the right way. (1986:333–334, my emphasis)

Thus ordered sexuality and regulated sexual relations are of prime importance to the regeneration of healthy life. In the Meru case, an increasing number of young women see the old way of life as unsustainable and "outdated" (*ya zamani*) and are forging new livelihoods – albeit with constraints. By pursuing new life trajectories they are moving in new directions and are challenging the "proper" combination of the sexual and reproductive order. To move out of their natal homes, to refer to Douglas, these women get rid of tedious constraint, but they are also, as we have seen, becoming exposed and vulnerable.

With AIDS in their midst, life-producing sexual activity has become potentially both a life-bringing and a death-bringing activity. Hence, sexuality and the life-giving fluids of semen, blood and mother's milk have also become potential death-producers. The sexually active generation and, thus, the future of the next generation, are in danger. AIDS is therefore a demanding disease both for the individual (body) and for the community (body) at large.

Once women cease to practise their "culture" (Meru traditions) and, even worse, pick up foreign and modern ways of living from the "outside", such ways of life become dangerous, as we have seen, both to themselves and to Meru society at large. Young and mobile women are outside male control and "drive the men like a car", people argue, they "milk them" and finally "skin" them. Men are lured by such sexually active and attractive women and get trapped and lose their own will and mind. Men like Paul forget all that is socially and morally good and turned into zombie-like beings – their wealthy and healthy bodies are targeted – milked, and sapped for their life force. Finally they are "skinned" before they are left for another healthy and wealthy body.

These are some of the reasons why AIDS is seen like a woman who, after sapping a wealthy and healthy man of his life force, then moves on to another. Both are moving around and target the healthy individuals of a population and drain them of their life force.

Acknowledgement

Grateful acknowledgement of funding is extended to the Tanzanian-Norwegian AIDS Project (1989–1992), the Norwegian Research Council (1992–1995) and the Nordic Africa Institute (2000–2005). I am especially grateful to my informants who have generously let me into their lives and to Jehovaroy Kaaya who has assisted me whenever I have been in the field over the past 20 years.

References

Bloch, Maurice, and Jonathan P. Parry (eds), 1987, *Death and the regeneration of life.* Cambridge: Cambridge University Press.

Bujra, Janet M., 2000, "Risk and trust: unsafe sex, gender and AIDS in Tanzania", in P. Caplan (ed.), *Risk revisited.* Anthropology, Culture and Society. London: Pluto Press, pp. 59–84.

Day, Sofie, 1988, "Prostitute women and AIDS: anthropology", *AIDS,* 2(6):421–428.

Dilger, Hansjörg, 2003, "Sexuality, AIDS, and the lures of modernity: reflexivity and morality among young people in rural Tanzania", *Medical Anthropology,* 22(1):23–52.

Douglas, Mary, 1980, *Purity and danger: an analysis of concepts of pollution and taboo.* London: Routledge and Kegan Paul.

—, 1994, *Risk and blame: essays in cultural theory.* London: Routledge.

Emanatian, Michele, 1996, "Everyday Metaphors of Lust and Sex in Chagga", *Ethos,* 24(2):195–236.

Foster, H.D., 2003, "WHY HiV-1 has diffused so much more rapidly in Sub-Saharan Africa than in North America", *Medical Hypotheses,* Vol. 60, Issue 4, April 2003, pp. 611–614

Green, December, 1999, *Gender violence in Africa: African women's responses.* New York: St. Martin's Press.

Haram, Liv, 1995, "Negotiating sexuality in times of economic want : the young and modern Meru women", in K.-I. Klepp, P.M. Biswalo and A. Talle (eds), *Young people at risk: fighting AIDS in Northern Tanzania.* Oslo: Scandinavian University Press, pp. 31–48.

—, 1999, "Women out of sight : modern women in gendered worlds : the case of the Meru of northern Tanzania". PhD dissertation, University of Bergen.

—, 2005a, "AIDS and risk: the handling of uncertainty in northern Tanzania", *Culture, Health & Sexuality,* 7(1):1–13.

—, 2005b, "'Eyes Have No Curtains': The Moral Economy of Secrecy in Managing Love Affairs among Adolescents in Northern Tanzania in the Time of AIDS", *Africa Today,* 51(4):56–73.

—, 2008, "Assessment of Health-Care Seeking Behaviour: The Case of Co-Infection of TB and HIV/AIDS in Temeke, Tanzania", The Norwegian Heart and Lung Patient Organization, May 2008.

—, 2009, (Forthcoming) "'We are tired of morning!' The Economy of Death and Bereavement in a Time of AIDS", in Hansjoerg Dilger and Ute Luig (eds), *Anthropologies of AIDS. The Morality of Illness, Treatment and Death in Africa.* Oxford/New York: Berghahn Books.

Harjula, Raimo, 1976, "The institutions of the Medicine-Men and the Encounter of Religions in Tanzania", *Temenos*, 12:149–162.

Ingstad, B., 1990, "The Cultural Construction of AIDS and its Consequences for Prevention in Botswana", *Medical Anthropology Quarterly,* 4(1):38–40.

Middelthon, Anne-Lise, 1992, *De farlige andre: om anti-struktur og metaforiserings – og metonymiseringsprosesser i HIV-epidemien.* Oslo: Universitetet i Oslo.

Mnyika, Kagoma S. et al., 1994, "Prevalence of HIV-1 infection in urban, semi-urban and rural areas in Arusha region, Tanzania", *AIDS,* 8(10):1477–1481.

Moore, Sally Falk, 1986, *Social facts and fabrications: 'customary' law on Kilimanjaro 1880–1980.* Cambridge: Cambridge University Press.

Ngubane, Harriet, 1977, *Body and mind in Zulu medicine: an ethnography of health and disease in Nyuswa-Zulu thought and practice.* London: Academic Press.

Obbo, Christine, 1995, "Gender, age and class : discourses on HIV transmission and control in Uganda", in H. Brummelhuis and G.H. Herdt (eds), *Culture and sexual risk: anthropological perspectives on AIDS.* Australia and United States: Gordon & Breach Publishers.

PlusNews, 2007, "Tanzania: Government to step up ARV rollout and VCT", Plus News Global HIV/AIDS news and analyses. http://www.plusnews.org/report.aspx?Report Id=73298

Shoepf, Brooke G., 2001, "International AIDS Research in Anthropology: Taking a Critical Perspective on the Crisis", *Annual Review Anthropology,* 2001(30):335–361.

Setel, Philip Wittman, 1999, *A plague of paradoxes: AIDS, culture, and demography in Northern Tanzania.* Chicago: University of Chicago Press.

Sontag, Susan, 1989, *AIDS and its metaphors.* Great Britain: Penguin Books.

Udvardy, Monica L., 1995, "The lifecource of property and personhood : provisional women and enduring men among the Giriama of Kenya", *Economic Anthropology,* 16:325–348.

UNAIDS/WHO, 2002, *Epidemiological fact sheets on HIV/AIDS and sexually transmitted infections.* United Republic of Tanzania.

—, 2003, *Epidemiological fact sheets on HIV/AIDS and sexually transmitted infections.* United Republic of Tanzania.

—, 2008, *Epidemiological fact sheets on HIV/AIDS and sexually transmitted infections.* United Republic of Tanzania.

Walker, Liz, and Leah Gilbert, 2001, "Women pay the price: HIV/AIDS and social inequalities", *South African Labour Bulletin,* 76–82.

Weiss, Brad, 1993, "'Buying her grave': money, movement and the AIDS in the North-West Tanzania", *Africa,* 63(1):19–35.

—, 1996, *The making and unmaking of the Haya lived world: consumption, commoditization, and everyday practice.* Durham, NC: Duke University Press.

Whyte, Susan Reynolds, 1990, "The widow's dream: sex and death in Western Kenya", in M. Jackson and I. Karp (eds), *Personhood and agency: the experience of self and other in African cultures.* Uppsala Studies in Cultural Anthropology, 14. Uppsala: Uppsala University.

Epilogue

Susan Reynolds Whyte

In their introduction to this volume, the editors Liv Haram and Bawa Yamba leave the concept of uncertainty open, allowing the contributors to reveal its potentialities in the different settings where they have worked. And the authors have done so through a series of topically compelling and ethnographically rich essays, which exactly fulfil the promise of the book's title: to *situate* uncertainty in contemporary Africa. The situations described and analysed here are so varied and thought-provoking that the decision not to impose a single conceptual framework seems wise. Yet an epilogue ("a speech or short poem addressed to the audience by an actor at the end of a play") might be the occasion to review the "lessons learned", as development discourse puts it, in order to consider possible ways forward.

Haram and Yamba explain that they are concerned with uncertainty on two levels: how researchers "conceive of phenomena that result in uncertainty in the lives of the groups they studied" and "how the people under study deal with problems of uncertainty", My remarks in this short "speech" are mainly about the first concern, even though my own work has been much occupied with the second.

The terms uncertain, insecure and contingent are often used more or less synonymously to describe living with war, poverty, disease and social disorder. Uncertainty, insecurity and contingency are indeed closely related, so closely that we might say that they are three aspects of the same unforeseeability that people in Uganda capture when they describe life as "just gambling". But it may be helpful to try to distinguish between them so that we can sharpen our discussions of phenomena that are by their nature rather vague.

We can think of uncertainty as a state of mind and minding: mind as a noun in the broad sense of intellect, will, intention, feelings; and minding as a verb meaning to care or feel concern. The uncertainty that matters is that which pertains to things we mind about, our situated concerns. Uncertainty refers to a lack of absolute knowledge: inability to predict the outcome of events or to establish facts about phenomena and connections with assurance. The contributors to this volume treat this as a negative state, but John Dewey (1929), one of the fathers of pragmatism, saw it as fruitful too. For uncertainty is the basis of curiosity and exploration; it can call forth considered action to change both the situation and the self. Yet in the contemporary African context, uncertainty is a source of anxiety and fear because of the prevailing conditions of insecurity.

If uncertainty is a state of mind, then insecurity is a social condition. It refers to a lack of protection from danger, weakness in the social arrangements that provide some kind of safety net when adversity strikes. It is insecurity that characterises so many of the situations described in the foregoing pages: the unreliability of health care systems, the undependability of livelihoods, the fragility of relationships, the inability of public authorities to protect citizens against violence. Insecurity itself gives rise to uncertainty, yes. But it is also a state of limited resources for action. Dealing with uncertainty is perhaps not so much about making certain, as it is about trying to make more secure. It is security that people seek to strengthen in their efforts to exert some degree of control, drawing on the social and cultural resources at hand – whether they be the forms of therapy or the kinship relations that feature strongly in many of the contributions to this volume. (Nearly 50 years ago M.J. Field [1960] chose as the title for her book on mental illness in Ghana, *The Quest for Security*.) Dewey played on the difference between assurance and insurance. Assurance is a state of certainty, but insurance (building security) is a measure taken to provide for a possible contingency.

If insecurity is a social condition, then contingency is an existential one. To be contingent is to be dependent on, or affected by, *something else* that cannot be fully foreseen or controlled. Conditions arise, events occur, and people act in ways that impinge upon us unexpectedly. Plans and the resources earmarked for realising them are suddenly destroyed by an unexpected death in the family or the need to pay bail for your brother who has been arrested. Insecurity and contingency are closely related concepts. The difference I see is that contingency more acutely emphasises dependence and interrelatedness, key themes in these essays. It can be argued that the lives of women are particularly marked by contingency (Bledsoe 2002).

Distinguishing between these three concepts may help us in setting further empirical questions, as we pursue the lines laid out here. For instance, under what circumstances is uncertainty denied in favour of assertions about truth? The new Charismatic churches provide one example, but are there other knowledge-claims (James 1995) being made in Africa today that would bear scrutiny? How do cultures locate uncertainty by focusing attention on issues people should mind about? I have suggested that divination and medical tests do this (Whyte 2005), but there are certainly many more examples of cultural formulations of the visible and invisible, the hidden and the secret. Soori Nnko's research in Tanzania explores ambivalence about public health interventions for malaria control, showing how people are both attracted by the promise of health technology and doubtful about it, especially these days when everything is "just business" (Nnko 2008; see also Kamat 2008 for a similar analysis). The issue here is uncertainty and ambivalence as states of mind: how they are expressed and how they are maintained by experience.

Insecurity may be the key concept for further work with attempts to control uncertainty. At the level of the social actor, attempts to control are not about mastery; if we follow the pragmatists, uncertainty is always a property of engagement in the world – it cannot be eradicated. Rather, control is about trying to secure what can be secured in the face of adversity. The possibilities for such control depend on the societal resources that exist, and on who has access to them. So the practices of social actors must be seen in the context of institutions and political economy. Research questions about human security should address the unequal distribution of the means of dealing with difficulty. Herbert Muyinda (2009) was concerned with this in his research on disability in war-torn northern Uganda. Everyone in Acholiland lived amidst insecurity, especially those with impaired mobility. But landmine survivors who lived in town were much better able to secure their livelihoods than polio survivors in the rural IDP camps. Mobility devices (wheelchairs, tricycles) were the resources that allowed disabled people to engage more easily in petty trade; they were provided by NGOs based in the urban area, whose target group was people maimed by the war. The social distribution of resources for security was biased.

Contingency as a concept can easily lead to a focus on vulnerability; to be dependent is to be susceptible, easily affected, readily wounded. Vulnerability is a central theme in much health, social and development work. EVP (extremely vulnerable people) and OVC (other vulnerable children) are categories used by agencies to classify those needing extra entitlements because they are at risk. But if we hold on to the notion that contingency is about interrelatedness, then it should guide research towards a closer analysis of the specific dependencies and interdependencies that characterise a situation. It should draw attention to relationships, not categories or individuals. In her study of very young mothers in Tanzania, Mette Ringsted (2008) showed how early motherhood created early grandmotherhood and how adults tried to save their own moral standing by condemning the girls they were responsible for. She emphasises that young girls' pregnancies disturb the plans and life trajectories of others. While painting detailed, often disturbing, pictures of the girl-mothers' vulnerability, she keeps their insecurities in a framework of interrelationships. This seems to me a fruitful use of the notion of contingency.

If the differentiation of these three terms is to be more than a pedantic exercise, then we must put them to work by putting them back together again, showing how contingency may feed into insecurity, and how the insecurity of some may affect the contingent situation of others. That the contingencies and insecurities of life give rise to uncertainty for millions of people is all too terribly obvious. What is less obvious, and deserving of much more attention, is that efforts to make life more secure, or to (pro) claim certainties, may have unexpected consequences. The work presented in the preceding pages offers striking examples of the interplay of states of mind, social conditions for securing life, and contingent existences.

References

Bledsoe, Caroline H., 2002, *Contingent Lives: Fertility, Time and Aging in West Africa*. Chicago: Chicago University Press.

Dewey, John, 1929, *The Quest for Certainty: A Study of the Relation of Knowledge and Action*. New York: Minton, Balch & Co.

Field, M.J., 1960, *The Quest for Security: An Ethno-Psychiatric Study of Rural Ghana*. London: Faber & Faber.

James, Wendy (ed.), 1995, *The Pursuit of Certainty: Religious and Cultural Formulations*. London: Routledge.

Kamat, Vinay, 2008, "This is not our culture! Discourse of nostalgia and narratives of health concerns in post-socialist Tanzania", *Africa* 78(3): 359–383.

Muyinda, Herbert, 2009, "Limbs and Lives: Disability, Violent Conflict and Embodied Sociality in Northern Uganda". PhD. Series no. 50. Department of Anthropology, University of Copenhagen.

Nnko, Soori, 2008, "Malaria, Modernity and the State: Ambivalence towards Public Health Interventions in Tanzania". PhD. Series no. 48. Department of Anthropology, University of Copenhagen.

Ringsted, Mette Line, 2008, "Collisions in life-courses: teenage motherhood and generational relations in north-east Tanzania", in E. Alber, S. van der Geest and S.R. Whyte (eds), *Generations in Africa: Connections and Conflicts*. Münster: LIT.

Whyte, Susan Reynolds, 2005," Uncertain undertakings: practicing health care in the subjunctive mood", in V. Steffen, R. Jenkins and H. Jessen (eds), *Managing Uncertainty: Ethnographic Studies of Illness, Risk and the Struggle for Control*. Copenhagen: Museum Tusculanum Press.

Notes on Contributors

Ezra Chitando is Professor of Theology at the University of Zimbabwe and Theological Consultant for the World Council of Churches' Ecumenical HIV and AIDS Initiative in Africa (EHAIA). Chitando has published widely on the Church's response to HIV and AIDS in Africa and the mainstreaming of gender and HIV in theological programmes. Among his many publications are "'Down with Devil, Forward with Christ!' A study of the interface between religious and political discourses in Zimbabwe", (*African Sociological Review*, 2002); *A Study of Gospel Music in Zimbabwe* (2002); *Living with Hope: African Churches and HIV/AIDS 1* (2008); and *Acting in Hope: African Churches and HIV/AIDS* (2008)

Catrine Christiansen is writing up a PhD thesis on Christian churches and development in Uganda at the Department of Anthropology, University of Copenhagen. She was the Nordic Research Fellow for Norway at the Nordic Africa Institute, Uppsala, Sweden, in 2002–2005. Her principal research interests include religion, development, health and social organisation. Her publications include: "Positioning children and institutions of childcare in contemporary Uganda" (*African Journal of AIDS Research*, 2005); "The New Wives of Christ: Paradoxes and Potentials in the Remaking of Widow Lives in Uganda" (in *Aids and Religious Practice in Africa*, 2009, Berghahn); and the co-edited book *Navigating Youth, Generating Adulthood: Social Becoming in an African Context* (2006).

Liv Haram is Associate Professor at the Department of Social anthropology, Norwegian University of Science and Technology, Trondheim. She has held academic positions at the University of Bergen and the Nordic Africa Institute in Uppsala. Her principal research interests are problems of modernisation, changing modes of livelihoods, gender relations and sexuality. Her current interest includes the problematic standardisation of mental illness. Besides doing fieldwork in Tanzania since 1989, she has conducted long-term field studies in Botswana. Her publications include "Tswana Medicine in Interaction with Biomedicine" (*Social Science and Medicine*, Vol. 33, No. 2, pp. 167–175, 1991); "AIDS and risk: the handling of uncertainty in northern Tanzania" (*Culture, Health & Sexuality*, Vol. 7, No. 1, pp. 1–13); and "'We are tired of morning!' The Economy of Death and Bereavement in a Time of AIDS" (in Dilger, Hansjoerg and Ute Luig, eds,

Anthropologies of AIDS: The Morality of Illness, Treatment and Death in Africa, Oxford/New York: Berghahn Books, forthcoming).

Simeon Mesaki retired from the University of Dar es Salaam, Tanzania, in November 2007, having taught in the Department of Sociology and Anthropology since 1973. Dr. Mesaki wrote a thesis on witchcraft and witch killings in Tanzania for the Graduate School of the University of Minnesota, USA, where he obtained his doctorate in anthropology in 1993. Since then he has been writing, teaching and giving lectures on witchcraft in and out of Tanzania. He is also engaged in a wide range of research projects and consultancies on various aspects of Tanzania society.

Mary Ann Mhina is currently Executive Director of *AbleChildAfric,* an NGO that works with disabled children and disabled young people in Africa. Mhina received a first-class degree in Swahili and Social Anthropology from the School of Oriental and African Studies (SOAS), University of London, in 2001 and an MA in Anthropological Research from Goldsmiths College, University of London, in 2003. She conducted research on mental health and illness in Tanzania, between 2002 and 2004 when she was a research associate at the Department of Psychiatry, Muhilibili College of Health Sciences (MUCHS), University of Dar es Salaam, Tanzania. Previously associated with BasicNeeds UK Trust, Mhina was involved in researching and establishing the organisation's first mental health and development projects in Tanzania (2002) and Uganda (2003).

Hanne O. Mogensen is Associate Professor at the Department of Anthropology, University of Copenhagen. She has done extensive research on medical anthropology and international health in various African countries and has also participated in research collaborations on reproductive health and AIDS in Vietnam and in Denmark. She has followed the AIDS epidemic since the early 1990s and her publications on AIDS in Africa include: *AIDS is a kind of kahungo that kills* (Scandinavia University Press, 1995); "The narrative of AIDS in Zambia" (*Social Science and Medicine,* 1997, Vol. 44, No. 4); and "New hopes and new dilemmas: Disclosure and recognition in the time of antiretroviral treatment" (in Dilger, Hansjoerg and Ute Luig, eds, *Anthropologies of AIDS: The Morality of Illness, Treatment and Death in Africa.* Oxford/New York: Berghahn Books, forthcoming).

Knut Christian Myhre is currently the Nordic Research Fellow for Norway at the Nordic Africa Institute, Uppsala, Sweden. He studied at the University of Oslo, and at the University of Oxford, where he received his D.Phil. in Social Anthropology. He previously served as a post-doctoral research fellow at the Department of Social Anthropology, Norwegian University of Science and Technology, Trondheim. His principal interests are in the fields of anthropological theory, epistemology and the dynamics of relationality. He is currently conducting research on property relations in Kilimanjaro Region, Tanzania. Among his publications are: "The truth of anthropology: epistemology, meaning and residual positivism" (*Anthropology Today*, Vol. 22, No. 6, pp. 16–19); "Family resemblances, practical interrelations and material extensions: understanding sexual prohibitions, production, and consumption in Kilimanjaro" (*Africa*, Vol. 77, No. 3, pp. 307–330); and "Divination and experience: explorations of a Chagga epistemology" (*Journal of the Royal Anthropological Institute*, N.S., No. 12, pp. 313–330).

Noah K. Ndosi is Associate Professor of Neuro-psychiatry at the Department of Psychiatry, Muhimbili University College of Health Sciences (MUCHS), Dar es Salaam. His research interests are suicide, schizophrenia and substance abuse. Currently he is engaged in research on childhood disorders. He has published on mental disorders in Tanzania, the nature of suicides, and the challenges of psychiatry in developing countries. Among his publications are: "The nature of attempted suicide in Dar es Salaam" (*Social Science and Medicine,* 1997, No. 44, pp. 55–61); "The Nature of Puerperal Psychosis at Muhimbili National Hospital; Its Physical Co-morbidity, Associated Main Obstetric and Social Factors" (*African Journal of Reproductive Health*, 2004, Vol 6, No. 1, pp. 41–49); "Profile of Suicide in Dar es Salaam" (*East African Medical Journal*, No. 81, 2004, pp. 207–211); "The Challenges of Psychiatry Amidst Economic Deprivations and Social Change in Dar es Salaam Tanzania" (in Lugalla, Joe and Kris Heggenhougen, eds, *Social Change and Health in East Africa*, Dar es Salaam University Press Ltd., pp. 196–208).

Todd Sanders is Associate Professor of Anthropology at the University of Toronto, Canada, and a Research Associate at the Cambridge Centre of African Studies, UK. He has written on anthropological theory, knowledge and epistemology; transparency; and rainmaking, witchcraft and neoliberalism in Tanzania. His most recent books are: *Beyond Bodies: Rainmaking and Sense Making in Tanzania* (University of Toronto Press, 2008); *Anthropology* *in Theory: Issues in Epistemology* (with H. L. Moore, Blackwell, 2006), *Transparency and Conspiracy* (with H. West, Duke, 2003); *Magical Interpretations, Material Realities: Modernity, Witchcraft and the Occult in Postcolonial Africa* (with H. L. Moore, Routledge, 2001); and *Those Who Play with Fire: Gender, Fertility and Transformation in East and Southern Africa* (with H. L. Moore and B. Kaare, Athlone, 1999).

Susan Reynolds Whyte is Professor at the Department of Anthropology, University of Copenhagen, has carried out fieldwork in Tanzania, Kenya, and especially Uganda, where she has a long-term collaboration with Makerere University. Her research falls mainly in the areas of family, generation and gender, misfortune, health, disability, medicines and international development, topics on which she has published widely. Among her works are: *Questioning Misfortune: The Pragmatics of Uncertainty in Eastern Uganda* (Cambridge University Press, 1997); *Disability in Local and Global Worlds* (co-edited with Benedicte Ingstad, University of California Press, 2007); and *Generations in Africa: Connections and Conflicts* (co-edited with Erdmute Alber and Sjaak van der Geest, LIT Verlag, 2008).

C. Bawa Yamba is Associate Professor at Diakonhjemmet University College, Oslo, where he teaches at the Department of Social Work. He has held academic appointments at the Karolinska Institute, Stockholm, and the Nordic Africa Institute, Uppsala, Sweden. His current interests include orphans and vulnerable children, and the socio-cultural impact of the HIV and AIDS pandemic in Africa. His publications include: *Permanent Pilgrims: The Role of Pilgrimage in the Lives of West African Muslims in Suda* (Edinburgh University Press, 1995); "Cosmologies in Turmoil: Witchfinding and AIDS in Chiawa, Zambia" (*Africa*, Vol. 67, 1997; "The Vindication of Chaka Zulu: Retreat into the Enchantment of the Past" (*Social Analysis*, Vol. 49, No. 3, Winter, 2005).

Index

and social relationships, 127–8,
133–8, 195
Sukumaland, 72–90
traditional goods, 104–8, 112
traditional methods of dealing with,
77–8
and wealth, 21–2, 107–12
women
changing role, 79–80
disadvantaged living conditions, 161
early motherhood, 215–16
educational level, 169
female sexuality and men, 205–8
fertility, 38–9, 107–8
and HIV/AIDS, 198–9, 202–4
HIV/AIDS carers, 40
HIV/AIDS and suicide, 164, 165,
172
and infidelity, 25, 170–1

prophetic activities, 38–41
rape, 39, 200
sexual partnerships, 201–5
suicide, 160–1, 164–6, 169–72
violence against, 25–6, 164, 171,
172–3
witch killings, 21, 73, 78–84
World Bank, 91, 92

Zambia, 13, 154, 157
Zimbabwe, 29–47
economic and social situation, 29,
41–2
emigration, 19, 43–4
female suicide, 166
health services, 37, 43
passports, 19, 44, 45
Pentecostalism, 15, 29, 32–3, 35–6
Zviratidzo ZveVapostori Church, 41

www.ingramcontent.com/pod-product-compliance
Lightning Source LLC
Chambersburg PA
CBHW071050280326
41928CB00050B/2163